WAGERING ON AN IRONIC GOD

WAGERING ON AN IRONIC GOD
Pascal on Faith and Philosophy

Thomas S. Hibbs

BAYLOR UNIVERSITY PRESS

© 2017 by Baylor University Press
Waco, Texas 76798

All Rights Reserved. No part of this publication may be reproduced, stored in a retrieval system, or transmitted, in any form or by any means, electronic, mechanical, photocopying, recording, or otherwise, without the prior permission in writing of Baylor University Press.

Cover Design by Alyssa Stepien
Cover image: *Les Pensées de Pascal,* 1924 (oil on canvas), Matisse, Henri (1869–1954) / Minneapolis Institute of Arts, MN, USA / Gift of Ruth and Bruce Dayton / Bridgeman Images. © 2016 Succession H. Matisse / Artists Rights Society (ARS), New York

This book has been cataloged by the Library of Congress.

Printed in the United States of America on acid-free paper with a minimum of 30 percent post-consumer waste recycled content.

For David Solomon

CONTENTS

Acknowledgments   ix

One

IRONY, PHILOSOPHY, AND THE CHRISTIAN FAITH   1

§1. Pascal and the Ancient Quarrel over the Best Way of Life   2
§2. Irony Rehabilitated   11
§3. The Figure of Socrates in Early Modern Philosophy: Montaigne, Descartes, and Pascal   18
§4. Divine Irony as an Alternative to Deism and Voluntarism   30

Two

SOCRATIC IMMANENCE: MONTAIGNE'S RECOVERY OF PHILOSOPHY AS A WAY OF LIFE   39

§1. Socratic Self-Knowledge and the Art of Living   42
§2. Against Speculative Philosophy   46
§3. Montaigne's Confessions   54
§4. Death, Diversion, and the Supernatural   60

Three

THE VIRTUE OF SCIENCE AND THE SCIENCE OF VIRTUE: DESCARTES' OVERCOMING OF SOCRATES — 67

§1. The Arts of Writing and the Science of Living — 69
§2. Recovering and Overcoming Socrates — 73
§3. Descartes' New Science of Virtue — 81
§4. Theology, Philosophical Irony, and the Arts of (Re-)Writing — 88

Four

THE QUEST FOR WISDOM: PASCAL AND PHILOSOPHY — 101

§1. Socrates and the Quest for the Good Life — 102
§2. Ironic Reversal: The Reduction of Cartesian Certitude to Socratic Amazement — 106
§3. Philosophy Deconstructed? Pascal Deconstructed? — 113
§4. The Restless Heart: Pascal's Residual Teleology — 122
§5. Pascal's Methods and the Quest for a Synoptic Vision — 132

Five

WAGERING ON AN IRONIC GOD — 143

§1. Rereading the Wager — 145
§2. Wagering as Self-Emptying — 163
§3. The Problem of Hope — 169
§4. Neither Deism nor Voluntarism — 175
§5. Christ as Eucharistic Cipher — 183

Bibliography — 193
Index of Names and Authors — 203

ACKNOWLEDGMENTS

I first read Pascal in a modern philosophy class at the University of Dallas in 1981. We read only the Wager. I don't recall being moved one way or the other by the assignment. I began thinking seriously about Pascal in the fall of 1987 when I began teaching the *Pensées* in the Junior Great Books Seminar as a tutor at Thomas Aquinas College. That exercise forced me to try to read the text as a unified whole or at least to strain to make connections among the variegated themes and fragmented style. Because we were reading numerous other early modern texts from a variety of disciplines, it also prodded me to begin to think about Pascal in relation to his contemporaries, especially Descartes and Montaigne. That in turn led me to read not just widely in Montaigne's *Essays* but also in the works of Descartes not typically studied in philosophy classes: *The Geometry*, *The Principles of Philosophy*, and especially *The Passions of the Soul*. But it was not until I arrived at Baylor University, after having spent thirteen years in the philosophy department at Boston College, that I took up this comparative study in a serious way. A single lecture by, and a few subsequent conversations with, the great French scholar Pierre Manent had given me a strong sense of the direction I wanted to pursue. Pierre gave a lecture at Boston College in the Bradley Lecture Series on Socrates and Pascal. This prodded me to think about the role of the figure of Socrates not just in Pascal but also in Montaigne and Descartes. It also began my thinking about Pascal's novel way of construing the relationship between faith and reason in terms of ironic discourse: "Philosophers astonish ordinary people. Christians astonish philosophers."

At Baylor University, where my principal duties are administrative, Mike Beaty, chair of the philosophy department, has encouraged me to teach when and what I want. A graduate seminar on Pascal in relation to Montaigne and Descartes launched the current project in earnest.

Along the way, numerous colleagues have made helpful suggestions and valuable criticisms either in written form or in conversation. Among them are my Baylor colleagues David Corey, Phil Donnelly, Michael Foley, Alan Jacobs, David Jeffrey, and Robert Miner, as well as colleagues from other universities: Paul Griffiths (Duke), Gerry Wegemer (University of Dallas), and Marc Guerra, Dan Maher, and Dan Mahoney (Assumption College). It goes without saying that the views expressed herein are mine, not theirs. Indeed, I cannot recall a single conversation with any of the above that was characterized by anything more than partial agreement. And that is to the good, as the disagreements and questions forced me to rethink numerous parts of the argument. Sabrina Little proofread the final version and constructed the index.

I have been at work on this book so long that an entire generation of graduate assistants has participated in its various iterations, including John Spano, Jay Bruce, Janelle Klaupisik, John Bishop, Brandon Dahm, and Adam Myers. A polyglot undergraduate, now in medical school, Elizabeth Luper, provided guidance on some of the French texts.

It is commonplace in spaces such as these to express gratitude toward family members for their patience and understanding. But my bouts of writing—inconstant, at odd hours, and for unpredictable periods of time—go largely unremarked by my wife, Stacey, and our three children, Lauren, Dan, and Sara, who have happily grown to discover their own favorite disciplines and texts.

I want to dedicate this book to someone who had absolutely nothing to do with its origins or development (at least he cannot be blamed for the result!) but who has been a nearly constant presence in my life and work since my time as a graduate student at the University of Notre Dame in the mid-1980s: David Solomon.

David introduced me to twentieth-century analytic ethics and helped me to see the significance of the projects of MacIntyre and

Hauerwas. A Texan, raised as a Baptist and an alumnus of Baylor University, he introduced me, a Yankee Catholic with degrees from the University of Dallas and Notre Dame, to Baylor. We have been members of one another's advisory boards. David's presence, often after lengthy periods of silence, calls to mind Belloc's famous refrain—dear to his dear friend and my mentor Ralph McInerny: "Wherever the Catholic sun doth shine, there's always lots of laughter and good, red wine." In David's case, splendid conversation, from raucous to rigorous, always ensues. He and his wife, Lou, have welcomed our family, as they have done countless others, into their homes and lives.

Certainly not all but a good deal of what I know—and a larger percentage of what is good and true in what I know—about philosophy, teaching, and friendship have been taught to me by David Solomon.

One

IRONY, PHILOSOPHY, AND THE CHRISTIAN FAITH

"Philosophers: they astonish the ordinary run of men. Christians: they astonish the philosophers" (613).[1] With its allusion to both Socrates and St. Paul, Pascal's pithy aphorism contains the key to understanding his conception of philosophy and its relationship to divine revelation. Revelation's mode of pedagogy is ironic; disrupting the ordinary and expected flow of events, it occasions surprise. Irony seizes upon incongruity, on the gap between what we think we know and what we actually know, between what we anticipate and what actually comes to be, and between what we think we are and what we in fact are. To ordinary human beings, the philosopher, who eschews what the many esteem in favor of some other, less apparent good, seems at best comical and at worst threatening. Alternately mocked and reviled, Socrates is ultimately put to death for practicing a philosophical way of life. Similarly, many have been put to death for practicing the Christian

---

[1] "*Les philosophes. Ils étonnent le commun des hommes. Les chrétiens, ils étonnent les philosophes*" (443). French quotations are taken from Blaise Pascal, *Pensées*, ed. Dominique Descotes and Léon Brunschvicg (Paris: Flammarion, 1976). The English translation is that of A. J. Krailsheimer (New York: Penguin Classics, 1995). I will cite the Krailsheimer numbering parenthetically at the end of each English quotation and the Brunschvicg, where necessary, in notes. I have altered the translation here to replace "surprise" with what I take to be a stronger sense in the original French.

life, which seems absurd or hazardous both to conventional life and the life of philosophy. Thus Paul speaks of the cross of Christ as folly.

In Pascal as in Paul, the praise of folly is ironic.[2] It is not the result of a crude anti-intellectualism; rather, it reposes on a recognition of human beings' "ignorance of an unseen or unexpected order."[3] Irony does not confine the intellect but awakens it, insofar as it is capable of grasping the irony, to "liberating depth."[4] The order or plane of knowledge on which an individual operates determines what he sees—or fails to see—in other orders or planes. Much more will be said below about irony, especially about the similarities and differences between philosophical and theological modes of ironic pedagogy. Interpreting Pascal from the perspective of ironic teaching has clear advantages; it suggests that his writings contain a much richer conception of the relationship between faith and reason than what interpreters typically recognize.

Pascalian irony, as we shall see in some detail below, is not to be confused with the ironic posture of the jaded, detached, postmodern nihilist; nor is it merely a self-protective tool of the philosopher or scientist attempting to shield himself from the threatening censure of church and state. Instead, it is a pedagogical tool inviting, castigating, bewildering—all with the intention of awakening dormant human souls to a quest for the good life.[5]

§1. Pascal and the Ancient Quarrel over the Best Way of Life

Reading Pascal in terms of the debate over the good life has a number of advantages; it offers a corrective to entrenched misreadings of his

---

[2] The phrase is from Erasmus, of course. See his *Praise of Folly* (New York: Penguin Classics, 1994) and M. A. Screech's *Erasmus: Ecstasy and the Praise of Folly* (London: Duckworth, 1980).

[3] Anthony Esolen, *Ironies of Faith: The Laughter at the Heart of Christian Literature* (Wilmington, Del.: ISI Books, 2007), 17.

[4] Esolen, *Ironies of Faith*, 28.

[5] Irony is, of course, a literary device. Pascal was a master of rhetoric and satire, as is clear from his masterful *Provincial Letters*. Our interest is rather limited. We will focus not on rhetoric broadly but on the role of irony in his conception of the relationship of faith and reason, with attention given almost exclusively to his *Pensées*. See, for example, Nicholas Hammond, "Pascal's *Pensées* and the Art of Persuasion," in the *Cambridge Companion to Pascal*, ed. Nicholas Hammond (New York: Cambridge University Press, 2003), 235–52.

work and established misinterpretations of early modern philosophy. First, as a corrective to the tendency, especially prominent in Anglo-American philosophy, to focus almost exclusively on isolated segments of the apology, particularly on the "wager" argument, the approach via the good life enables us to see the parts in light of a coherent and comprehensive whole. Such a synthetic approach to Pascal's apology has been on the rise, especially under the influence of leading Pascal scholar Jean Mesnard, whose work is credited with detecting an "underlying unity of heretofore disconnected fragments."[6] The various and seemingly unrelated elements have a place in the articulation of the debate between the philosophical and the religious ways of life. The wager, the only argument in Pascal that receives regular treatment from philosophers, is best read not as an isolated piece of reasoning but as one moment within a comprehensive defense of the Christian way of life. Thus, the wager, which is an invitation to a specific type of interlocutor to adopt the Christian way of life, can be properly understood only when recognized as part of a larger whole. As we shall see in detail in the last chapter, the wager is complex not only in its argument but also in its rhetoric. It is in fact a dialogue, replete with ironic reversals.[7]

Second, it shows how misleading and unhelpful is the reading of Pascal as an anti-intellectual fideist. As Thomas Carroll points out, the application of the term "fideist" to Pascal and other early modern figures is anachronistic. Moreover, there is no clear consensus about the meaning of the term.[8] Now, in Pascal's writings, there are indeed

---

[6] See the translators' preface, entitled "Pascal Rediscovered," to Jean Mesnard's *Pascal*, trans. Claude and Marcia Abraham (Tuscaloosa: University of Alabama Press, 1969), 9.

[7] As Virgil Martin Nemoianu astutely shows, the standard treatments, by critics and defenders alike, of the wager treat it as a self-contained argument and thus ignore Pascal's rich account of the human condition and his nuanced conception of rational persuasion. See Nemoianu, "The Insufficiency of the Many Gods Objection to Pascal's Wager," *American Catholic Philosophical Quarterly* 84, no. 3 (2010): 513–30. Nemoianu offers a nice summary and analysis of the extant literature, including Charles Natoli's *Fire in the Dark* (Rochester, N.Y.: University of Rochester Press, 2005), 8–12, which is one of the exceptions to the general rule of examining the wager in isolation from everything else Pascal wrote.

[8] Carroll identifies six different definitions. See Thomas Carroll, "The Traditions of Fideism," *Religious Studies* 44 (2008): 1–22. Also see Richard Amesbury, "Fideism," in *The Stanford Encyclopedia of Philosophy*, ed. Edward N. Zalta, Fall 2009 ed., http://plato.stanford.edu/archives/fall2009/entries/fideism/; Terence

passages containing negative appraisals of reason and philosophy. To take these to entail a hasty dismissal of philosophy is to miss Pascal's nuanced engagement of philosophy as a distinctive way of life. Moreover, highlighting the role of irony in Pascal's theological teaching brings to the fore a significant and enduring analogy between reason and revelation.

Third, reading Pascal in terms of the great debate over the best way of life helps us to recover what is most compelling and most interesting about early modern philosophy, as such a reading sheds new light on Pascal's relationship to his two most important interlocutors: Montaigne and Descartes. The standard narrative of these three early modern French thinkers is that Montaigne's skepticism generates a response in the form of Descartes' foundationalism, both of which give rise to Pascal's fideism. As is typically the case with established narratives, there are reasons for the labels bestowed upon philosophers. Pascal himself will locate Montaigne among the skeptical school and Descartes among the dogmatists. But he also sees them, more broadly, as engaging in two distinct styles of writing and thinking: the spirit of *finesse*, which discerns patterns in disparate, concrete experiences, and the spirit of geometry, which operates in abstraction from the here and now and seeks a demonstrative certitude that eludes us elsewhere. Beyond these matters of epistemology and style, he reads them both as offering, in quite divergent ways, defenses of the sufficiency of the philosophical life as the best way of life.

From this perspective, we can see the debates between various early modern philosophers as conflicts over the best way of life and thereby recover a sense of the deep connections among philosophy, science, and ethics in the early modern period. Matthew Jones detects in seventeenth-century philosophy, and even in many of the scientific and mathematical texts of the time, a pervasive concern with "spiritual exercises," which offer "practices and objects of knowledge held to

---

Penelhum, *God and Skepticism: A Study in Skepticism and Fideism* (Dordrecht: D. Reidel, 1983); and Richard Popkin, *The History of Skepticism from Savonarola to Bayle* (Oxford: Oxford University Press, 2003). Any discussion of these matters in Pascal must take its primary orientation from Pascal's clearest and most direct remarks about faith and reason in the fragments grouped under the subtitle "Submission and the Use of Reason" (frr. 167–88 in the Krailsheimer edition). Also germane here is the way in which Pascal deploys skepticism. See Robert Miner, "Pascal on the Uses of Scepticism," in *Logos: A Journal of Catholic Thought and Culture* 11, no. 4 (2008): 111–22.

be intellectually and affectively appropriate for living well."[9] On this account, Montaigne, often dismissed by philosophers as merely a literary figure, can be seen as a philosopher in the fullest sense of the term. Meanwhile, Descartes becomes a much more interesting writer than the standard textbook treatments of modern philosophy have allowed.[10] The quest for certitude is subordinate in early modern philosophy, even according to Descartes himself, to the vital question of the best way of life. Descartes can thus be recovered as a philosopher in conversation with classical antiquity, particularly with the figure of Socrates, and with his contemporary, Montaigne. Focusing on that question helps us to see better what is at stake in early modern philosophy.

On the standard account of modern philosophy, Descartes looms large, while Montaigne and Pascal are but footnotes. Montaigne's style, his penchant for the anecdote and the essay form, combined with his seemingly insouciant skepticism, render him an immature modern, eclipsed by the hard reasoning and demonstrative clarity of Descartes. If the sixteenth century, the century of Montaigne, breaks decisively with much of the past, particularly with the medieval past, it is only with the seventeenth century, the century of Descartes, that humanity sets "aside all doubts and ambiguities about its capacity to achieve its goals here on Earth, and in historical time, rather than deferring human fulfillment to an Afterlife in Eternity."[11] Only in the latter period, according to the standard view as described by Stephen Toulmin in his revisionist history *Cosmopolis: The Hidden Agenda of Modernity*, is the modern spirit of progress born with an "optimism" that leads to "major advances not just in natural science but in moral, political and social thought as well." But Toulmin shows that this picture is misleading and dangerous, as it assumes that there is no dark side to the

---

[9] Matthew Jones, *The Good Life in the Scientific Revolution: Descartes, Pascal, Leibniz, and the Cultivation of Virtue* (Chicago: University of Chicago Press, 2006), 6.

[10] Such a reassessment would be a welcome change in the historiography of early modern philosophy. "Tortuously decreasing interest": that's how Susan Neiman in her book *Evil in Modern Thought: An Alternative History of Philosophy* (Princeton, N.J.: Princeton University Press, 2003), describes the standard story of modern philosophy, as told in the dominant Anglo-American departments of philosophy. This is a story about the quest for certitude. It seems that "philosophy, like some people, was prepared to accept boredom in exchange for certainty as it grew to middle age" (23).

[11] Stephen Toulmin, *Cosmopolis: The Hidden Agenda of Modernity* (Chicago: University of Chicago Press, 1990), ix.

Enlightenment goal of transparent rationality. Through a reading of Montaigne, Toulmin argues that there are in fact "two distinct starting points" of modernity: "a humanistic one grounded in classical literature, and a scientific one rooted in natural philosophy."[12] The latter is abstract and theoretical and operates by an "analysis of the abstract core of theoretical concepts," while the former is concrete and practical and operates through an "accumulation of concrete details of practical experience."[13] The contrast works so far as it goes, although Descartes, who repudiates mere theory as much as Montaigne, certainly claimed that his method would produce practical results, going so far as to claim that it will render us "masters and possessors of nature."[14] Without that part of Descartes, we cannot make sense of the seventeenth century as optimistic or progressive. But there is also much that Toulmin gets wrong, especially when it comes to Pascal, who is admittedly a minor character in his reconstruction of modernity. Toulmin locates Pascal with Descartes because Pascal rejects casuistry and thus, on Toulmin's view, must also opt for the abstract over the concrete, the universal over the particular. But this is to ignore the predominance of rhetoric over science in Pascal's apology and his penchant, even more pronounced than in Montaigne, for what Toulmin calls the "accumulation of concrete details of practical experience." Moreover, Toulmin seems innocent of the knowledge that Pascal had already articulated Toulmin's own template for the twofold source of modernity as a contrast between the spirit of *finesse* and that of geometry.[15]

---

[12] Toulmin, *Cosmopolis*, 43.

[13] Toulmin, *Cosmopolis*, 43.

[14] René Descartes, *Discourse on Method*, in *The Philosophical Writings of Descartes*, trans. John Cottingham, Robert Stoothoff, and Dugald Murdoch (Cambridge: Cambridge University Press, 1985), 1:142.

[15] When Toulmin tries to interpret twentieth-century American history in terms of his template, things come undone. For example, when he turns to late twentieth-century higher education (*Cosmopolis*, 184), he discovers a contrast between "excellence," which involves conserving the wisdom of the past, and "relevance," which involves "putting knowledge to use for the human good." One might have thought that the humanists wanted to conserve the wisdom of the past, but Toulmin demurs. He locates the humanists in the latter camp. But in the modern university, the group that is focused on problem solving is precisely the one that comes out of Descartes' hope that we could be masters and possessors of nature through productive knowledge. By contrast, Montaigne was deeply skeptical of the professions, including medicine and law.

As much as Toulmin rightly urges a rethinking of the origins of modernity through a rereading of Montaigne and Descartes, his own interpretation rests on a superficial acquaintance with the texts of these authors. Thus, he misses their and Pascal's common preoccupation with the question of the good life, the recovery of which is crucial to a proper appreciation and appraisal of their writings.

Such a recovery is already underway in the exegesis of ancient philosophy, as is evident from the writings of thinkers as diverse as Pierre Hadot and Leo Strauss. In his discussion of Socrates in *What Is Ancient Philosophy?*, Hadot identifies "the existence of a philosophical life—more precisely, a way of life—which can be characterized as philosophical and which is radically opposed to the way of life of non-philosophers."[16] The philosophical life is not a matter of "knowing this or that, but of *being* in this or that way," especially of being in a way that is a preparation for death, indeed an "exercise of death."[17] It "is a way of life, which corresponds to the highest activity which human beings can engage in and which is linked intimately to the excellence and virtue of the soul."[18] Wisdom itself is a "way of being."[19] Now, such a conception of the philosophical life proved quite congenial, as Hadot notes, to many early Christians, who described the following of Christ as "the way," a distinctive path embodying the communal practice of certain virtues and oriented to a contemplation of Wisdom. Indeed, some go so far as to appropriate the term "philosophy" and to adopt some of philosophy's "spiritual exercises."[20]

Both philosophy and theology concern ways of life informed by authoritative texts, patterned after exemplary figures, and modeled on distinctive accounts of the human good.[21] As Matthew Jones observes,

---

[16] Pierre Hadot, *What Is Ancient Philosophy?*, trans. Michael Chase (Cambridge, Mass.: Harvard University Press, 2004), 172. Also see idem, *Philosophy as a Way of Life: Spiritual Exercises from Socrates to Foucault*, ed. Arnold Davidson (Malden, Mass.: Wiley-Blackwell, 1995).

[17] Hadot, *What Is Ancient Philosophy?*, 29, 67, and 207.

[18] Hadot, *What Is Ancient Philosophy?*, 220.

[19] Hadot, *What Is Ancient Philosophy?*, 18 and 44.

[20] Hadot, *What Is Ancient Philosophy?*, 237–52.

[21] In his biographical study of Pascal, *Reasons of the Heart*, Marvin O'Connell notes that, at a certain point after his conversion, Pascal no longer refers to himself as a mathematician or a scientist. His sister Jacqueline observed that Blaise was "no longer a mathematician." Another sister, Gilberte, testified that he came to see that the "Christian religion obliges us to live only for God and to have no other objective

when Pascal uses the term "philosophers" he includes "thinkers concerned with ways of life, with modes of caring for the self."[22] In one arena, various philosophical schools contend with one another over visions of the good life. In another, they share the assumption that reason or philosophy is the highest authority in the investigation of the good. In the latter, there is a chasm between philosophy and theology. In its authoritative texts (scripture, the church fathers, and the councils), exemplary figures (apostles, martyrs, and saints), and highest source of authority (*Deus revelans*, "God revealing"), Christianity precludes the possibility of its adherents being philosophers. This does not mean that Christians cannot offer philosophical arguments or that they cannot be lovers of wisdom and thus, in their own way, engage in philosophy. But as philosophy comes to be associated with a set of schools from antiquity, with their texts, authorities, and ways of living in accord with reason, Christians come to be associated with a different way of life and its distinctive set of authorities and texts. Pascal considers philosophy both in its complexity of schools and in its unity.

The question of the best way of life is inseparable from the question of who teaches authoritatively concerning that life, and that is a

---

in life but to serve him; and that this truth appeared so clear to my brother, so necessary and so useful, that he stopped all his researches." Now, the facts contradict the notion that he abandoned all research in things experimental, physical, and mathematical. At this time, he had not yet begun his work on the nature of the vacuum, nor had he ceased work on his calculating machine, and his treatise on conic sections was two years away. What seems indisputable is that Pascal's life—at this point a mixture of worldly ambition, intellectual curiosity, and conventional piety—began to be reordered in light of a more serious practice of the Christian faith. In this sense, the remark that he was no longer a mathematician may be perfectly accurate. In response to the questions, "What does he do? How does he live? What sort of person is he?"; one would no longer call him a mathematician as if that were the inquiry that most preoccupied him and about which he was most passionate. Denial in this case means that his life is no longer ordered according to a certain set of pursuits; its standards, goals, and practices no longer constitute the highest aspiration of his life. See Marvin O'Connell, *Blaise Pascal: Reasons of the Heart* (Grand Rapids: Eerdmans, 1997), 51. See the discussion of the geometer in A. W. S. Baird's *Studies in Pascal's Ethics* (The Hague: Martinus Nijhoff, 1975), 15–20. Baird discusses Pascal's growing realization of the limits to the mathematical path to reality and his increased appreciation for the *honnete homme*, the man of *finesse*, who is able to engage in conversation about a variety of matters concerning human life.

[22] Jones, *Good Life in the Scientific Revolution*, 159.

question, ultimately, of whether reason or faith is the supreme authority on the good life. Leo Strauss puts the point succinctly:

> Man cannot live without light, guidance, knowledge; only through knowledge of the good can he find the good that he needs. The fundamental question, therefore, is whether men can acquire that knowledge of the good without which they cannot guide their lives individually or collectively by the unaided efforts of their natural powers, or whether they are dependent for that knowledge on Divine Revelation. No alternative is more fundamental than this: human guidance or divine guidance.[23]

This is precisely the question that informs Pascal's apology for the Christian faith. One of the many paradoxes concerning Pascal's disposition toward philosophy can be seen in the formulation of the central question, a question to which, for Pascal, the only adequate answer is theological. Yet, the manner of framing the question, even in the hands of a Christian apologist, is philosophical. Indeed, Pascal aims, as do classical philosophers, for an understanding of the whole and for a way of life at once wise and blessed.

As noted in the opening quotation, Pascal conceives of three ways of life: that of the ordinary man, that of the philosopher, and that of the Christian. In a related passage, he describes three orders of things: "There are three orders of things: the flesh, the mind, and the will" (933).[24] A. W. S. Baird comments, "Pascal conceives of the three orders, not only as orders of being, . . . but also as moral categories, in which individuals range themselves according to the nature of the end which they pursue as the goal of existence."[25] That activities and ways of life are ordered to certain ends is integral to Pascal's account of the human condition; it is also the basis upon which he engages both ordinary folks and philosophers. The wager, for example, presupposes that happiness

---

[23] Leo Strauss, *Natural Right and History* (Chicago: University of Chicago Press, 1953), 74.
[24] *Il y a trois ordres de choses: la chair, l'esprit, la volonté* (460).
[25] Baird, *Studies in Pascal's Ethics*, 4. See also the chapter entitled "Pascal's Teleological Approach to Ethics in the *Pensées*," 56–84. Of course, "teleological" in Pascal applies only to ways of life, to rational practices, and to the fundamental goal of human desire, not to the order of nature, as it does in Aristotle and Thomas Aquinas. The result is a vastly circumscribed role for teleology, but a crucial role nonetheless.

and truth are naturally recognized goods or ends. Pascal embraces the premodern affirmation of the universal human desire for happiness:

> All men seek happiness. There are no exceptions. However different the means they may employ, they all strive towards this goal. The reason why some go to war and some do not is the same desire in both, but interpreted in two different ways. The will never takes the least step except to that end. This is the motive of every act of every man, including those who go and hang themselves. (148)[26]

Among the many false and imperfect ends pursued by human beings, there is, within and beneath them all, a longing for the true good and final end: "God alone is man's true good" (148).[27] In this respect, as in others, Pascal is an eccentric modern. Like other moderns, he repudiates the classical, Aristotelian notion of purposiveness in natural, nonhuman beings. Much less would he affirm any cosmic teleological harmony. He thinks, writes, and lives in the wake of the shattering of ancient and medieval cosmology. And yet, unlike many of his contemporaries, he retains the notion of a telos of human desire. He affirms both the broadly classical notion of happiness as the end or goal of human life and the specifically Augustinian notion that our heart is restless until it rests in God. Without this affirmation, Pascal's project of presenting the Christian faith as "promising true good" could have no purchase on his interlocutors.

If Strauss and Hadot are correct about the meaning of philosophy in antiquity, then the writings of Pascal, along with those of Montaigne and Descartes, might well be seen as marking a return to the classical problematic, a return to a debate for which the figure of Socrates is central.[28] Before turning to Socrates in the writings of Montaigne, Des-

---

[26] *Tous les hommes recherchent d'être heureux; cela est sans exception; quelques différents moyens qu'ils y emploient, ils tendent tous à ce but. Ce qui fait que les uns vont à la guerre, et que les autres n'y vont pas, est ce même désir, qui est dans tous les deux, accompagné de différentes vues. La volonté ne fait jamais la moindre démarche que vers cet objet. C'est le motif de toutes les actions de tous les hommes, jusqu'à ceux qui vont se pendre* (425).

[27] *Lui seul est son véritable bien* (425).

[28] Both in his book on ancient philosophy and in his earlier text, *Philosophy as a Way of Life*, Hadot identifies the High Middle Ages, the time of scholasticism, as the epoch in which philosophy in the classical sense disappears. Essentially a matter of a set of propositions, philosophy is "no longer a way of life"; it is rather a "purely theoretical and abstract activity" (270). We need not pause here

cartes, and Pascal, we need to consider briefly the immensely useful recent literature on the rehabilitation of irony.

§2. Irony Rehabilitated

As Charles Griswold suggests in his seminal essay "Irony in the Platonic Dialogues," the concealment and enigmas associated with irony can have either of two functions.[29] The point might be that within "every philosophical position there is a puzzle, within which there awaits a riddle, one that in turn conceals an enigma, and so forth ad infinitum." The implication would be that the "universe is intrinsically unknowable." But there is another possibility. "The function of irony in the dialogues is to encourage us to become philosophical by rightly appropriating for ourselves the dialogic search for knowledge," a search focused on a "multi-faceted question: what is the good life for a human being?" On this interpretation, irony mirrors not the "absurdity of the

---

to determine whether Hadot's sweeping claims about the Middle Ages apply to all Christian thinkers of the period. (There is reason to think he is wrong about early scholastic figures such as Anselm, Bonaventure, and Aquinas.) We need only note that Pascal's stylistic distance from early modern scholastic modes of argument and his repudiation of natural theology are intimately connected to his recovery of the ancient notion of the pursuit of wisdom as a way of life.

[29] Charles Griswold, "Irony in the Platonic Dialogues," *Philosophy and Literature* 26, no. 1 (2002): 84–106. Griswold's essay contains important discussions of, and correctives to, some of the most important treatments of irony in Plato. See especially Gregory Vlastos, *Socrates: Ironist and Moral Philosopher* (Ithaca, N.Y.: Cornell University Press, 1991); C. Rowe, "Platonic Irony," in *Nouva Tellus: Anuario del Centro de Estudios Clasicos* 5 (1987): 83–101; Alexander Nehemas, *The Art of Living: Socratic Reflections from Plato to Foucault* (Berkeley: University of California Press, 1998); E. L. Burge, "The Irony of Socrates," *Antichthon* 3 (1969): 5–17. Other relevant works include Wayne Booth, *A Rhetoric of Irony* (Chicago: University of Chicago Press, 1974); D. C. Muecke, *The Compass of Irony* (London: Methuen, 1969); C. Stephen Evans, "The Role of Irony in Kierkegaard's Philosophical Fragments," in *Kierkegaard on Faith and the Self* (Waco, Tex.: Baylor University Press, 2006), 67–80; idem, "Kierkegaard's View of Humor: Must Christians Always Be Solemn," in *Kierkegaard on Faith and the Self* (Waco, Tex.: Baylor University Press, 2006), 81–92; Brad Frazier, *Rorty and Kierkegaard on Irony and Moral Commitment* (New York: Palgrave Macmillan, 2006); and Esolen, *Ironies of Faith*. For a reading of Plato skeptical of the very notion of irony, see Melissa Lane, "Reconsidering Socratic Irony," in *The Cambridge Companion to Socrates*, ed. Donald R. Morrison (Cambridge: Cambridge University Press, 2011), 237–59.

universe" but the "limitations to the human ability to understand."[30] The latter befits Pascal's use of irony.

From the sophisticated to the crass, skeptical and even nihilistic versions of irony abound in our culture. The most influential defender of irony, as a mood or posture befitting our age, is the philosopher Richard Rorty. He writes, "Once upon a time we felt a need to worship something which lay beyond the visible world . . . [and now we have arrived at] the point where we no longer worship anything, where we treat nothing as a quasi-divinity, where we treat everything—our language, our conscience, our community—as a product of time and chance." The result for Rorty is ironic detachment from what he calls our "final vocabulary," the language we use to talk about our ultimate aims and fundamental commitment. Encountering rival vocabularies and alternative systems of belief engenders "radical and continuing doubts" about one's own vocabulary.[31]

As we shall see, Pascal's account of irony is closer to that of Griswold's Socrates than it is to that of Rorty. From Socrates to Kierkegaard, irony has been construed in a rich and positive manner, not just as a figure of speech but as what Kierkegaard calls an "existential determination," or way of life. In *A Case for Irony*, the text of his Tanner Lectures in Human Values at Harvard University, the philosopher Jonathan Lear derives from Socrates and Kierkegaard a positive account of irony as essential to a good human life. Lear marvels at the fact that so much of what passes for commentary on Socratic irony has to do exclusively with the question of whether Socrates dissembles, whether he wears a mask of unknowing behind which lurks either certainty about important matters or skepticism, perhaps even nihilism. By contrast, Lear sees the function of Socratic irony in Plato's dialogues as aiming to move readers in "the direction of virtue."[32] As he puts it, "It is constitutive of human excellence that one develop a capacity for appropriately disrupting one's understanding of what excellence consists in. This is what it means to get the hang of it, the erotic uncanniness of

---

[30] Griswold, "Irony in the Platonic Dialogues," 99.

[31] Richard Rorty, *Contingency, Irony, and Solidarity* (Cambridge: Cambridge University Press, 1989), 73.

[32] Jonathan Lear, *A Case for Irony* (Cambridge, Mass.: Harvard University Press, 2011), xi. Lear notes that Kierkegaard's views shifted from an early conception of irony as infinite negation to a mature judgment that Socrates' whole existence was irony and that irony is a human excellence.

human existence."[33] Such disruption of one's pre-existing understanding of excellence opens the path to a recovery of a deeper and more adequate understanding, which is itself susceptible to further episodes of ironic disruption.

Lear sees Rorty's conception of irony, which entails "radical and continued doubts about one's final vocabulary," as symptomatic of modernity's weary skepticism. On Rorty's view, irony presupposes and fosters detachment from any set of ends or goals. Beyond the initial, perhaps disorienting, recognition of contingency, there is nothing especially disruptive about Rorty's irony. It is the smug and self-congratulatory irony of the liberal academic. By contrast, Lear supposes that irony is the capacity for ongoing disruption; irony involves "cultivating the experience of oneself as uncanny, out of joint."[34] This is not disruption for its own sake, a romantic celebration of the sublime, or a postmodern accentuation of discontinuity. Instead, irony involves both detachment and attachment; it is a "peculiar form of detachment from the social pretense," combined with a "more robust attachment to the ideal."[35] This is neither skepticism, which simply puts into question the social pretense, nor is it Descartes' methodical doubt that seeks systematically to put into question whatever is not utterly indubitable. There is both a putting into question of what one thought one understood up to this point and an orientation toward an as-yet-to-be articulated more adequate account of things. According to Lear, irony entails an enduring attachment to an ideal. This presupposes ongoing fidelity. As Kierkegaard trenchantly observes, "From the fact that irony is present, it does not follow that earnestness is excluded. That is something only assistant professors assume."[36]

---

[33] Lear, *Case for Irony*, 37.

[34] Lear, *Case for Irony*, 37. Making a similar point about the difference between Socratic and Kierkegaardian irony, on the one hand, and contemporary irony, on the other, David Walsh states that the "crucial characteristic of modern irony is that it holds back from the opening toward existence that [classical] irony invites." See Walsh, *The Modern Philosophical Revolution: The Luminosity of Existence* (New York: Cambridge University Press, 2008), 398.

[35] Lear, *Case for Irony*, 19. In his use of the term "pretense," Lear is not speaking pejoratively. He has in mind simply the conventional standards operative within a certain practice.

[36] Lear, *Case for Irony*, 19.

Another way to put the contrast with Rorty is to note that for Lear there is an erotic dimension to irony, which is characterized by a "longing to grasp," in a "pretense-transcending direction."[37] One might well call irony the capacity for transcendence, which combines negation with an upward trajectory. There can be no genuinely human life without irony, without an openness to putting into question fundamental suppositions concerning practices in which one is engaged. This is an important point. Irony might seem to target only those who unreflectively or hypocritically participate in a social practice. But they are precisely the sorts of folks who are unlikely to be capable of irony. Only someone who is deeply and reflectively committed to the ideals of a particular practice can be afflicted with irony.[38]

Pascal would concur with Lear's emphasis on the connection between irony and cognitive disruption; he would also agree that the disruption is not merely negative, that it includes an aspiration for transcendence, an erotic longing for understanding and happiness. But he might be skeptical about Lear's confidence that irony will give rise to recovery, to deeper insight. In an interview about the book, Lear notes the intimate connection between ironic disruption and anxiety, but he has little say about why we should experience hope, rather than merely anxiety, in the face of ironic experience. For Pascal, one of the great questions about philosophy concerns hope, the motivation to continue the quest in light of ever-deepening conundra about the human condition. It might well be the case that the psychic vertigo induced by irony could permanently destabilize the human soul or at least atrophy the power of the intellect. Pascal might wonder whether Lear's view is not inherently unstable and thus liable to degenerate into the irony of Rorty. That is precisely why Pascal speaks in much more blunt and disconcerting terms about the effects of irony, the upshot of which is vertiginous fear and the realization that man is a monster that passes all understanding.

Of course, for Pascal, the philosophical inducement of fearful wonder is not an end in itself. Instead, it is instrumental, functioning as a theological protreptic. But the theological use of irony raises at least two important questions. The first is whether irony is appropriate to

---

[37] Lear, *Case for Irony*, 20.
[38] See Alan D. Pichanick, "A Case for Irony: An Interview with Jonathan Lear," *Expositions* 6, no. 1 (2012): 1–8.

theological speech, which is proclaimed publicly for all and which is rooted in the claim that God is truthful, not deceptive. The second has to do with whether irony, even if appropriate in a theological mode, could ever have the vertiginous impact that Lear describes. After all, the life of faith is about holding fast to the truth of revealed teachings. As the entire tradition affirms, the gift of faith has a certitude that eclipses even that of natural knowledge.

A complete response to these objections will be provided in the chapters to follow on Pascal. For now, it suffices to note the relevance of the distinction between irony as active deception and irony as concealment or indirection. The God of Abraham is, as Scripture and Pascal attest, a hidden God, a God who even as he is active in history remains obscure and concealed. Even in the incarnation, Christ remains veiled in the flesh and is selective about to whom and under what conditions he manifests his divinity. After the resurrection, moreover, on the road to Emmaus he appears to his disciples "in another countenance," and they fail to recognize him even as he interprets Scripture for them (Luke 24:11-35). When they finally come to recognize him in the breaking of the bread, he immediately vanishes from their presence. Already at the time of Pascal, Erasmus had compared Socrates and Christ as Sileni, "figures hiding divine wisdom within unpromising exteriors."[39] Indeed, Scripture itself is a kind of Silenus, with both surface and depth meanings. Pascal calls Scripture a "cipher," requiring the presence of Christ and his grace to be read aright.

Moreover, there is a long Christian tradition of ecstasy and wondrous bafflement, not just as a prelude to the life of faith but also as an ongoing experience within it. Indeed, the entire tradition of icons highlights the way in which human agency is decentered in an encounter with the face of the icon. Instead of a rationalist and idolatrous distancing of the observer from the comprehended object of the gaze, vision here undergoes a reversal in which the achievement of the inquiring heart is realized precisely in a recognition of the distance between observer and observed and of the subversive process whereby the one seeking and looking finds himself discovered and beheld. As Jean-Luc Marion puts it:

---

[39] Screech, *Ecstasy and the Praise of Folly*, 35. Screech is glossing Erasmus' work *Sileni Alcibiadis*.

> Here our gaze becomes the optical mirror of that at which it looks only by finding itself more radically looked at: we become a visible mirror of an invisible gaze that subverts us in the measure of its glory.... Thus, as opposed to the idol, ... the icon displaces the limits of our visibility to the measure of its own—its glory. It transforms us in its glory by allowing this glory to shine on our face as its mirror.[40]

The experience of the divine through icons is a synecdoche for the Christian life. In underscoring the way that wonder is exacerbated in the life of faith, Pascal stands in the mainstream of the Christian tradition. His famous mystical experience in the "night of fire," captured in his famous "Memorial," which he kept with him throughout his life, is but one of many instances of faith-filled ecstasy.[41] From Augustine to Bernard, Thomas to Dante, and John of the Cross to Theresa of Avila, the experience of the shattering of our sense of self in the presence of the divine is common to the saints and mystics. Of course, there is a context for this experience: divine revelation, its teachings about human sin and redemption; its dogmatic assertions concerning God, creation, redemption, and resurrection; and its liturgical practices of worship. If the mode of revelation can be said to be ironic, the doctrines themselves are not ironic statements but illuminating truths. Theological irony, it would seem, is an indispensable but always subordinate and merely instrumental tool. But that is not quite right. Faith is not simply or even primarily a matter of belief in a set of propositions but rather or at least primarily a matter of faith in a personal God; thus, faith is inseparable from hope in and love for God. Our encounter with a transcendent, personal God involves an ongoing condition of amazement.

So, the link Griswold and Lear detect between irony and the question of the good life informs Pascal's thought as well. His apology has less in common with modern apologetics, in either its rationalist or fideist forms, and more in common with Socrates' apology, understood as a defense of a way of life. Pascal makes a distinctive contribution to the ancient debate over the best way of life. Approaching Pascal's thought through the pedagogy of irony and the question of the good life aids the reading of Pascal in numerous ways. The focus on irony sheds new light

---

[40] Jean-Luc Marion, *God without Being*, trans. Thomas A. Carlson (Chicago: University of Chicago Press, 1991), 22.

[41] See Pascal, *Pensées*, trans. Krailsheimer, xii and 913.

on irony itself, on Pascal, and on the relationship of faith and reason. First, the rehabilitation of a positive, pedagogical role for irony helps us to sort out not only defensive, negative, even cynical conceptions of irony from positive ones but also to sort out different applications of the term. The original notion of irony is as a figure of speech that deceives or at least conceals. In Aristotle's *Ethics*,[42] irony is a vice that violates the mean of truthfulness. Located at the opposite end of the spectrum from the excess of boastfulness, it marks a deficit, a practice of self-deprecation and self-belittlement, and an unwillingness to say all that one knows or to admit all that one is in terms of virtue. There is sufficient ambiguity in Aristotle's discussion to warrant the conclusion that the practice of ironic speech need not necessarily be vicious, since such dissembling would seem to be appropriate in speech of a superior to an inferior who is incapable of understanding the superior on his own terms.[43] Thus does the analysis of irony move from consideration of a figure of speech, through a habit or disposition, to a question of suitable rhetorical or pedagogical practice. It is a further step to construe irony, as Griswold does, as part of a protreptic in the turning of souls to the pursuit of the good life. Pascal, as we shall see, embraces this and develops it in rich and surprising ways as a means of construing the mode of divine speech in relation to mortal men. Second, the construal of the relationship of faith to reason in ironic terms, analogous to the ironic stance of philosophy in relation to ordinary life, constitutes a novel contribution both to the reading of Pascal and to the discussion of faith and reason. Neither in the literature on Pascal nor in the even vaster literature on faith and reason is there any sustained treatment of Christian irony. That may well be related to another neglected theme: the explication of faith and reason, theology and philosophy as ways of life.

---

[42] Aristotle, *Ethics* 1108^{a}23.

[43] On irony as a figure of speech and habit of character and for a careful analysis of the limited set of cases in which the term surfaces in Plato's dialogues, see Ronna Burger, "Socratic Eironia," *Interpretation*, 143–49. Burger shows that in each case in which Socrates is accused of irony, he is faulted for deliberate deceit, of masking an inner truth or knowledge that his surface speech or conduct belies. In each case, Socrates turns the tables on his accusers, demonstrating that they harbor hidden motives, especially motives of the desire for mastery, a desire that marks not so much their liberation from convention as their enslavement to it. Burger also has some astute observations about irony in Aristotle.

§3. The Figure of Socrates in Early Modern Philosophy: Montaigne, Descartes, and Pascal

As we have noted, Pascal's engagement of philosophy works on two levels. On one, he analyzes the claims of the various schools of philosophy concerning the nature of the good life and the means to its attainment. On another, as is clear from the discussion of the three orders and the passage quoted at the outset above, Pascal sometimes speaks of philosophy in the singular. In the latter case, he is interested in a version of Strauss' question, whether the guidance of reason, however embodied, is sufficient for the good life. With regard to that topic, the philosophers speak with one voice. Pascal's supple understanding of philosophy has been mostly neglected in contemporary accounts, in part because his teleological language has been overlooked and in part because the centrality to his project of the Socratic question has been ignored. Before Pascal, Montaigne and Descartes invoke Socrates as they take aim at the pretenders to the name of philosophy; in castigating the professional philosophers of their time, they present Socrates as a counterexample.[44] As we shall see in the next two chapters, both recur to Socrates as the standard by which other claimants to philosophy are to be judged. The difference between the two approaches to Socrates is that Montaigne thinks of Socrates as an insuperable exemplar, while Descartes treats him as the figure to be surpassed. Yet both are doing something new with Socrates.

---

[44] On Pascal and his predecessors, see B. Jean and F. Mouret, *Montaigne, Descartes et Pascal* (Manchester: Manchester University Press, 1971); Henry Phillips, "Pascal's Reading and the Inheritance of Montaigne and Descartes," in *The Cambridge Companion to Pascal*, ed. Nicholas Hammond (Cambridge: Cambridge University Press, 2003), 20–39; Léon Brunschvicg, *Descartes et Pascal lecteurs de Montaigne* (Neuchâtel: A la Baconnière, 1942); Frank Chambers, "Pascal's Montaigne," *PMLA* 65, no. 5 (1950): 790–804; K. Christodoulou, "Socrate chez Montaigne et Pascal," *Diotima: Review of Philosophical Research* 7 (1979): 39–50; Graeme Hunter, "Motion and Rest in the *Pensées*: A Note on Pascal's Modernism," *International Journal for Philosophy of Religion* 47, no. 2 (2000): 87–99; Vlad Alexandrescu, "Descartes and Pascal on the Eucharist," *Perspectives on Science* 15, no. 4 (2007): 434–49; Roger Ariew, "Descartes and Pascal," *Perspectives on Science* 15, no. 4 (2007): 397–409; Vincent Carraud, "Pascal's Anti-Augustinianism," *Perspectives on Science* 15, no. 4 (2007): 450–92; and Douglas Michael Jesseph, "Descartes, Pascal, and the Epistemology of Mathematics: The Case of the Cycloid," *Perspectives on Science* 15, no. 4 (2007): 410–33.

Montaigne praises Socrates for his exemplary life, his union of contemplation and action, and his unending quest for self-knowledge.[45] The problem, as Montaigne sees it, is that, after Socrates, philosophers try to advance beyond his learned ignorance; they attempt to solve the problems of philosophy, to answer the highest questions, and thus they expose philosophy as a failed project. But this is only because the original Socratic self-understanding has been lost.

For Montaigne, the philosophical life is essentially zetetic, a matter of understanding the problems rather than resolving them. It involves an ever-deepening realization that one does not know. Far from undermining the philosophical life, the paradoxes inherent in the pursuit of the good life confirm its value. Precisely because the question of the best way of life is not resolvable in any peremptory fashion, asking after the best way of life is the best way of life. The true philosopher, who loves but does not possess wisdom, is committed to the view that this pursuit constitutes the best way of life available to the human soul.

Still, Montaigne's Socrates is a fictional construct, much more attuned than is Plato's Socrates to the insuperable lack of unity, the sheer flux of experience, and the irreducible singularity of each individual life. Thus, Montaigne's reflections evince the limits of philosophy, the way in which it too can be an evasion of an honest accounting of human life. Wisdom itself is no longer a transcendent ideal but rather an immanent achievement, an accommodation to the limits of the human condition. To his particular way of reviving Socrates corresponds an

---

[45] On Montaigne and Socrates, see Raphael Arteau-McNeil, "L'apologie de Raymond Sebond: Ignorance, savoir et confiance," *De Philosophia* 17, no. 1 (2001): 13–32; Azar Filho, "Montaigne e Sócrates: Cepticismo, conhecimento e virtude," *Revista Portuguesa de Filosofia* 58, no. 4 (2002): 829–45; Christodoulou, "Socrate chez Montaigne et Pascal," 39–50; Nehemas, *Art of Living*, contains an entire chapter on Montaigne and Socrates; James Hans, "Alexander Nehamas and *The Art of Living*," *Philosophy Today* 44, no. 2 (2000): 190–205; Timothy Hampton, "Montaigne and the Body of Socrates: Narrative and Exemplarity in the *Essais*," *Modern Language Notes* 104, no. 4 (1989): 880–98; Margaret McGowan, *Montaigne's Deceits: The Art of Persuasion in the "Essais"* (London: Hodder & Stoughton, 1974); Ann Hartle, *Michel de Montaigne: Accidental Philosopher* (New York: Cambridge University Press, 2003); David Schaefer, "Montaigne's Intention and His Rhetoric," *Interpretation: A Journal of Political Philosophy* 5 (1975): 57–90; idem, *The Political Philosophy of Montaigne* (Ithaca, N.Y.: Cornell University Press, 1991); and Lawrence D. Kritzman, "The Socratic Makeover: Montaigne's 'De la physionomie' and the Ethics of the Impossible," *L'Esprit Createur* 46, no. 1 (2006): 75–85.

art of writing, operating through indirection, contradiction, and irony. Montaigne replaces the inquiries of the dialogues into a specific set of philosophical problems with an autobiographical essay, a series of tests or trials of the self. The result of these tests is a suspicion about the claims of philosophical/spiritual exercises to effect that which they promise. Montaigne's allusions to Socrates, which increase exponentially with each new edition of the *Essays*, provide him with a suitable means, as Hugo Friedrich puts it, of "describing himself."[46] Montaigne does not go beyond Socrates in the sense of trying to complete or transcend him. But he does differ from Socrates: in his willingness to criticize not just received opinions of the many and the wise, but the philosophical life itself; in his focus on himself, rather than on philosophical puzzles; and especially in his curtailing of the longing for transcendence. As Pierre Manent shows in his recent book on Montaigne, the novelty of the project has to do with envisioning human life apart from, independent of, any standard, external or internal, divine, natural, or human. As Manent puts it, "life without law."[47]

If the prominence of Socrates in Montaigne's writings is apparent, his significance for Descartes is much less obvious.[48] Yet, in his brief discussion of the history of philosophy in the preface to the *Principles of Philosophy*, Descartes sets Socrates and Plato in opposition to the entire tradition of philosophy. Following his teacher Socrates, Plato admitted his ignorance, his uncertainty, about the most important questions. Plato "ingenuously confessed that he had never yet been able to discover anything certain."[49] With Aristotle, who duplicitously asserted

---

[46] Hugo Friedrich, *Montaigne*, ed. Philippe Desan, trans. Dawn Eng (Berkeley: University of California Press, 1991), 52. For a summary, and assessment, of the literature on the various ancient sources of Montaigne's presentation of Socrates, see Nehemas, *Art of Living*, 101–9.

[47] "*La vie sans loi.*" Pierre Manent, *Montaigne la vie sans loi* (Paris: Flammarion, 2015).

[48] On Descartes and Socrates, see Gail Fine, "Descartes and Ancient Skepticism: Reheated Cabbage?" *Philosophical Review* 109, no. 2 (2000): 195–234. Zahi Zalloua, "Montaigne, Skepticism and Immortality," *Philosophy and Literature* 27, no. 1 (2003): 40–61. Ann Hartle, *Death and the Disinterested Spectator: An Inquiry into the Nature of Philosophy* (Albany: State University of New York Press, 1986). Catherine Osborne, "Successors of Socrates, Disciples of Descartes, and Followers of Freud," *Apeiron: A Journal for Ancient Philosophy and Science* 34, no. 2 (2001): 181–93. Roger Wertheimer, "Socratic Scepticism," *Metaphilosophy* 24, no. 4 (1993): 344–62.

[49] Descartes, preface to the *Principles of Philosophy*, in *Philosophical Writings*, 1:181.

that he had answers to the most important philosophical questions, philosophy took a wrong turn from which it has yet to recover. The return to Socrates, however, is insufficient. Descartes wants not the love of wisdom but its possession. The recovery of Socrates is but a prelude to the surpassing of Socrates.

A similar, although implicit, acknowledgment of Socrates can be found in a key passage in Descartes' *Discourse on Method*, the point at which he concludes his summary of what his education afforded him: "I found myself beset by so many doubts and errors that I came to think I had gained nothing from my attempts to become educated by increasing recognition of my ignorance."[50] Of course, this is the Socratic insight, the one beyond which Socrates was unable to move. Descartes' goal is to go beyond the recognition of ignorance and achieve knowledge, to turn the pursuit or love of wisdom into its possession. Descartes' systematic method is designed not just to discover truths but to habituate the soul of the inquirer so that it is increasingly able to rise from opinion to knowledge, from wonder to wisdom. A subtle critique of the limits and danger of Socratic philosophy is evident in Descartes' discourse *The Passions of the Soul*, in which he counsels against excessive wonder, what he calls astonishment, a passion that keeps us from moving beyond wonder to knowledge. A vice of excess, "astonishment" is a rapture of the soul in which the "whole body remains as immobile as a statue."[51] The image calls to mind Plato's depiction of Socrates as caught up in, immobilized by, philosophical wonder in the midst of the active lives of his fellow citizens.[52] Descartes' counsel to overcome wonder is, in the language we have already introduced from Jonathan Lear, an attempt to eliminate irony as a virtuous condition of soul. In contrast to Lear, Descartes sees the cultivation of "the experience of oneself as uncanny, out of joint," not as a condition of the good life but as an obstacle to it.

Descartes detects in this classical, philosophical way of life neither certainty nor utility, neither the knowledge at which philosophy aims nor any great benefit to human life. He deems his own education, which issues in the awareness of his own ignorance, a thoroughgoing

---

[50] Descartes, *Discourse on Method*, in *Philosophical Writings*, 1:113.
[51] Descartes, *On the Passions*, in *Philosophical Writings*, 1:354.
[52] See Plato, *The Symposium*, in *The Dialogues of Plato*, trans. Benjamin Jowett (Chicago: Encyclopaedia Britannica, 1952), 150.

disappointment. Thus, he seeks to discover a method that would supply both. The very intractability of intellectual problems in the inherited tradition motivates Descartes to pursue another path. The most interesting query facing the reader of Descartes concerns the connection between his philosophical method and his account of the sovereign good, the latter of which consists in a kind of contentment of soul. Virtue consists in judging rightly and then executing resolutely on the basis of judgment.[53] As we shall see in a subsequent chapter, Descartes' writings exhibit a striking unity of purpose, the fundamental goal of which is an articulation and defense of the self-sufficiency of the philosophical life. They also exhibit some of the characteristics of ironic composition.[54]

Now, for Pascal, Socrates is an equally important figure. In a telling autobiographical remark about his conversion from physical science to the study of the human things, Pascal mimics Socrates' own conversion:

> I spent a long time studying abstract sciences, and I was put off them by seeing how little one could communicate about them. When I began the study of man I saw that these abstract sciences are not proper to man, and that I was straying further from my true condition by going into them than were others by being ignorant of them.... I thought I should... find many companions in my study of man, since it is his true and proper study. I was wrong. Even fewer people study man than mathematics. It is only because they do not know how to study man that people look into all the rest. (687)[55]

---

[53] In the *Principles of Philosophy*, he offers a unified account of the "pure and genuine virtues, which proceed solely from knowledge of what is right," which have "one and the same nature," and which "are included under the single term 'wisdom.'" Descartes, *Philosophical Writings*, 1:191.

[54] See, for example, Richard Kennington, "Descartes," in *History of Political Philosophy*, ed. Leo Strauss and Joseph Crospey, 2nd ed. (Chicago: University of Chicago Press, 1981).

[55] "*J'avais passé longtemps dans l'étude des sciences abstraites; et le peu de communication qu'on en peut avoir m'en avait dégoûté. Quand j'ai commencé l'étude de l'homme, j'ai vu que ces sciences abstraites ne sont pas propres à l'homme, et que je m'égarais plus de ma condition en y pénétrant que les autres en les ignorant. J'ai pardonné aux autres d'y peu savoir. Mais j'ai cru trouver au moins bien des compagnons en l'étude de l'homme et que c'est la vraie étude qui lui est propre. J'ai été trompé; il y en a encore moins qui l'étudient que la géométrie. Ce n'est que manque de savoir étudier cela qu'on cherche le reste*" (144). On the various strands in this tradition of the turn, see Walter Nicgorski, "Cicero's Socrates: Assessment of the 'Socratic Turn,'" in *Law and Philosophy: The Practice of Theory*, ed. J. Murley, R. Stone, and

Philosophy, which is about matters nearest and most significant to us, is surprisingly the least pursued. If Pascal embraces Socrates' sense of the source and subject matter of philosophy, he also affirms Socrates' (and Montaigne's) insistence that philosophy is about an ever-increasing awareness of the limitations to human knowledge. Echoing Socrates, he writes:

> Knowledge has two extremes which meet; one is the pure natural ignorance [*la pure ignorance naturelle*] of every man at birth, the other is the extreme reached by great minds who run through the whole range of human knowledge, only to find that they know nothing and come back to the same ignorance from which they set out [*trouvent qu'ils ne savent rien et se rencontrent en cette même ignorance d'où ils étaient partis*], but it is a wise ignorance which knows itself. (83)

The paradoxical note here signals not so much a repudiation of reason as a deepening of self-knowledge. The passages in Pascal most critical of reason are all intended to foster in readers a sense of their own wretchedness. But wretchedness itself is inexplicable without a concomitant apprehension of greatness. Conversely, the accent on human life as a quest for the good necessitates an account of the cultivation of reason. One might speak here of Pascal's ethics of thought, "All our dignity consists in thought.... Let us then strive then to think well; that is the basic principle of morality" (200).[56] Pascal is not celebrating a model of disengaged reason, about which so much has been made in the literature on modernity. Instead, Pascal insists that thinking well has much to do with the reorientation of our passions in light of a rationally discerned conception of the good, however dimly and fleetingly that good may be apprehended. Even if contemporary commentators might want to locate Pascal on one side of the dividing line between a premodern belief in the intelligibility of nature and its modern repudiation, it is clear that he couches his ethics of thought within a teleological

---

W. Braithwaite (Athens: Ohio University Press, 1992), 1:213–33. Nicgorski argues that both Plato and Cicero had reservations about the turn, about what they took to be its chief consequence: a parochial and exclusively practical conception of philosophy. Nicgorski attempts to provide "what one might call a metaphysics of the Socratic turn that clearly shows Socratic moral questions opening to and entailed with ultimate questions" (233).

[56] *Toute notre dignité consiste donc en la pensée.... Travaillons donc à bien penser: voilà le principe de la morale.* (347).

context. In Augustinian language, he writes, "Man is obviously made for thinking. . . . The proper order of thought is to begin with ourselves, and with our author and our end [*l'ordre de la pensée est de commencer par soi, et par son auteur et sa fin*]" (620).

One of the longest fragments of the *Pensées*, "Against Indifference," urges upon every human being the task of seeking for knowledge concerning his nature, his condition, and his ultimate destiny. Pascal bases this argument on assumptions concerning human dignity and self-interest. Indeed, he goes out of his way to insist that the shape of human life as a quest is evident not from principles of piety but from ordinary human reason. To see this, he says, we need "only see what the least enlightened see." Philosophy would seem to function as a salutary corrective to the forgetful way in which most human beings pass their lives. It raises, in a serious way, questions about serious matters, and it initiates the search for answers. It exhibits the nature of human life as a search concerning its end, telos, or destiny. There is an overlap here with the Socrates of the *Phaedo*, who in the face of uncertainty about what, if anything, comes after death continues to examine the arguments concerning the soul and immortality. In his study of the text, Hans-Georg Gadamer argues that the entire discussion of the soul and its immortality is framed by the threat posed by developments in the physical sciences to religious belief in immortality:[57]

> Plato certainly does not want to say that he has proved the same immortality of the soul which is basic to the religious tradition. But what he does want to say is that the spreading skepticism resulting from the scientific enlightenment does not at all affect the sphere of our human life and our understanding of it. The growing scientific insight into the causes of coming-into-being and passing-away, into the course of natural processes, does not obviate the need for thinking beyond the reality of this world, and it has no authority to contest religious convictions.[58]

This has similarities to Pascal's own project. Moreover, Pascal would concur with Gadamer's reading of the *Phaedo*, according to which the

---

[57] Hans-Georg Gadamer, "The Proofs of Immortality in Plato's *Phaedo*," in *Dialogue and Dialectic: Eight Hermeneutical Studies on Plato*, trans. P. Christopher Smith (New Haven, Conn.: Yale University Press, 1980), 21–28.

[58] Gadamer, "Proofs of Immortality in Plato's *Phaedo*," 37.

attempt to allay "our fear of death is never completed."[59] Precisely because the arguments are inconclusive and because death is imminent, Socrates proposes that we act on the hypothesis that is at once probable and most noble. He thus urges a kind of wager on immortality that would inform how we live here and now.

We should notice here the prominence of the notion of an end to be desired, a true and sovereign good to which human beings naturally incline. Although Pascal accuses the philosophers of taking a part of the human good and exaggerating it to the detriment of other parts, he sometimes speaks of philosophers as approaching nearer to the complete truth, even if the proximity leaves them with a perplexity rather than an answer:

> Some seek their good in authority, some in intellectual inquiry, some in pleasure.
>
> Others again, who have indeed come closer to it, have found it impossible that this universal good, desired by all men, should lie in any of the particular objects which can only be possessed by one individual and which, once shared, cause their possessors more grief over the part they lack than satisfaction over the part they enjoy as their own. They have realized that the true good must be such that it may be possessed by all men at once without diminution or envy, and that no one should be able to lose it against his will. Their reason is that this desire is natural to man, since all men inevitably feel it, and man cannot be without it, and they therefore conclude.... (148)[60]

Philosophy is left with a tantalizing question, a frustrating aporia. Even as he reveals the failure of philosophy, Pascal engages it dialectically on its own terms. In this respect, Pascal might be said to restore to Socratic philosophy the central role of erotic longing for wisdom and

---

[59] Gadamer, "Proofs of Immortality in Plato's *Phaedo*," 37.

[60] *Les uns le cherchent dans l'autorité, les autres dans les curiosités et* [var. ed.: *dans*] *les sciences, les autres dans les voluptés. D'autres, qui en ont en effet plus approché, ont considéré qu'il est nécessaire que le bien universel, que tous les hommes désirent, ne soit dans aucune des choses particulières qui ne peuvent être possédées que par un seul, et qui, étant partagées, affligent plus leur possesseur, par le manque de la partie qu'il n'a pas* [var. ed.: *qu'ils n'ont pas*], *qu'elles ne le contentent par la jouissance de celle qui lui appartient. Ils ont compris que le vrai bien devait être tel que tous pussent le posséder à la fois, sans diminution et sans envie, et que personne ne le dût* [var. ed.: *pût*] *perdre contre son gré. Et leur raison est que ce désir étant naturel à l'homme puisqu'il est nécessairement dans tous, et qu'il ne peut pas ne le pas avoir, ils en concluent . . .* (425).

happiness, both of which exceed its grasp. Yet, the restoration involves reassessment: seemingly insoluble questions about the good are not contemplated with detached pleasure but with growing unease, with the painful realization that the deepest longing of the heart appears subject to violent and tragic frustration.

Philosophy, the pursuit of wisdom about our condition, functions, according to Pascal, as a protreptic. Yet, when it goes beyond initiation and tries to deliver answers to the questions that afflict the human heart, it exceeds its capacity, even if the pursuit of truth is its very telos. In this, Pascal parts not only with Descartes but also with Montaigne, who supposes that the cultivation of Socratic ignorance is sufficient. For Pascal, this is to curtail the natural telos of philosophy, its orientation toward wisdom and happiness. Such a telos remains unrealized in the discursive activity of questioning. The very activity of inquiry becomes distorted if its goal-directed character, whose primary intention is to know the truth, is replaced with the counsel to be content with the questions themselves.

Pascal's ambivalence toward philosophy surfaces repeatedly. In an early fragment, entitled "Letter to Induce Men to Seek God," Pascal urges, "Then make them look for him among the philosophers, sceptics and dogmatists, who will worry the man who seeks" (4).[61] Given other passages in which Pascal commends to all rational animals the quest for answers to life's most important matters, he cannot here be attempting to undermine the quest. The philosophers are a source of weariness not because they pursue the quest but because the most gifted and most capable minds fail to answer the great questions or claim to have answered them without actually having done so.

For the Socratic philosopher, the opinions of the many provide the dialectical starting points of philosophical inquiry. Although the philosopher investigates the adequacy of these opinions and seeks to move from what is immediately accessible to us to what is most knowable in itself, the dialectic between opinion and knowledge is never completely overcome. The philosopher seeks to refine ordinary language but not to eradicate it. Instead, the shared world of ordinary experience and language endures as the source of philosophy and as that which it aspires to understand. Like the philosophers, Pascal wants to move beyond

---

[61] *Et puis le faire chercher chez les philosophes, pyrrhoniens et dogmatistes, qui travaillent celui qui les recherche* ("Lettre pour porter à rechercher Dieu," 184).

unreflective common sense; conversely, he finds merit in the common sense resistance to philosophy. Here Pascal echoes Montaigne, himself a follower of Socrates. By contrast, Descartes' eagerness to eliminate from philosophical inquiry the influence of ordinary language and common experience signals a radical break from the tradition of philosophy.

Pascal's attacks on Descartes aim to restore Socratic ignorance and to exacerbate the sense that philosophy itself is forlorn, bereft of hope for the thing it most desires. In the face of an incomprehensible natural order, of lingering doubts about human knowledge, and of the mysteries of soul and body, Pascal leads the would-be Cartesian to an experience not of calming certitude but of baffling wonder. Pascal shares with Descartes an appreciation of the power of modern mathematics; indeed, as Matthew Jones has shown, both philosophers envision mathematical investigation as a kind of spiritual exercise capable of transforming the soul of the practitioner. Whereas Descartes sees in mathematics a clue to the methodical resolution of important questions, Pascal thinks that the new discoveries should "unsettle rarely interrogated beliefs about human nature." The result is not the celebration of reason's command but a heightened sense of its limits. Wonder becomes a "permanent affective state," the goal of which is to abase reason "without ever abandoning it."[62] Another way to describe Pascal's method here is as an ironic reflection on the Cartesian embrace of mathematics as a vehicle of certitude and utility. Pascal embraces it too but only to reverse it; rather than overcoming wonder, mathematics renders us more baffled than we were before we studied it.[63]

The greatest mystery is the human person: "What sort of freak then is man! . . . Judge of all things, feeble earthworm, repository of truth, sink of doubt and error, glory and refuse of the universe. . . . Man transcends man" (131).[64] After listing the inexplicable contradictions characteristic of the human condition, Pascal states, "I go on

---

[62] Jones, *Good Life in the Scientific Revolution*, 133 and 162.

[63] On this, see Tamás Pavlovits, "Admiration, Fear, and Infinity in Pascal's Thinking," in *Philosophy Begins in Wonder: An Introduction to Early Modern Philosophy, Theology, and Science*, ed. Michael Funk Deckard and Péter Losonczi (Eugene, Ore.: Pickwick, 2010), 119–26.

[64] *Quelle chimère est-ce donc que l'homme. . . . Juge de toutes choses, imbécile ver de terre, dépositaire du vrai, cloaque d'incertitude et d'erreur: gloire et rebut de l'univers. . . . L'homme passe l'homme* (434).

contradicting him until he understands that he is a monster that passes all understanding" (130). Instead of treating it as a vice capable of being eliminated by the cultivation of reason, astonishment for Pascal marks the peak experience of philosophy. In its engagement of both the few and the many, Christianity redoubles and exacerbates the incommensurable and stupefying gap between philosophers and ordinary folks: "Philosophers astonish ordinary people. Christians astonish philosophers" (613). The uncanniness of human existence pervades Pascal's philosophical reflection on the human condition. But then "uncanniness" is too mild a word for the experience of the monstrous character of human existence. Pascal urges his interlocutors to begin a quest, but the more progress one makes, the less one knows and the more disconcerting and agonizing the search becomes.

Here we confront the paradox of reason in Pascal; indeed, Pascal is prone, in his compelling observations about reason, to use paradoxical and tragic language. The human person is a "thinking reed," a "dispossessed king." His nobility, rooted in his ability to think, to know himself and his condition, consists in the paradoxical capacity to know that he is wretched. But the paradox is even deeper than this. On the one hand, Pascal states that, once this fine reason was destroyed, it destroyed everything, that reason is able to determine nothing, that the quest reveals only darkness and obscurity. On the other, Pascal insists that our dignity consists in thought, that we can know that we are wretched, that is, that we have inexplicably lost what is proper to us, and that reason judges that there are cases when it ought to submit, that is, that it does not submit in an arbitrary and blind way. Abdication is an act of sovereignty.[65]

The affirmation of the paradoxical character of the human condition recalls Montaigne, whose situating of man between angel and beast becomes a leitmotif of Pascal's thought. But as is the case in his engagement with Descartes, so too with Montaigne Pascal seeks to exacerbate the tensions rather than to assuage them. Precisely on the question of diversion, which Montaigne sees as a useful strategy for fending off all sorts of threats to equanimity, is Pascal's distance from Montaigne evident. Diversion, for Pascal, is the clearest sign of the disordered soul; it discloses the tragedy of the human condition, the inexorable desire for happiness, whose achievement constantly eludes our grasp. Pascal

---

[65] I am indebted to Pierre Manent for this nice formulation.

embraces Montaigne's digressive style as befitting the impossibility of bringing the protean self, the *ego cogito*, into view in any systematic or transparent manner. Yet he goes even further than Montaigne in questioning the unity of the self, whose splintering is mirrored in Pascal's own fragmentary, aphoristic style, a manner of writing even less unified than that of Montaigne. Yet the cumulative effect of Pascal's fragments is to construct a kind of theater of the human condition, in which individuals might recognize themselves, confront the disorder of their lives, and begin a quest for wisdom and happiness.[66] The theatrical dialogue of souls, which emerges from so many of the fragments, retains only a slight connection to the Platonic dialogue. As is true of Montaigne and Descartes, so too for Pascal the styles and genres in which his thought is embodied are novel.

What is striking about Pascal's embrace of Socrates is not just his affirmation of Socratic ignorance as the mark of philosophy but also his sophisticated appreciation of the pedagogical role of irony. Ironic pedagogy is designed in part to force upon an interlocutor a self-awareness that he would otherwise lack, an awareness of his own ignorance, of where he stands with regard to the pursuit of truth, of whether and to what extent he is equipped to pursue a particular line of inquiry. Instead of marching forward, confident in one's understanding and one's capacities, irony counsels a retreat. Irony is also a pedagogical tool that protects philosophy from the uninitiated, the incapable, and those who, if they understood it, would be deeply hostile to it.[67]

---

[66] On this, see Vincent Carraud, *Pascal et la philosophie* (Paris: Presses universitaires de France, 1992), 400: Pascal offers *"une mise en scene, un spectable, un théâtre de l'égarement. L'égarement est fondamentalement ce qui, de l'homme, se donne à voir."* One might call this the tragic theater of Pascal. On this, see Lucien Goldmann, *The Hidden God: A Study of Tragic Vision in the "Pensées" of Pascal and the Tragedies of Racine* (London: Routledge & Kegan Paul, 1964). Although, as we shall see, Goldmann's interpretation of Pascal and tragedy is a fertile resource for uncovering Pascal's view of philosophy, it is inadequate to the whole of Pascal's thought. Also see Leszek Kołakowski, *God Owes Us Nothing: A Brief Remark on Pascal's Religion and on the Spirit of Jansenism* (Chicago: University of Chicago Press, 1998).

[67] In this context, we might advert to Leo Strauss' understanding of irony as a "noble dissimulation of one's worth, of one's superiority." Irony is the "humanity peculiar to the superior man," who "spares the feelings of his inferiors by not displaying his superiority." Strauss adds, "If irony is essentially related to the fact that there is an order of rank among men, it follows that irony consists in speaking

§4. Divine Irony as an Alternative to Deism and Voluntarism

Commentators on Plato have noted that concealment is an essential component in irony. As Nehemas in particular has argued, concealment can constitute a path intermediate "between lying and truthfulness." It "shares features with both: like truthfulness, concealment does not distort the truth; like lying, it does not reveal it."[68] That fits with Pascal's account of divine pedagogy. As he repeatedly insists, God is hidden. Pascal speaks of the "boldness" of those who attempt to appeal to "works of nature" in an effort to move unbelievers from doubt to belief. The problem is not in nature but in us, at least in those of us who have not received grace, "those in whom this light has gone out and in whom we are trying to rekindle it, people deprived of faith and grace, examining with such light as they have everything they see in nature that might lead them to this knowledge, but finding only obscurity and darkness" (781).[69] Such an approach will give unbelievers "cause to think that the proofs of our religion are indeed feeble" (781).[70] Pascal prefers to use the language of Scripture, which states that God is a hidden God, and since nature was corrupted he has left men to their blindness, from which they can escape only through Jesus Christ. Pascal does not deny that the evidence is there in nature, but only that, without grace, we lack the requisite capacity to see it. By comparison, "those living with faith in their hearts can certainly see at once that everything which exists is entirely the work of the God they worship" (781). So, divine pedagogy, an ironic pedagogy, is designed precisely to include and to

---

differently to different kinds of people." Strauss, *The City and Man* (Chicago: University of Chicago Press, 1964), 51.

[68] Nehemas is taking issue with Vlastos' thesis (*Socrates*) that irony involves saying what one means by saying something directly contrary to it. In this way, someone alert to the irony can quite readily pick up the truth intended. Vlastos seems to think that anything else would be a form of lying. See Nehemas, *Art of Living*, 43–62. Griswold follows Nehemas here.

[69] *Mais pour ceux en qui cette lumière s'est éteinte, et dans lesquels on a dessein de la faire revivre, ces personnes destituées de foi et de grâce, qui recherchant de toute leur lumière tout ce qu'ils voient dans la nature qui les peut mener à cette connaissance, ne trouvent qu'obscurité et ténèbres* (242).

[70] *C'est leur donner sujet de croire que les preuves de notre religion sont bien faibles* (242).

exclude. As David Walsh comments, this form of irony intends not to entrap others or mock them but to "draw them out."[71]

Far from marking a tragic impasse in the human progress toward the divine, the insistence on divine hiddenness, on God at once present and absent, has a precise pedagogical and medicinal function in divine providence. It allows for the possibility that we can know God as redeemer. "It was . . . not right that [Christ] should appear in a manner manifestly divine and absolutely capable of convincing all men, but neither was it right that his coming should be so hidden that he could not be recognized by those who sincerely sought him" (149).[72] In the incarnation, Mesnard writes, God "dissimulated his divinity under a veil."[73] The incarnation is perhaps the chief example of the irony that characterizes divine pedagogy. As we look up to the heavens or contemplate the attributes of a transcendent being, he appears in our midst as an individual human being, born at a particular time and place in a little-known part of the world, occupies no public office, and leaves no writings behind. The scandal of particularity is a surprise and an affront to the philosophical approach to God.

The proper recognition of God as mediator presupposes certain dispositions on the part of the agent, a precedent acknowledgment of our own wretchedness and need for grace (189–91). In our fallen state, we vacillate between pride and despair. Knowing God merely as God and not as redeemer only exacerbates this condition, as it engenders the proud assumption that we have attained God by our own powers. True knowledge of God is inseparable from self-knowledge, a recognition of our own wretchedness. Yet true knowledge must not leave us despairing over our condition; it must offer the hope of a cure. "Knowing God without knowing our own wretchedness makes for pride. Knowing our own wretchedness without knowing God makes for despair. Knowing Christ strikes the balance because he shows us both God and our own wretchedness" (192).[74] The religion of a humiliated, crucified God—inconceivable

---

[71] Walsh, *The Modern Philosophical Revolution*, 447.

[72] *Il n'était donc pas juste qu'il parût d'une manière manifestement divine, et absolument capable de convaincre tous les hommes; mais il n'était pas juste aussi qu'il vînt d'une manière si cachée, qu'il ne pût être reconnu de ceux qui le chercheraient sincèrement* (430).

[73] Mesnard, *Pascal*, 78.

[74] *La connaissance de Dieu sans celle de sa misère fait l'orgueil. La connaissance de sa misère sans celle de Dieu fait le désespoir. La connaissance de JésusChrist fait le milieu, parce que nous y trouvons et Dieu et notre misère* (527).

to natural reason—explains the paradoxes of human nature. As Pascal writes of figurative statements in the Old Testament, a "figure includes absence and presence" (265),[75] but "once the secret" to the deciphering of the figure is revealed, "it is impossible not to see it" (267).[76] As Esolen remarks, God "swindles man into his restoration. He dupes man into the truth. He became flesh, to raise man to himself."[77] The truths of Christianity are not propositions that can be detached from a way of life that takes its bearings from the comprehensive narrative of creation, fall, and redemption. As Walsh observes, "Christian truth cannot be demonstrated because it can only be lived."[78] Ironic pedagogy is intimately linked to the notion of the pursuit of wisdom as a way of life.

Socrates' willingness to play along with those who claim to know allows for the initial formulation of philosophical problems; failure to make progress underscores the inability of certain character types to make progress in the pursuit of knowledge. Socrates' interlocutors find his irony painful, frustrating, and embarrassing, even as observers find it humorous and potentially liberating.[79] The clash between what is purportedly known and actually known is central to the dramatic action of Plato's dialogues. Irony involves a disjunction between planes or levels of awareness.

Irony, reflective of cognitive disparity, is woven into Pascal's teaching on the three orders: body, mind, and spirit. Although ranked in a hierarchy, the three orders are different in kind. The lower knows nothing of the higher and provides no access to what is above. "The greatness of intellectual people is not visible to kings, rich men, captains, who are all great in a carnal sense. The greatness of wisdom, which is nothing if it does not come from God, is not visible to carnal or intellectual people" (308).[80] Pascal underscores the incommensura-

---

[75] *Figure porte absence et présence, plaisir et déplaisir. Chiffre à double sens: un clair et où il est dit que le sens est caché* (677).

[76] *Dès qu'une fois on a ouvert ce secret il est impossible de ne le pas voir* (680).

[77] Esolen, *Ironies of Faith*, 27.

[78] Walsh, *The Modern Philosophical Revolution*, 447.

[79] The danger for readers, of course, is that while we note the various cognitive failures and ethical lapses of some of Socrates' interlocutors, we fail to attend to our own.

[80] *La grandeur des gens d'esprit est invisible aux rois, aux riches, aux capitaines, à tous ces gens de chair. La grandeur de la sagesse, qui n'est nulle sinon de Dieu, est invisible aux charnels et aux gens d'esprit* (793).

bility of the orders in unrestrained hyperbole: "The infinite distance between body and mind symbolizes the infinitely more infinite distance between mind and charity, for charity is supernatural" (308).[81] Here there emerges a hierarchy of wonder or bafflement, of wisdom mistaken for folly.[82]

The irony of the philosopher in relation to the rest of humanity is redoubled in the irony God exhibits toward the philosopher. The lowliness of the philosopher, exemplified in Socrates' uncomely physical appearance, his lack of public office, wealth, and political honor—all this renders him a comic absurdity to the common citizen. Of course, when he proceeds to unveil the superficial trappings of the lives of those deemed honorable by the standards of society, he is no longer laughable but threatening. Similarly, God's revealing of the life of wisdom to the lowly, to the foolish of this world, startles both those deemed honorable by worldly criteria and the philosophers. The philosopher, confident in his own way of life, is apt to be deceived by appearances; he is likely to equate the Christian religion with the sub- or pre- or merely protorational myths of classical paganism. In the case of Christianity, what seems lower is in fact higher. There is a note of comic reversal here. Such a reversal of expectation is also evident in the mode of revelation of the doctrine of original sin, the doctrine that explains the paradoxical duality of the human condition. Pascal writes, "God . . . hid the

---

[81] *La distance infinie des corps aux esprits figure la distance infiniment plus infinie des esprits à la charité, car elle est surnaturelle* (793).

[82] The rational satisfaction of the inquiry into the truth about man can be seen only from above and in retrospect; there is no possibility of a smooth transition or ascent from body to mind or from either of these to charity. As Jean-Luc Marion puts it in *On Descartes' Metaphysical Prism*, "In the course of descending the hierarchy . . . continuity is reestablished, since the superior order evaluates and judges the inferior orders. Thus is opened the possibility that charity might judge each and every thing." There is no dichotomy between knowing and loving, no gap between intellect and will or between inclination and apprehension. Pascal speaks of the "impulse" of charity and accentuates the role of the will and love at the third level, yet the teaching on the heart governs here especially. Charity "opens eyes so that the mark of truth is everywhere apparent." Or, again, "Faith is God apprehended by the heart." Marion, *On Descartes' Metaphysical Prism: The Constitution and the Limits of Onto-theo-logy in Cartesian Thought* (Chicago: University of Chicago Press, 1999), 314.

knot so high, or more precisely, so low, that we were quite unable to reach it" (131).[83]

The notes of surprise, paradox, and reversal are not sufficient to constitute a pedagogy, a teaching.[84] Pascal's ironic pedagogy is part of an ambitious explanatory project.[85] As Hugh Davidson notes, Pascal repudiates a "procedure that would address arguments to someone with the aim of producing conviction, apart from a logic of demonstrative sequences"; "nor will he espouse the notion of strictly contextual truths and goods, determined apart from a comprehensive scheme."[86] Throughout his apology, Pascal's goal is "integrative, synoptic thinking."[87]

As Davidson notes, Pascal's work in science and mathematics provides him with an ideal of what a complete explanation would look like. In an essay entitled "Pascal's Theory of Knowledge," Jean Khalfa argues for the centrality to Pascal's method of his novel treatment of conic sections, projective geometry. Instead of defining and constructing

---

[83] *D'où il parait que Dieu, voulant nous rendre la difficulté de notre être inintelligible à nous-mêmes, en a caché le nœud si haut, ou, pour mieux dire, si bas, que nous étions bien incapables d'y arriver* (434).

[84] Germane here is Wayne Booth's distinction in *A Rhetoric of Irony* between stable or controlled irony and unstable irony. Similarly, Griswold distinguishes between the irony that reflects the disorder of the universe and the irony that prompts to the quest for self-knowledge. Surprise, paradox, and reversal may be part of both types of irony, but only stable irony leads somewhere.

[85] Scholars have attended increasingly to the place of dialectic and rhetoric in Pascal's writing. Mesnard focuses on the dialectic of opposites, resolved by revelation. See Mesnard, *Pascal*, 38. Erec Koch argues against this static notion of dialectic and proposes instead a dynamic dialectic, an "infinitely productive" "sequential movement" that finally undermines the very intelligibility of the problems Pascal seeks to resolve. See Koch, *Pascal and Rhetoric: Figural and Persuasive Language in the Scientific Treatises, "The Provinciales," and the "Pensées"* (Charlottesville, Va.: Rookwood Press, 1997), 114–20. Essays by Paul de Man and Jacques Derrida inform Koch's study *Pascal and Rhetoric*, the argument of which is that Pascal's dialectical method ends up dissolving, rather than resolving, the very questions he thinks are most pressing. See Paul de Man, "Pascal's Allegories of Persuasion," in *Allegory and Representation*, ed. Stephen Greenblatt (Baltimore: Johns Hopkins University Press, 1981), 1–25; and Jacques Derrida, "Force of Law: The Mystical Foundations of Authority," *Cardozo Law Review* 11, no. 5 (1990): 920–1045. We will have occasion to consider Koch's critique in a later chapter.

[86] Hugh Davidson, *Pascal and the Arts of the Mind* (New York: Cambridge University Press, 1993), 219.

[87] Davidson, *Pascal and the Arts of the Mind*, 252.

each of the conic sections independently, Pascal treats the "different features of curves as variations of a singular point of view, not as the inner properties of ideal forms."[88] The problem of the apology is this: "Find a particular point of view from which all the effects (*divertissement*, irrationality of political and ethical systems, survival of the Jewish people, power of imagination and custom over reason, etc.) will make sense, and demonstrate its superiority over all other possible ones." Pascal has an ambitious explanatory goal in mind. Pascal's argumentation works "not by planned stages" or by "axioms and consequences" but "by relations that are seen immediately, in a light radiating from a central source."[89]

Thus Pascal seeks nothing less than the intelligibility of the whole, an intelligibility made manifest only retrospectively from the vantage point of the reception of the Christian hypothesis. Of course, none of this constitutes a philosophical demonstration of the truth of the Christian faith. To offer such a proof would be to deny the very nature of faith, whose doctrine and way of life are the result of an unmerited gift. Irony thus plays a crucial role in safeguarding the revealed character of the comprehensive truth about the human condition. That this truth startles the philosophers is a sign that it is not a doctrine dreamed of in human wisdom. Yet, unlike subrational myths, Christian faith does not evaporate in the face of, or retreat from, rational discourse.

From yet another perspective we can see the paradox of reason in Pascal. He embraces the philosophical and scientific goal of intelligibility, of a comprehensive account of things. Yet, on Pascal's view, the gap between reason's aspiration and its achievement is huge, startling, and horrifying. Reason degenerates into interminable debate, unresolved aporias. In this respect, faith, which is not susceptible to rational proof, is more reasonable than reason.

---

[88] Jean Khalfa, "Pascal's Theory of Knowledge," in *The Cambridge Companion to Pascal*, ed. Nicholas Hammond (Cambridge: Cambridge University Press, 2003), 128.

[89] Davidson, *Pascal and the Arts of the Mind*, 255. Nemoianu puts it this way: "The result [of the movement through various modes and levels of explanation] is a higher viewpoint which at once brings together and passes beyond the two prior perspectives through an awareness of their reciprocal partiality." He is quick to add, "comprehension is not subsumption." The other viewpoints remain and retain a validity on their own level. See Nemoianu, "The Order of Pascal's Politics," *British Journal for the History of Philosophy* 21, no. 1 (2013): 34–56.

The proper, pedagogical use of irony is a matter of deft rhetorical skill and prudential assessment. It is most fruitfully exhibited in the dialogue of two or three interlocutors, where the needs and capacities of each soul can be detected in the concrete flow of the conversation. It is thus a highly personal mode of communication, one that cannot be reduced to abstract principles or to a written text. Although Christian revelation takes shape in authoritative texts and doctrinal pronouncements, revelation itself is from, about, and to persons.

The exclusion of a personal God, active in history, is the target of Pascal's attack on Descartes: "I cannot forgive Descartes: in his whole philosophy he would like to do without God; but he could not help allowing him a flick of the fingers to set the world in motion; after that he had no more use for God" (11).[90] In contrast to Descartes, Pascal does not see voluntarism as the only alternative to deism. What else is there? Pascal's response involves a conception of God as practicing an ironic pedagogy, to which Socratic irony is analogous.

Before turning to Pascal's account of philosophy and divine irony, we will consider, in the next two chapters, the divergent defenses of the sufficiency of the philosophical life in Montaigne and Descartes. Little noticed in the comparisons of Montaigne and Descartes is a striking similarity in their approach to theology and revelation, philosophy's chief opponent in the debate over the best way of life. They also agree that, in the antecedent tradition of philosophy, Socrates achieved the highest expression of this way of life. After Socrates and by reference to him, philosophy falls off and suffers from a forgetfulness of itself as a way of life; it becomes a system of purported answers—a desiccated tradition. Yet, their judgments of Socrates differ vastly. Montaigne seeks to recover and reinvigorate in his own life the way of Socrates. Descartes holds that Socrates' pursuit of knowledge is a failure, a defeat readily acknowledged by Socrates himself. Montaigne wants to revive Socrates; Descartes, to overcome him.

The subsequent chapter will examine Pascal's account of the philosophical life—his interpretation of its origin, methods, nature, and goals. At the heart of Pascal's project in the *Pensées* is the persistent asking of the question Strauss identifies as fundamental, the question of

[90] *Je ne puis pardonner à Descartes: il aurait bien voulu, dans toute sa philosophie, pouvoir se passer de Dieu; mais il n'a pu s'empêcher de lui faire donner une chiquenaude pour mettre le monde en mouvement; après cela, il n'a plus que faire de Dieu* (77).

guidance about whether reason is able to teach authoritatively concerning the sovereign good and the means to its attainment. That question is a philosophical question, even if it is a question that philosophy could not ask unless it were aware of a challenge from a rival teaching on the good life. As we shall see, Pascal engages the conceptions of philosophy of both Montaigne and Descartes and in some measure uses one to correct the other. The figure of Socrates is no less significant for his understanding of the philosophical life than it is for his French predecessors. Pascal agrees with Montaigne against Descartes that Socrates is normative and insuperable for philosophy. But he agrees with Descartes against Montaigne that philosophy aspires to more than what Socrates can supply.

As we have indicated already, the influence of Socrates on Pascal extends beyond an appreciation of Socratic ignorance and the way of life congruent to it. The notion of an ironic pedagogy—the subject of our final chapter—informs Pascal's interpretation of the divine mode of communication. Structured as a detailed interpretation of the wager, the last chapter highlights the way in which revelation, which invites human persons to participate in a way of life that involves friendship with Wisdom Incarnate, communicates in and through irony. In this and other ways, revelation resists the attempts of philosophy to refute, dismiss, marginalize, or subordinate theology to philosophy. Willing and eager to engage philosophy on its own terms—on the basis of its claim to enact the best way of life—revelation both underscores the limits to philosophy's achievement of the sovereign good and proffers an alternative path. The "religion of a humiliated God" is certainly baffling to the philosophers, who are nonetheless invited to discern in that life the very wisdom of God, the satisfaction of that for which philosophy longs but which it cannot provide. Divine irony befuddles only to enlighten and accuses only to restore. Instructed in ironic pedagogy by Socrates and St. Paul, Pascal writes in praise of folly.

Two

SOCRATIC IMMANENCE
Montaigne's Recovery of Philosophy as a Way of Life

Of all the allusions to classical authorities in Montaigne's *Essays*, Socrates is perhaps the most prominent and most important.[1] Montaigne praises Socrates for his admission of his own ignorance, for his practice of philosophy as conversation, for his pursuit of self-knowledge, for his equanimity in the face of death, and especially for his subordination of the arts of inquiry to the art of living. The aim of Socrates, Montaigne writes in "On Physiognomy," was "to provide us with matter and precepts which genuinely and intimately serve our lives."[2] Following a tradition with roots in antiquity, Montaigne adds that Socrates "brought human wisdom back from the heavens where she was wasting her time and returned her to mankind, in whom lies her most proper and most demanding task as well as her most useful one."[3] Socrates "raised nothing but rather brought it down and back to

---

[1] The number of references to Socrates increases exponentially with each new edition of the *Essays*. See Pierre Villey, *Les sources et l'évolution des "Essais" de Montaigne* (Paris: Hachette, 1908), 2:423. Also see Elaine Limbrick, "Montaigne and Socrates," *Renaissance and Reformation* 9 (1973): 46.

[2] Michel de Montaigne, *The Complete Essays*, translated by M. A. Screech (New York: Penguin Classics, 2003), 1174. All quotations are from this edition. I will occasionally and parenthetically cite the French text: *Les essais de Michel de Montaigne: Nouvelle edition conforme au texte de l'exemplaire de Bordeaux* (Paris: Libraire Felix Alcan, 1931).

[3] Montaigne, *Essays*, 1174.

its natural and original level, by which he moderated vigour, hardships, and difficulty."⁴

In Montaigne's Socratic humanism, Stephen Toulmin detects a distinctively modern turn, prior to that of Descartes and the scientific revolution, a modernity rooted not in abstract theory and transparent rationality but in the order of practice, operating through an "accumulation of concrete details of practical experience."⁵ Falling outside the canon of Western philosophical authors, Montaigne's influence is vast, ranging from Shakespeare to Nietzsche. His influence on Descartes, encompassing their shared focus on the self as point of origin for philosophy and on the philosophical resources of the genre of the autobiography, and his influence on Pascal, present on nearly every page of the *Pensées*, not least in its digressive, aphoristic style, are enormous. Yet, in marked contrast to both Descartes and Pascal, Montaigne refuses to defend any fixed, comprehensive account of what is true or good. So reticent is Montaigne that he might seem to have opted out of philosophy itself. His pervasive attention to Socrates and the art of living belies that assumption.

Montaigne subordinates inquiry to self-knowledge and knowledge itself to living a certain kind of life. On the one hand, Montaigne relaxes the demands of the good life. He does not aspire to complete repose of soul; he is skeptical about the possibility of perfect virtue; and he does not pursue, let alone claim to have achieved, a unified, highest good. On the other hand, the quest for self-knowledge is a remarkably rigorous task, a matter of meticulous observation. Precisely because of the fluidity of experience and the opacity of the self to itself, self-reflection requires a vigorously active and adroit operation of the intellect, which seeks a fertile and mobile description of the human condition.

As much as he may cite Socrates as an authority, Montaigne's Socrates is something of a fiction, a construct that fits imperfectly any of the principal sources about his life and teachings.⁶ As Hugo Friedrich observes, when Montaigne describes Socrates, he "is describing

---

⁴ Montaigne, *Essays*, 1174.

⁵ Stephen Toulmin, *Cosmopolis: The Hidden Agenda of Modernity* (Chicago: University of Chicago Press, 1990), 43.

⁶ In the course of his analysis of dogmatism and various forms of skepticism in "An Apology for Raymond Sebond," Montaigne makes the case for an esoteric reading of Plato's metaphysical and theological teachings. See Montaigne, "Sebond," in *Essays*, 559–72.

himself."⁷ In that project of self-construction, Montaigne makes highly selective use of Socrates. Gone are the speculative elements in the dialogues, the metaphysical and epistemological investigations concerning the Ideas, the Good, recollection, and the correspondence of the hierarchy of powers in the soul to an order of intelligibility. Gone is the notion of philosophy as a dialectical investigation of received opinions in a quest for truth. Most notably, Montaigne purges Socrates of his eros or longing for wholeness or transcendence. In place of Socratic transcendence, he gives us Socratic immanence. Under the guise of a humanist reading, Montaigne provides a revolutionary exegesis of Socrates, whose art of living engages and subtly but unmistakably alters the classical traditions of the good life in the pagan thought of Plato and Aristotle and in the Christian thought of Augustine. In contrast to a traditional reading of Socrates, which saw in his life an invitation to conversation and debate about the highest things, Montaigne gives us a Socrates indifferent to theological matters.

We will begin with Montaigne's Socrates, with his embrace of the ancient philosopher's quest for self-knowledge and his conception of philosophy as an art of living. We will then turn to his critique of the philosophy of the schools, embodied in the texts of Aristotle. Montaigne's crafty engagement of Aristotle at once affirms and undermines Aristotle's notion of the quest for understanding. Yet Montaigne also finds much to embrace in Aristotle, particularly in the area of legal and ethical matters, particularly his attention to the concrete, contingent circumstances of human action. Montaigne also affirms Aristotle's account of the unity of soul and body, a teaching that is developed out of a critique of Plato's somewhat more dualistic account. Without drawing the inference, Montaigne here distances himself from Plato on a significant issue. Of course, the wedding of soul to body makes the possibility of transcendence of bodily conditions less likely and less plausible. Thus does the discussion of Aristotle prepare the ground for a tempering of Socrates' transcendental aspirations. Another premodern thinker whose impact can be felt at various points in the *Essays* is Augustine, whose reflections on his own life constitute one of the

---

⁷ Hugo Friedrich, *Montaigne*, ed. Philippe Desan, trans. Dawn Eng (Berkeley: University of California Press, 1991), 52. For a summary, and assessment, of the literature on the various ancient sources of Montaigne's presentation of Socrates, see Alexander Nehemas, *The Art of Living: Socratic Reflections from Plato to Foucault* (Berkeley: University of California Press, 1998), 101–9.

chief antecedents to Montaigne's self-reflections. Yet, as we shall see, in crucial ways, Montaigne rejects the fundamental tenets of Augustine's thought. If Augustine highlights pagan philosophy's incomplete longing for wisdom and happiness, Montaigne reads Plato, Aristotle, and Augustine in a way that undercuts their shared way of framing the debate over the good life.

§1. Socratic Self-Knowledge and the Art of Living

Read in relationship to the philosophy of the schools, Montaigne's *Essays* exhibit novelties of both style and subject matter. The very form of his writing is a deliberate provocation against the extended, systematic exposition of texts in the commentary tradition and the argument by analysis of propositions in the philosophical textbooks of his time. Montaigne's highly digressive style, with its initially inexplicable twists and turns, is not amenable to reduction to a set of propositions. He writes essays because that mode of investigative writing, writing by trial, best suits the object of his knowledge, himself. That is the second distinctive feature of his text, its subject matter. As he boldly proclaims, "I study myself more than any other object. That is my metaphysics; that is my physics."[8] As with so much else in Montaigne, the emphasis on self-investigation is both a revival of something that has fallen into desuetude and an advance or transformation into something novel. Socrates, after all, did not spend much time talking about himself. Moreover, Montaigne's style is neither Socratic nor Platonic. He does not resurrect the dialogue form, nor does he principally devote himself to a dialectical examination of philosophical theses.

In a lament common to early humanists in their critique of scholastic philosophy, Montaigne observes, "We know how to decline the Latin word for virtue; we do not know how to love virtue. Though we do not know what wisdom is from practice or from experience we do know the jargon by heart."[9] Instead of the "practice of familiarity or personal intimacy with virtue," we are content with its "definitions, divisions, and subdivisions." His style is intended to foster and deepen our own pursuit of self-knowledge; to follow his circuitous path

---

[8] Montaigne, *Essays*, 1217. "*Je m'estudie plus qu'autre subject. C'est ma metaphisique, c'est ma phisique.*" Montaigne, *Les essais*, 1072.

[9] Montaigne, *Essays*, 750. Montaigne, *Les essais*, 660.

of self-testing, one must test oneself.[10] Thus, Montaigne's texts operate as spiritual exercises informing a distinctively philosophical way of life.

Montaigne writes in the vernacular and in a nontechnical language. He is aware that his eccentric style will alienate a certain, academic audience: "The scholars whose concern it is to pass judgement on books recognize no worth but that of learning and allow no intellectual activity other than that of scholarship and erudition."[11] He finds the "morals and speech of the peasants more in conformity with the principles of true philosophy than those of the philosophers."[12] Montaigne's writing thus embodies a double irony. Baffling ordinary folks, he deploys an erudition and mode of writing opaque to the many, who "cannot perceive the grace and weight of sustained elegant discourse." Conversely, he gently mocks the learned, as he defends the wisdom of commoners and writes in a style not shared by academics. Irony here functions to underscore the gap between what each (the ordinary person and the learned) thinks it knows and what it actually knows. Montaigne is thus a baffling figure to both groups, the two types of human person, who together "occupy the whole world." A third sort, the true philosopher, with a mind "strong and well-adjusted," is exceedingly rare. But that does not trouble Montaigne, since he writes for and about himself: "Everybody looks before himself: I look inside myself."[13] He elaborates, "I who make no other profession but getting to know myself find in me such boundless depths and variety that my apprenticeship bears no other fruit than to make me know how much there remains to learn."[14] The recovery of Socratic unknowing, focused on endless exploration of the self, revives a Socrates in a new and distinctively modern key, an exemplar of the individual pursuit of authenticity.[15]

Like Socrates, the paradigm of the "strong and well-adjusted" human being, Montaigne arrogates to himself nothing more than amateur status; he is not a professional intellectual. He remains an

---

[10] For the meaning of *essai* as "test" or "trial," see Alan M. Boase, *Fortunes of Montaigne: A History of the Essays in France, 1580–1669* (London: Methuen, 1935), 2–3; and Richard A. Sayce, *The Essays of Montaigne: A Critical Exploration* (London: Weidenfeld & Nicolson, 1972), 20–22.

[11] Montaigne, *Essays*, 746.

[12] Montaigne, *Essays*, 750.

[13] Montaigne, *Essays*, 747.

[14] Montaigne, *Essays*, 1220.

[15] On this, see Nehemas, *Art of Living*.

"apprentice," never a master or authoritative teacher. Yet, he does offer guidance, of a sort. He invites his readers to live within the Platonic paradox of wisdom through learned ignorance. Those who already know need not seek; those who do not know do not know for what they are looking and hence can never find it. Of course, the paradox is introduced by the eponymous Meno in Plato's dialogue as a sort of excuse to avoid inquiry. Socrates invites his interlocutors to seek together with him to discover whether virtue can be taught. The paradox need not be self-defeating, however. It contains a deep truth: that everything we come to know, we come to know through something already known. Conversely, the wisdom of unknowing requires, in its very failure, at least an inkling of what it is that one does not know.

Ann Hartle detects in the paradox of inquiry a clue to Montaigne's philosophical method: "The movement of Montaigne's thought is first to open us to the possibility of the strange and foreign, then lead us back to the familiar and let us see the extraordinary in the ordinary, in the familiar and the common."[16] In this way, Montaigne puts skeptical doubt to good use, not to defeat all claims to knowledge or even to achieve the state of imperturbability sought by many ancient skeptics, but to foster "openness to the possible, to the unfamiliar," or at least to the marvels available to us when we take a second look at what we think we already know. The approach accords with Montaigne's recovery of Socrates as someone who ponders ordinary things in an extraordinary manner. It also fits with a central contention of Jonathan Lear's account of irony as involving an experience of the uncanny, the return of the familiar as unfamiliar.

Montaigne embraces Socrates' turn from the investigation of natural philosophy to the human things, particularly to a pursuit of self-knowledge. That which is nearest to us and therefore seems most obvious is in fact the hardest to know: "In the study that I am undertaking, the subject of which is Man, I find such extreme variation of

---

[16] Ann Hartle, "Montaigne and Skepticism," in *The Cambridge Companion to Montaigne*, ed. Ullrich Langer (Cambridge: Cambridge University Press, 2006), 183–206. Hartle's depiction bears some resemblance to Jonathan Lear's conception of irony and calls to mind Stanley Cavell's philosophical attention to the "uncanniness of the ordinary." On Cavell, see my essay "Stanley Cavell's Philosophical Improvisations," *Chronicle of Higher Education* 57, no. 8 (2010): B6–B9. For a developed interpretation of Montaigne, see Hartle's *Michel de Montaigne: Accidental Philosopher* (Cambridge: Cambridge University Press, 2007).

judgement, such a deep labyrinth of difficulties one on top of another, so much disagreement and uncertainty in the very School of Wisdom."[17] Establishing a precedent that will be followed by both Descartes and Pascal, although in quite different ways, Montaigne argues against philosophy on behalf of philosophy. The ironic upshot is that philosophy is most true to itself when it confesses its poverty and impotence.

Learned ignorance is neither a source of inordinate anxiety nor a basis for imperturbability, *ataraxia*, as the skeptics called it. Montaigne simultaneously embraces ancient skepticism even as he voices his own skepticism about its claims to supply perfect peace of mind.[18] We need to recall here that the goal of ancient philosophy was to pursue a certain way of life, the best way of life available to human beings, a way of life promising human flourishing. Ancient skepticism was less an epistemological doctrine than a way of life. Curtailing one's ambitions in the arena of knowledge has the salutary effect of allowing one to live in accord with the natural limits of the human condition. Errors in argument and fallibility in our memory serve not so much to move us toward a better apprehension of this or that particular matter as to "learn" of our "infirmity in general" and of the "treacherous ways" of the intellect. Self-knowledge, which consists at least in part in recognizing the

---

[17] Montaigne, *Essays*, 721.

[18] Richard H. Popkin, *The History of Scepticism from Erasmus to Spinoza* (Berkeley: University of California Press, 1979), 42–54. Popkin argues that the reading of ancient skeptics precipitated a crisis that led to Montaigne adopting skepticism. In response to Popkin's thesis, Zachary Shiffman argues, on the contrary, that the encounter with ancient skepticism did not so much cause as resolve a crisis. It freed Montaigne from the burden of a serious quest for answers. See Zachary S. Shiffman, "Montaigne and the Rise of Skepticism in Early Modern Europe: A Reappraisal," *Journal of the History of Ideas* 45, no. 4 (1984): 499–516. As Shiffman puts it, "Aristotle had originated the technique of arguing *in utramque partem* [on both sides of an issue] in order to establish verisimilitude in matters where truth could not be ascertained. . . . This technique was later adopted by the Academic skeptics, the most influential of whom was Cicero. Unlike Aristotle, Cicero denied that one could ever attain truth or certainty. . . . Montaigne used the discourse *in utramque partem* to demonstrate that one could not even establish verisimilitude in human affairs; for any given question, the diversity of human reality provided too many contradictory answers. In other words, Montaigne transformed the instrument of Academic skepticism into that of an even more radical skepticism" (502).

types and effects of our ruling passions, enables us to "see them coming and slow down a little the violence of their assault."[19]

If this sort of skepticism foregoes ultimate answers to the big questions, it nonetheless proffers a specific wisdom about the human condition, what Montaigne calls a "gay and companionable wisdom." Montaigne is under no illusions about reason's ability to control, let alone eliminate, the contingent elements of the human condition. Reason cannot eradicate the attachment of our minds and passions to other things or persons. The best it can do is to monitor and anticipate; it cannot rest in universal notions or in settled indifference to what happens to the soul or the body. Yet it can achieve a kind of "peace in the midst of restlessness" precisely because it no longer identifies human happiness with bliss or with the cessation of movement, desire, or even affliction and because it has developed a practice of "thankful self-awareness."[20]

§2. Against Speculative Philosophy

Montaigne exercises irony not just with the opinions of the many but also with those of the philosophers who exhibit a comical lack of self-knowledge, a humorous and instructive gap between what they think they know and what they actually know. The essay "On Experience" begins by repeating the opening line of Aristotle's *Metaphysics*: "No desire is more natural than the desire for knowledge." Yet the quotation is ironic, as the remainder of the essay serves to undermine the entire possibility of metaphysics.

The vast erudition of scholars derails the pursuit of self-knowledge, wisdom that informs life. Before Descartes, Montaigne is eager to throw off the weight of the commentary tradition: "All we do is gloss each other."[21] Further, "Can anyone deny that glosses increase doubts and ignorance [*les glosses augmentent les doubtes et l'ignorance*], when there can be found no book which men toil over in either divinity or the humanities whose difficulties have been exhausted by exegesis?"[22] The principal source of this tradition is the corpus of Aristotle, on which a series of lengthy detailed commentaries had been produced. Aristotle

---

[19] Montaigne, *Essays*, 1219. "*Il les verroit venir, et ralantiroit un peu leur impetuosité et leur course.*" Montaigne, *Les essais*, 1074.

[20] Friedrich, *Montaigne*, 324–25.

[21] Montaigne, *Essays*, 1212.

[22] Montaigne, *Essays*, 1210. Montaigne, *Les essais*, 1067.

wrote on nearly every discipline and offered a broad account of the principles, methods, and conclusions of each. Thus, the easiest way to get out from under the weight of the entire desiccated tradition is to combat Aristotle.

In keeping with his moderate skepticism about philosophical knowledge, Montaigne rejects any systematic conception of philosophy. The most direct and most potent attack on such a conception of philosophy can be found in "On Experience," where he describes the relationship of reason to experience in the following way:

> We assay all the means that can lead us to it. When reason fails us we make use of experience. . . .
> Reason has so many forms that we do not know which to resort to: experience has no fewer. The induction which we wish to draw from the likeness between events is unsure since they all show unlikenesses. When collating objects no quality is so universal as diversity and variety.[23]

The initial affirmation of Aristotle is ironic. Instead of following Aristotle's pattern of ascent from sensation through memory and experience and on to science and art, Montaigne starts with reason and descends to experience. He thus subjects Aristotle's text to ironic reversal. Instead of underscoring the way similarities in features of our experience lend themselves to rational insight and universal abstraction, Montaigne highlights the diversity of experience, its resistance to generalization. Experience is too diverse and varied to be brought under systematic study: "reason has so many shapes [*la raison a tant de formes*] that we do not know which to take hold of; experience has no fewer. . . . Events are always unlike."[24] Speculative philosophy, scientific inquiry, and even certain types of theology cannot establish a basis in experience for their universal assertions.

For Aristotle, the greatest of human desires, felt profoundly by those of a philosophical nature, is to contemplate the whole, the cosmos, its order, and, ultimately, the source of that order, the first principles and highest causes of what is. The desire is to contemplate what is eternal. Before Aristotle, Plato affirmed a version of that ascent. After him, in the Neoplatonists and early Christian authors, the movement from the external to the internal and from the internal to the superior becomes

---

[23] Montaigne, *Essays*, 1207.
[24] Montaigne, *Essays*, 344. Montaigne, *Les essais*, 1065.

the standard path to God, to the satisfaction of the ineradicable human longing to know and delight in the source of the whole. Montaigne repudiates all this as a kind of illness afflicting human souls. He embraces the notion of Socrates' descent from the study of astronomy to the study of human things but ignores or dismisses the numerous places in the dialogues in which Socrates ascends to a contemplation of the highest things.[25] As Friedrich observes, for Montaigne, reason does not move in a hierarchical order or in any kind of predictable order; instead, it moves "elastically in chance ideas."[26]

The selection of Aristotle's *Metaphysics* as the focus of the attack on knowledge is astute. Montaigne takes aim at the culminating book in Aristotle's hierarchy of philosophical disciplines, a book which opens with broad claims about the foundation, nature, and goal of human inquiry. Aristotle's account of human knowing traces an ascent from the singular to the universal, from the sensible to the intelligible. By attacking the opening of the *Metaphysics*, Montaigne undoes the very possibility of speculative philosophy. He also thereby undermines the entire commentary tradition that reposes on the assumption that Aristotle's approach simply needs elaboration and clarification.

There is a Baconian thrust to Montaigne's insistence on the ways in which experience resists conformity to abstract universals. Receptive attentiveness rather than a desire to comprehend and control is what nature asks of us. In this respect, Montaigne's Baconian sense of the rich particularity of experience fails to give rise to the Baconian (and Cartesian) boast that a better method will overcome these problems and enable us to master nature. Montaigne is not the "lord of nature, but rather its protégé."[27]

The critique extends beyond the realm of theoretical knowledge to that of practical wisdom; it touches the foundations of both philosophy

---

[25] As noted in chap. 1, Walter Nicgorski, in "Cicero's Socrates: Assessment of the 'Socratic Turn,'" in *Law and Philosophy: The Practice of Theory*, ed. J. Murley, R. Stone, and W. Braithwaite, vol. 1 (Athens: Ohio University Press, 1992), argues that both Plato and Cicero had reservations about the turn, about what they took to be its consequences: a parochial and exclusively practical conception of philosophy. Nicgorski attempts to provide "what one might call a metaphysics of the Socratic turn that clearly shows Socratic moral questions opening to and entailed with ultimate questions" (233).

[26] Friedrich, *Montaigne*, 22.

[27] Friedrich, *Montaigne*, 141.

and politics: "There is hardly any relation between our actions (which are perpetually changing) and fixed unchanging laws."[28] He expatiates:

> Since the moral laws that we apply to individuals are so difficult to establish (as we see that they are), not surprisingly those laws which govern collections of all those individuals are even more so. Consider the form of justice whch has ruled over us: it is a true witness to the imbecility of Man, so full it is of contradiction and error.[29]

Montaigne does not attempt to ground the conventional laws of regimes in a natural or divine law. His only defense of law, the only one he deems possible, is that it is law: "Now laws remain respected not because they are just but because they are laws. That is the mystical basis of their authority. They have no other."[30] Custom itself bestows upon law the semblance of being much more than merely conventional. Indeed, it inclines us to think of the law as standing above the conventions, as timeless and absolute.

As some commentators have observed, Montaigne's critique of universal rules, whether in philosophy, science, or law, is anticipated in Aristotle's own teaching on equity, which involves the "rectification of the law where law is defective because of its generality." In such instances, a "special ordinance is made to fit the circumstances of the case."[31] Ian Maclean proposes that the "scornful tone of Montaigne's description of the faculty of reason disappears if reason is seen as flexible and subject to circumstance, and hence closer to the particulars of human lives."[32] There is indeed a connection between Montaigne's objection to abstract universals and Aristotle's doctrine of equity or, even more strikingly, Aristotle's notion of prudence as the perception

---

[28] Montaigne, *Essays*, 1208. "*Il y a peu de relation de nos actions, qui sont en perpetuelle mutation, avec les loix fixes et immobile.*" Montaigne, *Les essais*, 565.

[29] Montaigne, *Essays*, 1213–14.

[30] Montaigne, *Essays*, 1216.

[31] Aristotle, *Nicomachean Ethics* 5.10.1137b, in *The Complete Works of Aristotle*, ed. Jonathan Barnes, vol. 2 (Princeton, N.J.: Princeton University Press, 1984).

[32] Ian Maclean, "Montaigne and the Truth of the Schools," in *Cambridge Companion to Montaigne*, 156. For an argument that Montaigne came increasingly to cite Aristotle approvingly, at least in matters ethical, see Edilia Traverso, *Montaigne e Aristotele* (Florence: Le Monnier, 1974).

of singular circumstances.³³ Yet, the attempt at reconciliation of Montaigne and Aristotle must overlook any number of Aristotelian teachings, for example, on the intelligibility of natural substances, of human nature, and of the role of general knowledge in the practical order. Montaigne's account of experience is what remains of Aristotle's teaching once one has subtracted his metaphysics, anthropology, and broad ethical teaching on human nature, its telos, and the virtues.

As always, for Montaigne the chief goal is to deepen self-knowledge. The place to start is with oneself, with a reflective appropriation of what is nearest to us, indeed, in many cases, within us. What is most obvious to us is precisely that which we are most inclined to ignore. To see what is immediate takes a cultivated sensibility, which Montaigne identifies with virtue:

> Whatever we may in fact get from experience, such benefit as we derive from other people's examples will hardly provide us with an elementary education if we make so poor a use of such experience as we have presumably enjoyed ourselves; that is more familiar to us and certainly enough to instruct us in what we need.³⁴

The pursuit of self-knowledge, in which Socrates excels, aims to understand not human nature but oneself in one's individuality. As Jean Starobinski puts it, "Manifesting their own uniqueness, *exempla* point to a world composed of unique, dissimilar entities. . . . They testify to their singular existence."³⁵ The study of the lives of others, even that of Socrates, is useful only to the extent (a) that we see in those lives their irreducible particularity and (b) that we take others' lives as prompts for the investigation of our own lives.

At the same time that he elevates the status of the study of the self, he tempers the self's sense of its own power: "We have to grope through a fog even to understand the very things we hold in our hands."³⁶ He con-

---

[33] Similarly, according to George Hoffmann, Montaigne's dismissive attitude toward medicine conceals "his very real affinity with its descriptive function." See Hoffmann, "The Investigation of Nature," in *Cambridge Companion to Montaigne*, 169. Also pertinent is Jean Starobinski, "The Body's Moment," in *Montaigne: Essays in Reading*, ed. Gerard Defaux (New Haven, Conn.: Yale University, 1983), 273–305.

[34] Montaigne, *Essays*, 1217.

[35] Jean Starobinski, *Montaigne in Motion*, trans. Arthur Goldhammer (Chicago: University of Chicago Press, 1985), 89.

[36] Montaigne, *Essays*, 204.

cludes this short essay by reflecting on the twin vices of vainglory and curiosity: "The former makes us stick our noses into everything; the latter forbids us to leave anything unresolved or undecided."[37] These vices render us restless and anxious, always wanting that which eludes us or that which we have no business pursuing. Cupidity applies as much to the thirst for knowledge as it does to the longing for sensual pleasure.

Montaigne is not arguing that we ought to cease questioning or searching. On the contrary, he observes, "There is no end to our inquiries; our end is in the next world [*nostre fin est en l'autre monde*].... No powerful mind stops within itself: it is always stretching out and exceeding its capacities. Its inquiries are shapeless and without limits; its nourishment consists in amazement, the hunt and uncertainty [*son aliment c'est admiration, chasse, ambiguité*]."[38] Our quest for answers cannot be completed in this life. But it is striking that Montaigne is silent not only about what we learn in the other world but also whether we will learn anything. In fact, he does not even raise the question. That stands in contrast both to Socrates' wondering at the end of the *Apology* and throughout the *Phaedo* about the prospects for continued inquiry after death and to Augustine's claim that the pursuit of wisdom, begun here, will reach fruition in the contemplation of God in eternity. In both of these cases, there is an accent on the distance that separates our present inquiries from some sort of potential completion; moreover, these thinkers both assumed a hierarchical account of human knowledge. Montaigne depicts knowledge in a linear or even circular fashion. Finally, he downplays rather than highlights the erotic lack motivating the desire to know. His attitude toward endless ambiguity is one of resignation, while both Descartes and Pascal (as we shall see below) find the contradictions and paradoxes of our condition a cause for alarm, regret, even horror.

Vice, Socrates taught, is rooted in ignorance. For Montaigne, the most damaging ignorance is not knowing that our ignorance is insuperable. Montaigne counters the thrust toward divinization with an ironic redescription of divinization, the rare and noble achievement of accommodation to our condition:

---

[37] Montaigne, *Essays*, 204. "*Cette cy nous conduit à mettre le nez par tout, et celle là nous defant de rien laisser irresolu et indecis.*" Montaigne, *Les essais*, 182.

[38] Montaigne, *Essays*, 348. Montaigne, *Les essais*, 1068.

> It is an accomplishment, absolute and as it were God-like [*c'est une absolue perfection, et comme divine*], to know how to enjoy our being as we ought. We seek other attributes because we do not understand the use of our own; and, having no knowledge of what is within, we sally forth outside ourselves. A fine thing to get up on stilts: for even on stilts we must ever walk with our legs! And upon the highest throne in the world, we are seated, still, upon our arses.
>
> The most beautiful of lives to my liking are those which conform to the common measure, human and ordinate, without miracles though and without rapture [*au modelle commun et humain, avec ordre, mais sans miracle et sans extravagance*].[39]

Montaigne holds that the true mean of human life is found in Socrates; he unites what others have rent asunder: thought and action, soul and body. After a lengthy list of varied activities of Socrates, from his valor in battle to his habit of standing motionless in thought, Montaigne concludes, "Philosophy says that all activities are equally becoming in a wise man, all equally honour him."[40]

The egalitarianism with respect to the activities constitutive of the good life applies to Montaigne's account of the component parts of human nature. He identifies the task of wisdom: "to obtain and procure the common good" of soul and body "in fellowship."[41] On this point, Montaigne discerns a unity between Plato and Aristotle and compliments the latter for his insights into the union of soul and body. Montaigne's own way of putting the matter is this:

> We must command the soul ... not to despise and abandon the body (something it cannot do anyway except by some monkey-like counterfeit), but to rally to it, take it in its arms and cherish it, help it, look after it, counsel it, and when it strays set it to rights and bring it back home again. It should in short marry the body and serve as its husband.[42]

Montaigne offers a reading of Plato through the lens of Aristotle's critique, a reading that stands athwart the dominant lines of interpretation of Plato's texts. In contrast to the dualist position often attributed

---

[39] Montaigne, *Essays*, 1268–69. Montaigne, *Les essais*, 1116.

[40] Montaigne, *Essays*, 1258. Montaigne, *Les essais*, 1110.

[41] Montaigne, *Essays*, 727. "*De pourvoir et procurer en commun le bien de ces deux parties associées.*" Montaigne, *Les essais*, 639.

[42] Montaigne, *Essays*, 727.

to Plato, the unification of soul and body and a focus on the virtues harmonizing the two parts of human nature are, for Montaigne, the most important Platonic doctrines.

The union of soul and body does not involve an assertion that the two are equal in authority. Montaigne's teaching is in this respect modestly Aristotelian. Aristotle held the so-called hylomorphic theory of the soul and body. Soul is to body as form (*morphē*) is to matter (*hylē*). Soul is to body as act is to potency. For Aristotle, this is the highest type of unity: the union of an act and that of which it is the act. The soul makes the matter to be this or that sort of thing. It actualizes the matter by informing it, shaping it, and directing its activities. The soul is not just the principle of life in the body; it is its very form, establishing its organizational structure and its distinctive manner of functioning. The soul answers the question why it is that material substances are intelligible, that is, why they are more than mere lumps or material parts, why the parts or organs belong together and why they work in harmony in the precise manner they do. The ethical application of this argument from the *De Anima* can be found early in the *Ethics*, in the categorization of the types of virtue in accord with the chief division of the soul into its rational and nonrational components. He subdivides the latter portion into a part of the soul that is not subject to rational control and another part that is amenable to reason. The former is the vegetative part—what we might call biological and chemical processes in the bodies of living things. The latter is the realm of the passions, which can be persuaded and trained to obey reason, indeed to participate in its activities.

Were the passions not open to formation by reason in this way, that is, by habituation in activities in accord with practical reason or prudence, virtue would be impossible. The best one could hope for would be a kind of self-control that would involve a constant checking of the passions by reason. Aristotle certainly accepts the fact that for most individuals most of the time there is a fairly strong tension between reason and passion, but this is simply because most individuals are not virtuous. While the training that leads to virtue can be onerous, virtue itself is pleasant, indeed more pleasant than vice. Here we may detect both agreement and disagreement with Montaigne. For Montaigne, there is no possibility even among the best of human beings of achieving virtue but only of "drawing near to her." He denies any sort of dichotomy between a wearisome pursuit of virtue and its pleasant possession. Instead, the "very pursuit is pleasurable; the undertaking savours of the quality of the object it has in view.... There is a happiness and blessedness radiating from virtue [*l'heur et la beatitude qui reluit en la vertu*]."[43]

Aristotle would affirm this in part. The closer one approaches to virtue, the more pleasure and ease will characterize one's acts. But insofar as one remains distant from complete virtue, one's life will contain an element of want and displeasure. One will not flourish as much as one might because the telos of one's nature will not yet be fully actualized. Aristotle's teleological language plays a vastly diminished role in Montaigne. He does not stress the gap between human nature as-it-is and human nature as-it-might-be, if it were to realize its natural end. Montaigne's account of the complacency of the soul, with regard to its multiple and contradictory impulses, is ultimately incompatible with Aristotle's teleological account of the virtues. By offering a more relaxed standard of happiness and of virtue, Montaigne renders the good life more widely accessible even as he diminishes the potential sources of tragic failure. Montaigne's return to the ordinary differs from that of ancients, who saw in the ordinary desire to know, in the universal capacity for wonder, in the common appreciation of goodness and beauty the roots of the longing to behold the highest causes. For Plato and Aristotle, the roots of the telos of speculative philosophy are not alien to ordinary desires and affections; they have the same soil.

§3. Montaigne's Confessions

In support of his account of soul and body, Montaigne cites, beyond Aristotle, the Christian doctrine on the resurrection of the body. We can detect in this manner of introducing Christian theology a common practice of Montaigne. He cites Christian theology only as confirmation for conclusions established by other means and for topics introduced on the basis of considerations extrinsic to theology. Even this is rare.[44] If he does not typically cite Christian authors, he is nonetheless often in conversation with them. In crucial sections of his text, Montaigne is engaging not just Plato and Aristotle but also Augustine, who offers a criticism of the possibility of human achievement, unaided by grace, of

---

[43] Montaigne, *Essays*, 91. Montaigne, *Les essais*, 82.
[44] Friedrich's section on "Christian Sources" in the *Essays* is a mere two pages. See Friedrich, *Montaigne*, 81–82.

the good life.⁴⁵ But Augustine's critique reposes on agreement with the best of the pagan philosophers about the nature of happiness as something desirable for its own sake, satisfying all human desire, perfective of human persons, and, once possessed, incapable of being taken from us. The ancients had a notion of the goal or end but could not grasp the means. This is the upshot of Augustine's famous discussion of the ultimate end of human life in book 19 of the *City of God*. Augustine's entire account of the ultimate end of human life is encapsulated in his eloquent statement at the outset of the *Confessions*. Directly addressing God, he writes, "You have made us for yourself and our hearts are restless until they rest in you."⁴⁶

Although Montaigne occasionally cites Augustine, particularly the *City of God*, he nowhere cites the *Confessions*. This is an odd omission, given that he is writing a sort of autobiographical text, the chief antecedent to which might well be Augustine's narration of his own life. Montaigne more than once refers to his work as a confession, yet the meaning of that term undergoes, at Montaigne's hands, a reversal. Augustine talks about himself only to accuse himself or to discern in the interstices of the events of his life the providential hand of God. The very condition of confession for Augustine, namely, a personal communion with a God who judges and saves, has no place in Montaigne's confession.

As least as much as Montaigne, Augustine is in conversation with pagan philosophy, yet he highlights and criticizes in the pagans' work matters quite different from what Montaigne singles out for praise and blame. What makes possible Augustine's engagement of the ancients is their shared teleological conception of human nature, as ordered to certain ends. To reach the ends prescribed by Plato and Aristotle, Augustine urges, conversion is necessary, a reorientation of the intellect and will, made possible by divine grace. Augustine's peculiar literary invention of the genre of the confession is meant to reflect in its form this new path to the achievement of the sovereign good. An extended spiritual exercise, Augustine's *Confessions* traces the working of divine providence in the particular events of an individual life. Essential to

---

⁴⁵ Friedrich devotes nearly six pages to a comparison of Montaigne with Augustine. Friedrich, *Montaigne*, 214–19.

⁴⁶ "*Nam fecisti nos ad te; et inquietum est cor nostrum donec requiescat in te.*" Augustine, *Confessions* 1.1, Loeb Classical Library (Cambridge, Mass.: Harvard University Press, 2014).

that narrative is a conversion, prompted by grace and rooted in repentance for one's sinful disobedience of God. Of course, the process of conversion is precisely a matter of realizing the proper end for which God created the human person in the first place, the goal of the longing woven into every human heart.

Patrick Riley stresses Montaigne's departure from the Augustinian model: "What makes the *Essays* such a cogent counterweight to the Augustinian conversional model (and to Cartesian essentialism) is its refusal of both narrative and subjective hypostasis."[47] Riley points us to Montaigne's essay "On Repenting" as indicative of the contrast between the two. Without mentioning Augustine, Montaigne eschews fundamental Augustinian tenets. First, he rejects the "stability of his subject," namely, himself: "I grasp it as it is now, at this moment when I am lingering over it. I am not portraying being but becoming [*Je ne peints pas l'estre. Je peints le passage*]: not the passage from one age to another . . . , but from day to day, minute to minute."[48] If he could "find a firm footing," he would no longer be "assaying" but rather "resolving" himself. As it is, his soul is "ever in an apprenticeship and being tested [*tousjours en apprentissage et en espreuve*]."[49] Riley comments, "In this sense, the self undergoes a constant but unpredictable series of minor conversions: it has always just become something other than what it was and is about to become something new yet again."[50] These conversions never involve, nor are they ordered to, the discovery of the one thing to which one's entire life is ordered, unless that one thing is the ever-attentive tracking of unpredictable alterations.

Montaigne rejects the possibility of a perspective from which one might retrospectively see the parts of one's life as forming a unified whole. Moreover, temporality and depth do not disclose the self as soul, as *imago Dei*, in which the temporal and finite reflect the eternal and the infinite. Like Augustine, Montaigne encounters in his inner mind the flux of temporality and the unfathomable depths of the self. But this recounting of the moments of the self's story does not entail that the story has a plot, with a beginning, middle, and end. It has merely episodes. Montaigne adopts Augustine's self-reflective, digressive mode

[47] Patrick Riley, *Character and Conversion in Autobiography: Augustine, Montaigne, Descartes, Rousseau, and Sartre* (Charlottesville: University of Virginia Press, 2004), 61.
[48] Montaigne, *Essays*, 907–8. Montaigne, *Les essais*, 805.
[49] Montaigne, *Essays*, 908. Montaigne, *Les essais*, 805.
[50] Riley, *Character and Conversion in Autobiography*, 72.

of inquiry and writing not as a way of grasping images and likenesses of the divine or of catching key moments in the working of divine providence in his life. Instead, he pursues these serpentine paths for their own sake, without any sense of purpose or unity.

Montaigne eschews precisely the sort of classical teleology that Augustine shares with his pagan predecessors. Montaigne does not deny a certain type of universality, that of the human condition: "Every man bears the whole form of the human condition."[51] To capture that condition is a task for an exquisitely perceptive artistry. Patterns and themes may emerge from such a trial of one's self, but no clear telos. Thus, there is no need to determine how to bridge the gap between nature as-it-is-now and nature as-it-could-be, if it realized its end. The paradoxical implication of Montaigne's insistence on flux is a kind of stasis: "I am virtually always settled in place [*Je me trouve quasi tousjours en ma place*], as heavy ponderous bodies are. If I should not be 'at home,' I am always nearby."[52] The references to being settled in place, to being at home, and to ponderous bodies call to mind both Aristotle and Augustine. Aristotle's natural philosophy, which in some measure informs his ethical doctrine, treats the motion of natural bodies as ordered to a natural place, a point of rest to which motion itself, unless it be violent, is ordered. In the ethical order, that natural place or home for the human species is the end or telos of all human action, activity in accord with reason. Montaigne has his own version of the natural home of human beings, but it does not presuppose a teleology. Augustine speaks of his love as a weight that carries him, even against his conscious wishes, toward God, who is the ultimate object of love. Augustine's *Confessions* and *City of God* concur in defending the Pauline claim that we have here no lasting city, no home. Our home is in another city, the city of God.

There are indeed points of contact between Montaigne and Augustine. The former speaks, for example, of our end being in the other life. Yet Montaigne does not stress the distance of this life from the next, nor does he highlight the gap between the quest and its fulfillment. Reason's recognition of, and resignation toward, what exceeds its grasp make tranquility and the good life possible here and now. Similarly, Montaigne and Augustine share a view of the enduring presence of

---

[51] Montaigne, *Essays*, 908. "*Chaque homme porte la forme entiere de l'humaine condition.*" Montaigne, *Les essais*, 805.

[52] Montaigne, *Essays*, 914. Montaigne, *Les essais*, 811.

conflict in the internal working of the soul. Montaigne concedes Augustine's point—a key point in Augustine's critique of pagan antiquity—that reason is incapable of completely reordering the unruly passions. For Montaigne, there is a limited sense in which reason is, if not a slave of the passions, at least at their mercy. It cannot fully eradicate them, nor can it hope to control their influence in every case. Yet, once again, reason's recognition of its own limits is liberating for reason. Montaigne can boast that within him "judgment holds the rector's chair."[53] Judgment lets the passions go their own way "without being corrupted or worsened" by them. Judgment "plays its role apart."[54]

Montaigne here seems to adopt a revised Stoic version of the role of reason with respect to the passions. He does not go so far as to promote the dominance of the passions by reason. But he does hold to a segregation of reason from the passions, which allows reason to retain its own freedom from, and transcendence of, the passions. The limited freedom of reason in monitoring and tempering the effect of passion is crucial to Montaigne's promotion of equanimity. Even in the middle of the greatest internal conflicts, reason "plays its role apart." That is a significant alteration of Augustine's sense of sin as infecting the hidden depths of the soul, both passion and reason. It also introduces a questionable dualism into Montaigne's otherwise hylomorphic account of reason and passion.

As surprising as it may appear in light of his insistence on the unity of soul and body and the flux of experience, it may be that the lingering dualism in Montaigne is unavoidable. Given his repudiation of a unity established either by human nature or by a narrative account of the progress or failure of human persons in achieving ends, Montaigne might find it difficult to resist the dissolution of the self into a shifting series of events. Montaigne does not opt for the classical language of reason as a principle of order with respect to the passions; he prefers the language of navigation or negotiation. Yet it is hard to see how that enables him to circumvent the question of who or what is doing the navigating or negotiating. Is it one or more? If it is one, what accounts for its unity? If plural, then what sense can be made of the claim, concerning his whole enterprise, "I study myself"? Is the subject or the object stable

---

[53] Montaigne, *Essays*, 1219. "*Le jugement tient chez moy un siege magistral.*" Montaigne, *Les essais*, 1074.

[54] Montaigne, *Essays*, 1219. Montaigne, *Les essais*, 1074.

enough for the study not to dissipate into a series of fragmentary observations? However much Montaigne works by digression and diversion, he nonetheless wants to compose a whole, a book, that reflects his self. Can that claim be sustained? Does not Montaigne anticipate the fundamental tenets of deconstruction about language and the self while clinging to some of the classical tenets of philosophy and its texts?[55] As we will see in future chapters, these concerns will lead Descartes and Pascal to revive respectively the substantial unity of the self and an account of potential unity through narrative, both of which have their roots in Augustine. In this respect, the divisions among Montaigne, Descartes, and Pascal might reflect the legacy of Augustine as much as that of Socrates.

Rethinking Augustine is at the heart of the project of "On Repentance." Montaigne states directly, "I rarely repent and . . . my conscience is happy with itself."[56] Before Nietzsche's proclamation of eternal return, Montaigne says of his whole life, "If I had to live again, I would live as I have done; I neither regret the past nor fear the future."[57] Or again, "My doings are ruled by what I am and are in harmony with how I was made. I cannot do better: and the act of repenting does not properly touch what is not in our power—*that* is touched by regretting."[58] Montaigne can conceive of a kind of repentance or regret that arises from a desire for one's life to be quite different from what is has been or currently is, but he finds himself unable to treat that as a rational desire.

Without ever mentioning Augustine's *Confessions*, Montaigne undermines the very conditions for the possibility of the genre. "Confession" means accusation of self and praise of God; with the assistance of grace, the confession brings forth into the light of day the evidences of a disordered will, a monstrous turning of nature against itself. The response to that revelation is repentance. A condition of alienation from God, others, and oneself is a condition into which each human being is thrust at conception, but it is also a condition exacerbated by each person's own

---

[55] See Jerome Schwartz, "Montaigne and Deconstruction," in *Approaches to Teaching Montaigne's Essays*, ed. Patrick Henry (New York: Modern Language Association of America, 1994).

[56] Montaigne, *Essays*, 909. "*Je me repens rarement et que ma conscience se contente de soy.*" Montaigne, *Les essais*, 806.

[57] Montaigne, *Essays*, 920.

[58] Montaigne, *Essays*, 916.

sins. For these, indeed for the sins of the children of men, Augustine issues a call to repentance.

§4. Death, Diversion, and the Supernatural

Another dramatic contrast to Augustine can be seen in Montaigne's varied reflections on death. Nowhere is Montaigne's capacity for contradiction more evident than in his two quite different views on death and dying in the *Essays*. The first view fits rather neatly the classical philosophical project of preparing for death by means of spiritual exercises; the second adopts a critical stance toward all such exercises and comes close to siding with the practice of the many who assuage the fear of death by diversion. Thus does Montaigne engage in ironic contradiction, the assertion of opposed views. In an early essay devoted to Solon's ancient dictum "That we should not be deemed happy till after our death," Montaigne wonders at its meaning. He considers, only to set aside, the notion that Solon was commenting on the contingency of fortune or on the way a radical alteration of attitude can emerge in the last moments of life. Instead, he proposes that the saying highlights the last act of the play of life, which is indubitably the hardest. "When judging another's life I always look to see how its end was borne [*je regarde tousjours comment s'en est porté le bout*]: and one of my main concerns for my own is that it be borne well—that is, in a quiet and muted manner [*quietement et sourdement*]."[59]

Montaigne identifies philosophy itself as a preparation for dying. One of the chief effects of virtue is contempt for death. The dilemma death poses for the good life is this: "If death frightens us how can we go one step forward without anguish? For ordinary people the remedy is not to think about it; but what brutish insensitivity can produce so gross a blindness?"[60] Instead of fleeing from death or simply ignoring it, we should approach it directly, cultivate a habitual awareness of it, and thus deprive it of its force over us. We do so by the use of the imagination, which is no longer a source of unwelcome anxiety about death but a faculty that calls up images of death under the deliberate control of reason.

Intellectual clarity in this matter is paramount. We must focus on the question, what is death? We fear in death both the loss of life and

---

[59] Montaigne, *Essays*, 88. Montaigne, *Les essais*, 80.
[60] Montaigne, *Essays*, 92.

the uncertainty about what might come next. But it is just as absurd to lament that we shall not be alive in the future as to weep over the fact that we were not alive in some past, prior to our birth. The same principle applies to our naive preference for a long over a short life: These are "made one by death: long and short do not apply to that which is no more.... If we compare our own span against eternity or even against the span of mountains, rivers, stars, trees or, indeed, of some animals, then saying shorter or longer becomes equally ridiculous."[61] To enjoy one's life is a matter of virtue. As for the awareness of mortality, of the inevitable loss of all we now treasure, Montaigne observes, "Above all now, when I see my span so short, I want to give it more ballast; I want to arrest the swiftness of its passing by the swiftness of my capture, compensating for the speed with which it drains away by the intensity of my enjoyment. The shorter my lease of it, the deeper and fuller I must make it." Attending to a happy experience allows the soul to "take joy in it, not losing herself but finding herself in it; her role is to observe herself mirrored in that happy state, to weigh that happiness, gauge it and increase it."[62] This is the task of philosophy; paradoxically, the cultivation of happiness is indistinguishable from a training in death that liberates us to enjoy the present.

Personifying Nature, Montaigne affords her the opportunity to respond to the human resentment toward the natural necessity of human mortality. Among Nature's numerous arguments, including one based on equality, on the fact that everyone must die, is an appeal to ignorance. Fear of the uncertain or unknown is a primary source of trepidation concerning death. Nature counters, "It is very simple-minded of you to condemn something which you have never experienced either yourself or through another."[63] In this early essay on death, Montaigne seems quite close to ancient philosophical pedagogy and its practice of spiritual exercises, designed in part to free the individual from irrational fear, especially concerning death. Yet, in later essays, most notably "On Diversion" and "On Physiognomy," Montaigne explicitly warns against following the philosophical methods intended to help us overcome various passions and fears. They cause more torment than death

---

[61] Montaigne, *Essays*, 102.
[62] Montaigne, *Essays*, 1263.
[63] Montaigne, *Essays*, 106.

itself. Socrates alone looks squarely at the "phenomenon itself" and ponders death as a "natural and neutral event."

Having separated Socrates from the rest of humanity, Montaigne proceeds to diminish, even trivialize, the entire art of dying well. He insouciantly counsels, "If you do not know how to die, never mind. Nature will tell you how to do it on the spot, plainly and adequately."[64] Diversion, which seemed in the early essay on Solon's dictum to be the great enemy of the proper approach to death, is now seen as nature's way of assuaging fears and doctoring grief. Speaking of the hold any strong passion can have on us, Montaigne writes, "Change always solaces it, dissolves it and dispels it. If I cannot fight it, I flee it; and by my flight I made a diversion and use craft; by changing place, occupation, and company, I escape from it into the crowd of other pastimes and cogitations, in which it loses all track of me and cannot find me."[65] As David Lewis Schaefer puts it, "The term 'diversion' is actually a label for the enormous project . . . of redirecting human concerns from transcendent goods to earthly ones, so as to leave our souls with no leisure, so to speak, for the former." He adds, "Montaigne intends the energy of the passions which has previously been drawn in the direction of transcendental strivings to be redirected toward earthly concerns."[66]

Montaigne's strategy of ironic reversal, of arguing first on behalf of and then against philosophy, finds its most dramatic instantiation in the investigation of death. Hartle's "circular dialectic" is put to different use in Montaigne's treatment of death, in this case with the focus on a dialectical clash between the few and the many, between philosophical and common opinion. Much more than Socrates, Montaigne aims to harmonize philosophy and popular opinion. Indeed, he often abases or ridicules philosophical theories, as is the case in the later discussions

---

[64] Montaigne, *Essays*, 1190.

[65] Montaigne, *Essays*, 941.

[66] David Lewis Schaefer, *The Political Philosophy of Montaigne* (Ithaca, N.Y.: Cornell University Press, 1990), 308. Schaefer sees Montaigne as a "propagandist for the liberal way of life," who develops a rhetoric "deprecating the significance of public or political concerns as such, by comparison with private, pacific, and bodily good" (395). Whether Schaefer is right in thinking that Montaigne's fundamental goal was political and included making politics safe for philosophy is not germane to my reading of Montaigne. Schaefer's general point about Montaigne's promotion of diversion as a way of channeling energy formerly attuned to transcendent goods seems sound. For Schaefer's view of the relationship of Montaigne to Socrates, see 295–311.

of death in the *Essays*. If Montaigne never directly questions Socrates' equanimity in the face of death, much doubt is cast on the philosophical framework within which Plato depicts Socrates' death: the lengthy attention given in the *Apology*, *Crito*, and *Phaedo* to arguments concerning the nature of the soul, its immortality, and the condition in which a soul ought to live so as to be prepared for death. Montaigne equates theological preparation for death, of the sort practiced in the Christian churches, with the strategies advocated by philosophers: they are both diversions.[67] In his words, those

> poor wretches ... on our scaffolds, filled with a burning zeal to which they devote, as far as they are able, all their senses—their ears drinking in the exhortations they receive, while their arms and their eyes are lifted up to Heaven and their voices raised in loud prayer full of fierce and sustained emotion—are certainly performing a deed worthy of praise and proper to such an hour of need. We must praise them for their faith but not strictly for their constancy. They flee the struggle; they divert their thoughts from it (just as we occupy our children's attention when we want to use a lancet on them). ...
>
> Those who have to cross over some terrifyingly deep abyss are told to close their eyes or to avert them.[68]

The position that results from the dialectic between the many and the few leaves largely intact the beliefs of ordinary folks even as it gives philosophical readers a way back from idealized philosophical argument to a reflective embrace of the ordinary. Such dialectic is at the service of an ironic pedagogy, whose aims include purging philosophy of its inclination toward the supernatural.

The attempt to transcend death is a dangerous illusion, but the attempt to confront it directly can have equally dire consequences. We must aspire to rise above our own strength, but the scope of that aspiration is circumscribed by a properly human order. By accommodating ourselves to that condition, we can indeed be like gods, not in the sense that we reach a level of being proper to them but in the sense that we live happily in accord with our own limits. "The man who knows how

---

[67] In "Montaigne and the Rise of Skepticism in Early Modern Europe," Schiffman makes the case that only in the early essays does Montaigne hold that to philosophize is to learn to die. Later, he proposes that to philosophize is to doubt.

[68] Montaigne, *Essays*, 938.

to enjoy his existence as he ought has attained to an absolute perfection, like that of the gods. We seek other conditions because we do not understand the proper use of our own, and go out of ourselves because we do not know what is within us."[69] Montaigne repudiates the "inhumane wisdom which seeks to render us disdainful of and hostile to our bodies."[70] In a famous passage, and one dear to Pascal, Montaigne writes, "People try to get out of themselves and to escape from the man. This is folly; instead of transforming themselves into angels, they turn themselves into beasts; instead of lifting, they degrade themselves [*au lieu de se transformer en anges, ils se transforment en bestes; au lieu de se hausser, ils s'abattent*]."[71]

The distinctive features of Montaigne's natural theology emerge in this context. His natural theology differs markedly from that of the scholastics. It is not an attempt to prove by rational argument that God exists; it is rather an attempt to ground the human relationship to the divine in the experience of benevolent nature. Indeed, as some have noted, although Montaigne uses separate terms for God and nature, he writes in such a way as to obscure the distinction between them.[72] One might more accurately speak of a theological naturalism rather than a natural theology. In the midst of Montaigne's description of the sort of life we ought to live, there is a rich theological admonition against the vice of ingratitude. "I love life and cultivate it as it has pleased God to vouchsafe it to us. . . . You do wrong to that great and almighty Giver to refuse His gift, to nullify it or disfigure it [*refuser son don, l'annuller et disfigurer*]."[73] We must render "condign thanksgivinsg to Him who vouchsafes it to us."[74]

Even as he articulates an alternative theology, one that apparently has no need for doctrines of sin and redemption, he continues to affirm the truth of Christian theology. The strategy is instructive. It involves, on the one hand, verbal exaltation and, on the other, the theoretical and practical segregation of theology from the inquiry of philosophy. In the midst of the discussion of prayer, he considers an objection he has heard against those who write books on the "humanities or philosophy

---

[69] Montaigne, *Essays*, 406.
[70] Montaigne, *Essays*, 1256.
[71] Montaigne, *Essays*, 1268. Montaigne, *Les essais*, 1115.
[72] Friedrich, *Montaigne*, 315.
[73] Montaigne, *Essays*, 1264–65. Montaigne, *Les essais*, 1113.
[74] Montaigne, *Essays*, 1264.

without any admixture of Theology [*sans melange de Theologie*]."[75] Montaigne counters, with a position he describes as "not totally indefensible," "Christian Doctrine holds her rank better when set apart."[76] Divinity, he adds, is "regarded with more veneration and reverence when expounded on its style rather than when linked to human reasoning."[77]

One might wonder about the consequences for theology of its being sealed off from philosophy and its pursuit of wisdom. Could it be possible that theology has nothing important to say about how we ought to live? Does it shed no light on the human quest for self-knowledge? What accounts, for example, for the complete absence of any reference to religious instruction in Montaigne's celebrated "On the Education of Children"? At best, theology would become a set of teachings and commandments to which one gives public assent, but it is no longer a wisdom that nourishes the soul and informs its self-understanding. At worst, it would become a superfluous teaching about human life, perhaps even an unintelligible teaching, given the subtle ways in which Montaigne hints at its incongruity with the human condition. Might it be that one of the chief uses of irony in Montaigne pertains to religion?[78] He rarely addresses it directly; when he does, he is clear, perhaps too clear, about his own obedience. Yet his failure to engage directly its claims about self-knowledge and the human good creates perplexity. The mode of indirect speech reprises a central function of Platonic irony—to protect philosophy from conventional power even as doubt is cast on the authority of that power to govern souls.

In his new natural theology, Montaigne quietly distances himself from Socrates on the matter of the divine. He explains, "Nothing in the life of Socrates is so awkward to digest as his ecstasies and his daemonizings [*ses ecstases et ses demoneries*], and nothing about Plato so human

---

[75] Montaigne, *Essays*, 361. Montaigne, *Les essais*, 1.56:322.

[76] Montaigne, *Essays*, 361. "*La doctrine divine tient mieux son rang à part.*" Montaigne, *Les essais*, 322.

[77] Montaigne, *Essays*, 361.

[78] For interpretations of Montaigne that portray him as basically orthodox, see Hartle, *Michel de Montaigne*; and M. A. Screech, *Montaigne and Melancholy* (Selinsgrove, Penn.: Susquehanna University Press, 1984). Screech's defense runs from the extreme claim that "Montaigne is the authentic voice of post-Tridentine rigour" (96) to the laughably incredible assertion that Montaigne's "praise of suicide is quite orthodox" (46).

as what is alleged for calling him divine."[79] Montaigne articulates his reservation with such brevity that, were it not for the matters we have already touched upon in this chapter, it might be difficult to know what to make of it or even to determine its precise target. We have seen mention, as part of a catalog of Socrates' activities, his penchant for standing in rapt attention, caught up in contemplative thought, as others went about their business. And Socrates did of course attribute his actions to the inspiration of a daemon, who warned him when a course of action was not suitable. Montaigne surely also has in mind large sections of the dialogues of Plato in which Socrates puts forth arguments for the Idea of the Good, urges the transcendence of the Cave of ordinary human opinion, pursues an erotic longing to behold transcendent forms, or insists upon nonnegotiable moral principles, as Socrates does in the *Crito*. The circumscription of teleology, which we discussed earlier, might well exact a certain cost in Montaigne's purported fidelity to Socrates, an elimination of the erotic conception of philosophy as a love of wisdom, a yearning for that which escapes the grasp of rational inquiry. But Montaigne knows that already. His concern is less with reviving Socrates than with preserving the ancient skeptic focus on leading a life not utterly free from discontent but at least minimally troubled by the most perplexing of metaphysical and theological questions.

---

[79] Montaigne, *Essays*, 1268. Montaigne, *Les essais*, 1115.

Three

THE VIRTUE OF SCIENCE AND THE SCIENCE OF VIRTUE
Descartes' Overcoming of Socrates

If Socrates and his notion of philosophy as care of the self permeate the texts of Montaigne, that ancient philosophical authority and his way to wisdom would appear wholly irrelevant to the writings of Descartes, who seems to reverse the famous Socratic turn from natural philosophy and mathematics to human things. The pursuit of certitude and utility replaces the love of wisdom and the cultivation of the virtues constitutive of happiness. And yet the questions of happiness and the good life are not absent from Descartes' writings. In a letter to Princess Elizabeth, Descartes writes, "Beatitude, it seems to me, consists in perfect contentment of spirit and interior satisfaction."[1]

---

[1] "*La béatitude consiste, ce me semble, en un parfait contentement d'esprit et une satisfaction intérieure.*" Descartes goes on to write, "Each person can make himself content for himself without attending to any other, presuming that he observes three things, which can be traced back to the three rules of morality that I have provided in the *Discourse* [*Il me semble qu'un chacun se peut rendre content de soi-même et sans rien attendre d'ailleurs, pourvu seulement qu'il observe trois choses, auxquelles se rapportent les trois règles de morale, que j'ai mises dans le* Discours de la Méthode]." Réne Descartes, *Œuvres et lettres*, ed. André Bridoux (Paris: Bibliothèque de la Pléiade, Paris, 1937), 1199. The translations of the passage from the letter are my own. The passage addresses, even if it does not resolve, a famous debate in the literature on Descartes about the relationship between the "provisional morality" of the *Discourse* and what has come to be called the final or definitive morality. It indicates that, at a minimum, the provisional morality contains important elements in Descartes' mature understanding

The passage indicates that Descartes had determinate ideas about happiness; as we shall see, beatitude is much more of a preoccupation of Descartes than has usually been acknowledged. He speaks here, as elsewhere, of the sovereign good, "the theme or the end to which our actions tend."[2] He explains, "To achieve secure contentment, we must cultivate virtue, that is, we must possess a strong and unyielding will to execute all that we judge to be better and employ all our strength to judge well."[3] In what follows, we will take seriously Descartes' overlooked entrance into the classical debate over the best way of life. Since Descartes' treatment of this issue is often indirect and subtle, we shall have to attend to the arts of writing in his texts. He is as deliberate as Montaigne about stylistic matters, and, contrary to appearances, he is as serious about Socrates as is Montaigne.

To see Descartes' complex and paradoxical stance toward inherited philosophy, we need to consider the role of Socrates in Descartes' project, a role that is more prominent than is typically admitted. That neglect is at least partly attributable to another omission, regarding the influence on Descartes of Montaigne, for whom Socrates is the exemplar of the learned ignorance of the philosopher. The significance of

---

of the good life for human beings. On that debate, see Gary Steiner, *Descartes as a Moral Thinker: Christianity, Technology, Nihilism* (Amherst, N.Y.: Humanity Books, 2004), 15–49. Also see Etienne Gilson, *Discours de la méthode: Texte et commentaire*, 5th ed. (Paris: Vrin, 1976); Michele le Doeuff, *The Philosophical Imaginary*, trans. Colin Gordon (Stanford, Calif.: Stanford University Press, 1989), 62; Martial Geurolt, *Descartes' Philosophy Interpreted According to the Order of Reasons*, trans. Roger Ariew, 2 vols. (Minneapolis: University of Minnesota Press, 1984–1985), 2:192. M. H. Lefebvre, "De la morale provisoire à la générosité," in *Descartes, Cahiers de Royaumount*, Philosophie no. 2 (Paris: Les Éditions de Minuit, 1957); and T. Keefe "Descartes's 'Morale Definitive' and the Autonomy of Ethics," *Romantic Review* 64, no. 2 (1973): 85–98.

[2] "*Le motif, ou la fin à laquelle tendent nos actions.*" Descartes, *Œuvres et lettres*, 1199.

[3] "*Pour avoir un contentement qui soit solide, il est besoin de suivre la vertu, c'est-à-dire d'avoir une volonté ferme et constante d'exécuter tout ce que nous jugerons être le meilleur, et d'employer toute la force de notre entendement à en bien juger.*" Descartes, *Œuvres et lettres*, 1200 (transl. mine). In the dedicatory letter to the *Principles of Philosophy*, he offers a unified account of the "pure and genuine virtues, which proceed solely from knowledge of what is right," which have "one and the same nature," and which "are included under the single term 'wisdom.'" Descartes, dedicatory letter to the *Principles of Philosophy*, in *The Philosophical Writings of Descartes*, trans. John Cottingham, Robert Stoothoff, and Dugald Murdoch (Cambridge: Cambridge University Press, 1985), 1:191.

Descartes' engagement with Socrates is twofold. First, it serves, as it does in Montaigne, as the basis for a critique of the philosophy practiced in the schools, indeed in the entire history of philosophy since Plato. Second, it serves, as it does not in Montaigne, to establish a standard that must be overcome. For Montaigne, Socrates is the model of the philosophical life, a life devoted to unending inquiry, a life characterized by learned ignorance. For Montaigne, such a life constitutes the sovereign good for human beings. Descartes' attitude toward Socrates is quite different. Just as he presents his physics and his geometry as advancing beyond the ancients in their solution of problems the ancients deemed insoluble, so too Descartes' philosophy itself will now resolve the key questions, precisely the ones Socrates and Montaigne deem intractable. Descartes offers a new science of virtue isomorphic to his new method for the sciences. As we shall see, the character of that new science raises questions about the status of theology and role of the divine in the good life. Here again, Descartes' style of writing and his use of ironic discourse surface in telling ways.

§1. The Arts of Writing and the Science of Living

On the surface of his writings, Descartes apparently tables or ignores the question of the good; he certainly addresses it in a manner that leaves its relationship to his overall project unclear. Perhaps his most explicit treatment of the question of the good life in his new system occurs in his famous image of knowledge as a tree; that perfect morality will be the final fruit of his methodical approach to all knowledge:

> The whole of philosophy is like a tree. The roots are metaphysics, the trunk is physics, and the branches emerging from the trunk are all the other sciences, which may be reduced to three principal ones, namely medicine, mechanics and morals. By "morals" I understand the highest and most perfect moral system, which presupposes a complete knowledge of the other sciences and is the ultimate level of wisdom.[4]

But that would seem to delay indefinitely a philosophical knowledge of how to live well. Conversely, the knowledge of how to live would result from a technical knowledge supplied by experts—the prototypical Enlightenment dream. And yet in numerous other works Descartes

---

[4] Descartes, *Principles of Philosophy*, in *Philosophical Writings*, 1:186.

makes at least passing reference to the good life as something accessible to us through the cultivation of certain habits of mind. In these passages, his thought appears to be in line, or at least to invite comparison, with classical discussions of the sovereign good.

To discern the unity in his various projects, we need not only to display the connections between the different texts and parts of his philosophy, we also need to see the way the texts themselves operate as spiritual exercises, fields for the practice of the virtues constitutive of the sovereign good. As Matthew Jones convincingly argues in *The Good Life in the Scientific Revolution*, Descartes' most influential books, such as the *Discourse* and the *Meditations*, offer a "series of striking images and recondite reasoning intended to effect a moral and epistemic transformation of the attentive reader."[5] In a manner that calls to mind Plato even as it transforms the pedagogy of the Academy, Descartes' mathematical and natural-philosophical writings constitute "practices that can help one live the good life."[6] The goal of fostering in readers self-appropriation of the relevant practices involves at least a modest ironic pedagogy. Going beyond Jones, David Lachterman, in his groundbreaking *Ethics of Geometry*, argues that *The Geometry* is the key text in Descartes' corpus. The overcoming of the geometry of Euclid and Apollonius involves much more than a display of greater mathematical expertise. It demonstrates the success of the new method and reflects a divergent conception of the relationship of intellect to nature, body, and human community. Lachterman speaks of the "disparate ways (*mores*) and styles in which the Euclidean and the Cartesian geometers do geometry, comport themselves as mathematicians both toward their students and toward the very nature of those learnable items (*ta mathemata*) from which their disciplined deeds take their name."[7] As we shall see, the differences in posture or

---

[5] Matthew L. Jones, *The Good Life in the Scientific Revolution: Descartes, Pascal, Leibniz, and the Cultivation of Virtue* (Chicago: University of Chicago Press, 2006), 79. See also Matthew Jones, "Descartes's Geometry as Spiritual Exercise," *Critical Inquiry* 38, no. 1 (2001): 40–71.

[6] Jones, *Good Life in the Scientific Revolution*, 3. On philosophy and spiritual exercises, see Pierre Hadot, *Philosophy as a Way of Life: Spiritual Exercises from Socrates to Foucault* (Malden, Mass.: Blackwell, 1995).

[7] David Rapport Lachterman, *The Ethics of Geometry: A Genealogy of Modernity* (New York: Routledge, 1989), xi. The simplest way to put the contrast between the ancient Greek and the modern Cartesian conception of mathematics and science is to say that, while the ancients had a hypothetical awareness of *mathesis universalis*, they resisted its blandishments, for ontological, epistemological, and ethical

comportment of teacher and student with respect to the knowable will signal differences in pedagogical method.

As Amos Funkenstein has noted, in contrast to ancient Aristotelian science, Cartesian science opts for linguistic univocity and homogeneity of method.[8] Cartesian logic drops discourse through middle terms in favor of sequential ordering. Reasoning in terms of proportions or relations was not novel; it was part of ancient geometry. What is new is the application of this mode of reasoning to the knowable as such, its elevation to the status of *mathesis universalis*.[9] Another noteworthy feature of the universal science is its accentuation of construction over demonstration and its introduction of motion into the very operation of geometrical proof. In Euclidean geometry, theorems or proofs predominate over problems or constructions; the elegant use of the perfect passive participle, for both problems (*quod erat faciendum*) and theorems (*quod erat demonstrandum*), indicates that the geometrical object and its properties have always already existed. By contrast, in Cartesian geometry, the focus is on problems rather than theorems, and the constructions arise from temporal motion.

The transformations wrought within Cartesian geometry are crucial; in them can be found the roots and the promise of the fertility of a productive conception of human knowing.[10] Moreover, Descartes' geometry contains a sophisticated rethinking of the connections between geometrical objects and the natural world. In antiquity, geometry is often prized as the most rigorous form of reasoning. In the *Posterior Analytics*, Aristotle appeals to geometry as the paradigm of demonstrative reasoning. Even as it invites an ascent from the sensible to the intelligible, it remains anchored in the shared prescientific understanding of nature and imagined shapes. Incorporating into geometry

---

reasons. Descartes stakes his entire method on the establishment of just such a universal science of learning, with important repercussions for metaphysics, epistemology, and ethics.

[8] Amos Funkenstein, *Theology and the Scientific Imagination from the Middle Ages to the Seventeenth Century* (Princeton, N.J.: Princeton University Press, 1986), 72–76.

[9] On the antecedent, Greek discussions of *mathesis universalis*, see Lachterman, *Ethics of Geometry*, 177–78.

[10] Descartes indicates the significance of geometry at the end of the *Meditations* when he repeatedly speaks of considering physical objects as "objects of pure mathematics." Descartes, *Meditations on First Philosophy*, trans. Michael Moriarty (Oxford: Oxford University Press, 2008), Meditation 6.

the techniques of algebra, with their indifference to the objects under consideration, Descartes largely frees geometry from the constraint of imagined shapes. Comparison is now possible across all genera of beings, whose qualitative differences recede from view.[11] As we have noted, Descartes is more interested in constructions than in proofs, in the art of discovery (analysis) and making than in the art of the presentation (synthesis) of truths already known. Suspecting that the ancients hid the art of discovery from students, Descartes wants to reveal that art. But the art of discovery requires more than merely mimicking what has already been shown by a teacher; it requires the student to launch out on his own. Thus, Descartes' irony will sometimes involve silence or skipping over steps or not taking the next step so that students can make these themselves.

The reading of Descartes' scientific and mathematical writings by Jones and Lachterman suggests the possibility of a more intimate pedagogical and rhetorical connection between his more obviously stylized literary texts and his more technical writings. Descartes certainly stresses the virtues of his new science, but he also offers a new science of virtue, an account of the sovereign good and the means to its achievement. The topic of the good life, far from being unimportant or even secondary in Descartes, is a pervasive, if somewhat veiled, concern. In place of an endlessly puzzling, aporetic investigation of the good life, Descartes prefers to issue peremptory statements, as in his letter to Princess Elizabeth, concerning the nature of happiness. Recognizing its prominence helps us to relocate Descartes in the mainstream of classical philosophy, which takes its orientation from the great question of the good life for human beings. Yet Descartes is not simply building upon the giants who preceded him. Indeed, except for Socrates (and his Plato), Descartes seems to envision the history of philosophy as a series of dead ends. Neither here nor elsewhere does he work dialectically in and through the received opinions of the many and the wise about the good life. Nor does he pose the question of the good life in as direct or robust a fashion as do his predecessors. It is as if Descartes wants to resolve a question without ever allowing the question itself to arise.

---

[11] The most important philosophical study of the history of these transformations remains Edmund Husserl's *Crisis of European Sciences and Transcendental Phenomenology* (Chicago: Northwestern University Press, 1970).

§2. Recovering and Overcoming Socrates

Descartes wants to move philosophy from the love to the realization of wisdom. To do so, he must liberate human reason and the practice of inquiry from the kinds of dependency and limits that have previously been deemed insuperable. Consider the following passage:

> We were all children before being men and had to be governed for some time by our appetites and our teachers, which were often opposed to each other and neither of which, perhaps, always gave us the best advice; hence I thought it virtually impossible that our judgments should be as unclouded and firm as they would have been if we had had the full use of our reason from the moment of our birth, and if we had always been guided by it alone.[12]

The antecedent conditions of human rationality will not play a part in its free exercise. To achieve what Socrates could not, a radical departure from received opinion is necessary. It is not sufficient simply to recognize the deficiency in convention and the diversity of views about the big questions. Philosophy must uncover an indubitable foundation. Hence the necessity of radical doubt: "Regarding the opinions to which I had hitherto given credence, I thought I could not do better than undertake to get rid of them, all at one go, in order to replace them afterwards with better ones, or with the same ones once I had squared them with the standards of reason."[13] Here we find a revealing expression of Descartes' combination of revolution and tradition or, to be more precise, of the way he justifies a radical departure from tradition by reference to the tradition itself. Only through a severing can one realize the as yet unrealized telos of philosophy.

Descartes' understanding of the ultimate goal of philosophy is evident in the preface to the French edition of the *Principles*. Philosophy is a

> search for the first causes and the true principles which enable us to deduce the reasons for everything we are capable of knowing, both for

---

[12] Descartes, *Discourse on Method*, in *Philosophical Writings*, 1:117.
[13] Descartes, *Discourse on Method*, in *Philosophical Writings*, 1:117.

the conduct of life and for the preservation of health and the discovery of all manner of skills.[14]

It is difficult to imagine a more comprehensive philosophical vision, encompassing the traditional division into theoretical and practical and, within the practical, the orders of doing and making. As Richard Kennington observes, "Mastery is neutral between thinking and making, between philosophy and *techne*." Even as it calls to mind, it subverts ancient distinctions. Indeed, seen from the vantage point of medieval thought, Descartes' philosophy looks more like theology than philosophy.[15] Thomas Aquinas, we should recall, claimed that sacred doctrine, unlike speculative philosophy, was both theoretical and practical.[16] Moreover, the famous marks of the new science, certitude and utility, are, for Thomas, signs of the superiority of the believer's pursuit of wisdom over that of the philosopher.[17] In Descartes' project, philosophy subtly takes on the characteristics of theology.

Descartes goes on to provide a brief genealogy of philosophy, particularly of its roots in Plato and Aristotle. The former, following Socrates, "ingenuously confessed that he had never yet been able to discover anything certain."[18] By contrast, Aristotle was "less candid" and put forth a new method and proposed principles as "true and certain, although it seems most unlikely that he in fact considered them to be so."[19] As was true for the ancients, so too for Descartes, unlearning is often the first step in learning. The common practice of philosophy in the centuries separating Descartes from Socrates has only exacerbated the problem, inculcating bad habits and spreading erroneous opinion. The habit of passive reading and the substitution of commentary for

---

[14] Descartes, preface to *Principles of Philosophy*, in *Philosophical Writings*, 1:179. Descartes, *Œuvres de Descartes*, ed. C. Adam and P. Tannery (Paris: Vrin/C.N.R.S., 1964–1976), 9b:3.

[15] Richard Kennington, "Rene Descartes," in *History of Political Philosophy*, ed. Leo Strauss and Joseph Cropsey, 2nd ed. (Chicago: University of Chicago Press, 1981), 395–415. Kennington's essay is especially helpful on the political setting and implications of the *Discourse* (401, 408).

[16] Aquinas, *Summa Theologiae* 1.1.4.

[17] Aquinas, *Summa Contra Gentiles* 1.2.

[18] Descartes, preface to the *Principles of Philosophy*, in *Philosophical Writings*, 1:181. "A ingenuëment confessé qu'il n'auoit encore rien pu trouuer de certain." Descartes, *Œuvres*, 9b:5–6.

[19] Descartes, preface to the *Principles of Philosophy*, in *Philosophical Writings*, 1:181.

the active engagement with vital questions have made true philosophy nearly nonexistent. Here we detect a consonance between Descartes and Montaigne, the latter of whom crafts a new genre of philosophical writing as a way of circumventing the desiccated commentary tradition.[20] Descartes confronts Aristotle directly in order to clear the ground for his own science.

In the *Principles*, what stands in the way of philosophical progress is the authority of the texts of Aristotle: "The majority of those aspiring to be philosophers in the last few centuries have blindly followed Aristotle."[21] Descartes grants that much of the confusion has to do with poor readers who import claims into Aristotle's works that he would never recognize; the influence of Aristotle is so pervasive that even those who have not followed him are nonetheless "saturated with his opinions in their youth (since these are the only opinions taught in the Schools)."[22] Aristotle's influence must be extirpated because his starting points are insecure and misleading. The situation is so grave that, "among those who have studied whatever has been called philosophy up till now, those who have learnt least are the most capable of learning true philosophy."[23]

Socratic unknowing, in opposition to Aristotelian dogmatism, is thus the path to reawakening the possibility of true philosophy. But this suggests for Descartes a new type of reading and writing. As potentially positive sources of knowledge, Descartes includes only those books "capable of instructing us well; for in such cases we hold a kind of conversation with the authors."[24] The quest to discern a manner of composition that would provoke rather than enervate thought aligns Descartes, among the ancients, with Plato and, among his contemporaries, with Montaigne, and with their ironic modes of composition.

---

[20] On Descartes and Montaigne, see Carol Collier, "The Self in Montaigne and Descartes: From Portraiture to Indigence," *De Philosophia* 13, no. 2 (1997): 249–58; E. M. Curley, *Descartes against the Skeptics* (Cambridge, Mass.: Harvard University Press, 1978); John Lyons, "Descartes and Modern Imagination," *Philosophy and Literature* 23, no. 2 (1999): 302–12; Hassan Melehy, *Writing Cogito: Montaigne, Descartes, and the Institution of the Modern Subject* (Albany, N.Y.: State University of New York Press, 1998); Léon Brunschvicg, *Descartes et Pascal lecteurs de Montaigne* (Neuchâtel: A la Baconnière, 1942).

[21] Descartes, preface to *Principles of Philosophy*, in *Philosophical Writings*, 1:182.
[22] Descartes, preface to *Principles of Philosophy*, in *Philosophical Writings*, 1:182.
[23] Descartes, preface to *Principles of Philosophy*, in *Philosophical Writings*, 1:183.
[24] Descartes, preface to *Principles of Philosophy*, in *Philosophical Writings*, 1:181.

Like Plato and unlike Socrates, Descartes writes books. Like Plato and with the same note of irony, he writes a book to disabuse readers of the influence of books, both certain types of books and certain conventional ways of reading books. In one of the more perplexing statements in all of his writings, he describes his *Discourse on Method*, whose goal is to portray his "life as if in a picture," as a "history or, if you prefer, a fable [*une histoire, ou, si vous l'aymez mieux, que' comme une fable*] in which, among certain examples worthy of imitation, you will perhaps also find many others that it would be right not to follow."[25] Although Descartes is not typically given to poetic discourse, the genre to which he assigns his *Discourse* is closer to what Aristotle calls poetry than it is to what he calls history. In the *Poetics*, Aristotle says that poetry is more philosophical than history because the former has to do with the universal rather than the particular.[26] Descartes is writing about matters whose significance and pedagogical implications transcend the particular conditions of his own life. That is perhaps the point of the added reference to the genre of the fable, whose latent meaning must be deciphered by the reader. As he puts it in the course of reviewing his own education, "fables awaken the mind." But of course well-crafted fables need not make their lessons obvious. As is clear from Descartes' repeated claims that not everyone should follow his example, he needs to write so that his true meaning is grasped by his intended audience and so that the remaining readers will not do harm to themselves or others.

The proximate source of this mode of writing is not Plato but Montaigne. As Jonathan Rée notes in "Descartes's Comedy," the *Discourse* is a kind of autobiography, a "first-person narrative about a protagonist who the narrator used to be."[27] Complicating matters is that Descartes offers a critique of fables in the very work that he presents as a fable. If Montaigne's strategy is to reduce philosophy to autobiography as a means of dissolving philosophical systems into anecdote, Descartes puts Montaigne's technique to an opposite use: "building anecdote into philosophy."[28] The difference between the narrators of Montaigne and Descartes is reflected in their divergent attitude toward temporality. In

---

[25] Descartes, *Discourse on Method*, in *Philosophical Writings*, 112. Descartes, *Œuvres*, 6:4.

[26] Aristotle, *Poetics* 9.1451b6–7.

[27] Jonathan Rée, "Descartes's Comedy," *Philosophy and Literature* 8, no. 2 (1984): 153.

[28] Rée, "Descartes's Comedy," 154.

Montaigne, temporality dissolves into a flux that the narrator cannot reduce to order; the best he can do is to record its passing and remind himself and us in the present of its very passing. Temporality signifies "restless indeterminacy" and gives rise to an "unbridled irony" that undermines even the narrator. Temporality is also prominent in the *Discourse* and *Meditations*, but there is a striking difference between time as experienced prior to the discovery of the method and time as experienced after the mind has subjected itself to liberating spiritual exercises. Descartes thus tempers irony and directs it only toward those unaware of the method or toward the former self of the narrator. It is, as Rée puts it, the "irony of a confidently anticipated retrospect."[29]

Meeting Montaigne on his terms and deploying genres of writing that engage the style of Montaigne's essays, Descartes fashions a narrative whose telos is the transcendence of narrative. More than Montaigne, Descartes is a reformer, whose task is to improve nature, to move it from what it is now to what it might become if it were rendered docile to rational, methodic control. There is thus a surface resemblance to the old teleological understanding of nature. Yet the basic philosophical task of supplying a secure foundation for all knowledge is complete at the end of the *Meditations*. What remains is not the ongoing pursuit of a partially realized good through the further practice of a set of virtues constitutive of happiness. Rather, what remains is the pursuit of progress, the alleviation of the ills afflicting the human condition. That makes Descartes' account, as Riley indicates, a genuinely independent position, a novel theory, not easily assimilated to Augustine or Montaigne or any other classical or medieval predecessors. Descartes eschews the narrative of erotic longing for the divine even as he insists that philosophy needs precisely what Montaigne rejects, namely, "the stability of the subject."[30] As we have seen, Montaigne wants to have it both ways; he simultaneously repudiates any notion of a metaphysical subject even as he naively assumes the unity of his reflections on his own self. Moreover, he also holds that reason "plays its role apart" from the flux of experience and the force of the passions. Both thinkers are, in the words of Vincent Carraud, egologists, philosophers of the self. In the wake of Montaigne's own inconsistencies on the ego, Descartes

---

[29] Rée, "Descartes's Comedy," 162.

[30] Patrick Riley, *Character and Conversion in Autobiography: Augustine, Montaigne, Descartes, Rousseau, and Sartre* (Charlottesville: University of Virginia Press, 2004), 61.

opts to affirm the stability of the intellectual substance and defend its transparency and veracity against skeptical challenges.

From his youth, Descartes observes, he was "nourished upon letters."[31] He supposed that by means of such training he could acquire a "clear and certain knowledge of all that is useful in life." But the promise was not realized. "I found myself beset by so many doubts and errors that I came to think I had gained nothing from my attempts to become educated but increasing recognition of my ignorance [*découuert de plus en plus mon ignorance*]."[32] Of course, this is precisely the Socratic moment in education, the moment in which one comes to know that one does not know. The reference to Socrates is instructive not just because it reinforces the notion that Socrates' insight is superior to that of Descartes' teachers but also because Descartes moves past it so quickly. The key insight of Socrates' entire life, the awareness that made him wiser than others, provides for Descartes merely an occasion to underscore the defects of his own education. Of course, Descartes obliquely indicates his own superiority both to the tradition of philosophy since Plato and to his contemporary teachers, who are unaware of their own ignorance. But, in a masterful use of ironic understatement, Descartes asserts none of this directly; it is left for the deft reader to surmise.

There are other telling Socratic allusions in Descartes' writings, particularly in the *Discourse*. His reduction of extant philosophy to a rhetorical art of speaking reflects Socrates' denigration of the Sophists, who were able to give impressive speeches before large crowds but were incapable of responding in private to the perspicacious questions of a serious interlocutor. Later in that work he will speak of his own method as allowing light to flow into a cellar—an image that both calls to mind the allegory of the Cave and promises to deliver enlightenment of the most important human affairs. But, of course, Descartes is interested in much more than illumination; he is committed to transformation. Whereas Plato provides images and writes ironically about the reordering of society by reference to philosophical knowledge, Descartes rejects metaphors, or rather uses metaphors as a first stage in a philosophical pedagogy that will ultimately transcend metaphor. Descartes goes directly to what one might call, following Machiavelli, the

---

[31] Descartes, *Discourse on Method*, in *Philosophical Writings*, 1:113.

[32] Descartes, *Discourse on Method*, in *Philosophical Writings*, vol. 1. Descartes, *Œuvres*, 6:4.

"effectual truth of things." Moreover, in his reference to "ancient moral teachings as proud and magnificent palaces [*palais fort superbes & fort magnifiques*]," he echoes Machiavelli's critique of the "imagined republics" of the ancients.[33] Even in this passing reference we can detect Descartes' standard practice with respect to Socratic philosophy: cite its aspirations in order to demonstrate the path toward their fulfillment or overcoming—in this case by a jarring fusion of Plato and Machiavelli.

To transcend both Plato and Aristotle, Descartes introduces a novel accent on utility, which highlights the intimate connection between knowledge and the activity of production. Indeed, one of Descartes' principal objections to Aristotle has to do with the latter's failure to supply true knowledge of causes, a failure evident from the poverty of Aristotle's productive sciences. If he had known the causes, as Bacon would put it, he would have produced the effects. In the preface to the French edition of the *Principles*, Descartes writes, "The best way of proving the falsity of Aristotle's principles is to point out that they have not enabled any progress to be made in all the many centuries in which they have been followed."[34] There is much more operative here than a simple objection to stagnant technological progress. Basing his argument on a careful reading of *The Geometry* and the works on physics, Lachterman argues that Descartes shifts the balance from contemplative knowing to productive knowing, a model of knowing that discloses a more intimate connection between certitude and utility than might initially be apparent. This has far-reaching metaphysical implications: "Method, in Descartes, not only codifies rules of procedure; it constrains those 'objects' to which it is applied to such an extent that their very intelligibility becomes identical with their susceptibility to methodical treatment."[35] Objects owe their intelligibility to their mode of genesis; this means that the distinction between the natural and the artificial nearly vanishes. Descartes invites the "reader to regard the natural as a result of the artificial."[36] Consequently, the "*topos* of wonder," characteristic of the life of the philosopher, "now has a new home": "the artistry of the technician."[37]

---

[33] Descartes, *Discourse on Method*, in *Philosophical Writings*, 1:114. Descartes, *Œuvres*, 6:7–8. For Machiavelli, see *The Prince*, chap. 9.
[34] Descartes, preface to *Principles of Philosophy*, in *Philosophical Writings*, 1:189.
[35] Lachterman, *Ethics of Geometry*, 175.
[36] Lachterman, *Ethics of Geometry*, 172.
[37] Lachterman, *Ethics of Geometry*, 151.

Like Socrates, Descartes adopts a skeptical stance toward received opinion. His insistence upon doubting any opinion that admits in any way of being doubted can be seen as an exaggeration of Socrates' practice of questioning the deeply held beliefs of his fellow citizens. The need to go beyond Socrates is counseled by philosophy itself, which seeks knowledge and wisdom. On Descartes' view, the zetetic conception of philosophy—what Montaigne would call Socratic philosophy, that is to say, philosophy simply—subverts not just conventional opinion but philosophy itself. A promising protreptic, the ancient genre of speech that aimed to persuade potential philosophers to take up the life of wisdom, ends up as a reductio ad absurdum of the philosophical life. The pondering of variant and contradictory philosophical positions confirms only the futility of the attempts of the greatest intellects to give an account of nature and human nature. If Descartes had not discovered his method, he might well have concluded with Pascal that the philosophers "worry the man who seeks."[38]

Careful readers can pick up hints of Descartes' reservations about Socrates in odd places. Indeed, one of his more subtle uses of irony—an irony of understatement and indirection—is evident in the references to Socrates that fail to cite Socrates. Consider, for example, the discussion in *The Passions of the Soul* of the passion of wonder, which, first of all the passions, is a sudden surprise of the soul provoked by objects that seem "unusual and extraordinary." The use of wonder is to "make us learn and retain in our memory things of which we were previously ignorant."[39] It can also "dispose us to acquire scientific knowledge."[40] But Descartes seems most concerned with castigating excessive wonder, what he calls "astonishment," a kind of rapture of the soul in which the "whole body remains as immobile as a statue."[41] The problem with this state, to which those who have a low estimation of their abilities are most inclined, is that it precludes careful analysis of the subject matter in question. One cannot help but read in these passages an admonition against the classical understanding of philosophy as both arising

---

[38] Blaise Pascal, *Pensées*, trans. A. J. Krailsheimer, rev. ed. (New York: Penguin Classics, 1995), 4.

[39] Descartes, *On the Passions*, in *Philosophical Writings*, 1:353–54.

[40] Descartes, *On the Passions*, in *Philosophical Writings*, 1:353.

[41] Descartes, *On the Passions*, in *Philosophical Writings*, 1:354. "*Ce qui fait que tout le corps demeure immobile comme une statue.*" Descartes, *Œuvres*, 11:383; *Les Passions* part 2, article 73.

from and issuing in wonder. Even more pointedly, the passage directly, if silently, targets Socrates, whom Plato depicts in the *Symposium* as immobilized by thought. It treats as an obstacle to the good life what Jonathan Lear identifies as one of its constituents: the habitual art of the uncanny, of bafflement at what one thought one knew. Thus does Descartes deploy irony to transcend irony, just as he deploys narrative to transcend it.

§3. Descartes' New Science of Virtue

In a variety of contexts, Descartes refers to the life of virtue as the sovereign good, a life that breeds in the soul tranquility and harmony. Commentators have noted the resemblance between Descartes' account of virtue and the third rule in the provisional moral code in the discourse:

> Try always to master myself rather than fortune, and change my desires rather than the order of the world. In general I would become accustomed to believing that nothing lies entirely within our power except our thoughts, so that after doing our best in dealing with matters external to us, whatever we fail to achieve is absolutely impossible so far as we are concerned.[42]

The task of self-mastery with its attendant attitude of indifference toward what escapes our control calls to mind classical Stoic conceptions of the good life. What is novel in Descartes is his expansive, but not limitless, view of what lies within our control. Toward the end of the *Discourse*, he speaks of the fruits of his method and, before making the famous announcement of a new philosophy that would "replace the speculative philosophy taught in the Schools [*qu'au lieu de cette Philosophie speculatiue, qu'on enseigne dans les escholes*]," he describes the method as assisting both in resolving "certain difficulties in the speculative sciences" and in "governing his own conduct."[43] The method will have palpable, public benefits as well. Descartes proposes that it will contribute to the "general welfare of mankind." He amplifies:

> Through this philosophy, we could know the power and action of fire, water, air, the stars, the heavens, and all the other bodies in our

---

[42] Descartes, *Discourse on Method*, in *Philosophical Writings*, 1:123.
[43] Descartes, *Discourse on Method*, in *Philosophical Writings*, 1:142. Descartes, *Œuvres*, 6:61.

environment, as distinctly as we know the crafts of our artisans; and we could use this knowledge—as the artisans use theirs—for all the purposes for which it is appropriate and thus make ourselves, as it were, the masters and possessors of nature [*ainsi nous rendre comme maistres & possesseurs de la Nature*].[44]

This calls to mind the original title for the *Discourse*: "The Project of a Universal Science Which Can Elevate Our Nature to Its Highest Degree of Perfection."[45] Having counseled conformity in external matters to conventional laws and customs and indifference to the order of the world, he now engages in what he elsewhere calls "boldness," redefined against the tradition as a form of courage, rather than a vice, that "disposes the soul to carry out the most dangerous tasks."[46] The audacity of the goal is made feasible by a new conception of the relationships among the intellect, the body, and the external world: a new ethos, as Lachterman puts it, in the human inquirer's way of being in and toward other entities.

While not absolute or immediate, control over the external world is indeed possible. For example, the world to which we return in the final section of the *Meditations* is the world as understood by mathematical physics; the only features of things that are clearly and distinctly known are those susceptible to a quantitative description. There is, then, an important connection between the final meditation and Descartes' *Geometry*, which aims to provide "rules for the measurement of all bodies."[47] Some see Descartes' emphasis on mathematics as reprising a Platonic or Augustinian theme. In that tradition, mathematics occupies an intermediate and subordinate stage in the ascent to the Good; a partial overlap with that tradition is operative in the *Meditations*, where, for example, the second proof for the existence of God contains as one of its crucial steps an analogy to geometrical necessity. Descartes reshapes ancient philosophical pedagogy. Whereas, in the Platonic tradition, the notion of God as geometer is but a likely story, in need of supplementation by other likely stories or myths, Descartes takes this notion literally. Thus, the meditation ends not with a hierarchical reflection

---

[44] Descartes, *Œuvres*, 6:62.
[45] See Lachterman, *Ethics of Geometry*, 129.
[46] Descartes, *On the Passions*, in *Philosophical Writings*, 1:391.
[47] Descartes, *The Geometry of René Descartes*, ed. and trans. David Eugene Smith and Marcia L. Latham (New York: Dover, 1925), 43.

on the likenesses between image and exemplar but with the announcement of the infinite and linear project of mapping nature in mathematical terms. Descartes' method and its success in a variety of fields testify to the existence of resources at our disposal for the mastery of the external world.

The peculiar intelligibility that the world manifests when seen under the purview of mathematical physics might be said to constitute a new way of being in the world for rational beings. Some, such as Lachterman, have seen in Descartes' description of the new philosophy a thoroughgoing constructivist conception of knowledge. Yet Lachterman may go too far here. Despite Descartes' penchant for aligning knowledge to the model of the artisan, he also insists upon the indispensable role of the natural light, the claim that all knowledge must repose upon an indubitable foundation, a basis acknowledged but not constructed by human knowledge or will. Stanley Rosen thus speaks of a central ambiguity in Descartes. Descartes aims at two goals that may not be fully compatible with one another:

> The first is to identify the structure of nature, and so all of rational order, with mathematical properties of extension; the second is to give man mastery over this order, thanks to the new technique of mathematics. If order is to provide man with certitude and security, it must be eternal, regular, and independent of, although accessible to, subjective mental activity. Unfortunately, if man is to be master of this order, it must be subject to his will.[48]

The common picture of the relationship of the mind to its body and to the external world has given rise to the notion of Cartesian angelism, the abstraction of the mind from the world of matter. Yet, in other works, perhaps most importantly in the *Passions*, Descartes tempers the tendencies toward angelism. The key, to turn from physics to the cultivation of the virtues constitutive of the good life, is proper self-knowledge, ignorance of which is the gravest source of vice. We need, as Descartes tells us in the *Passions*, to distinguish what is in our power from what is not.

---

[48] Stanley Rosen, "A Central Ambiguity in Descartes," in *The Ancients and the Moderns: Rethinking Modernity* (New Haven, Conn.: Yale University Press, 1989), 22–36.

The discernment and negotiation of what is in our power is both a theoretical and an ethical task. The theoretical point echoes Bacon's claim that if we wish to master nature, we must first obey it. Without a clear sense of nature, the investigator of its powers is likely to suppose that she can do more or less than she actually can. But it is also ethical. Given the tension between aspiration and resistance, how can the soul dwell in the tranquility that Descartes prizes as the sovereign good of human life? The answer to this question has to do with the practice of virtue, especially the virtue of generosity.

In the course of his comments on generosity, a virtue rooted in proper self-esteem, Descartes observes that "no virtue is so dependent on good birth as the virtue which causes us to esteem ourselves in accordance with our true value, and it is easy to believe that the souls which God puts into our bodies are not all equally noble and strong."[49] Despite the disparities of nature, "a good upbringing is a great help in correcting defects of birth." Through training, "we may arouse the passion of generosity in ourselves and then acquire the virtue."[50] Generosity, which "causes a person's self-esteem to be as great as it may legitimately be," has two parts.[51] The first is an awareness that nothing truly belongs to us but the freedom to dispose our volitions. Following upon that knowledge, second, is a "firm and constant resolution to use it well—that is, never to lack the will to undertake and carry out whatever he judges to be best."[52] Descartes concludes, "To do that is to pursue virtue in a perfect manner."[53]

As for Montaigne, so too for Descartes the complete possession of virtue is not as relevant as a certain kind of determination, a sign of the success of which is that one remains "firm, constant, and always the same."[54] Irresolution, a kind of anxiety, results from "too great a desire to do well and from weakness of the intellect."[55] The remedy for this is "to believe that we always do our duty when we do what we judge to be best, even though our judgment may perhaps be a very bad one."[56] The

---

[49] Descartes, *Passions of the Soul*, in *Philosophical Writings*, 1:388.
[50] Descartes, *Passions of the Soul*, in *Philosophical Writings*, 1:388.
[51] Descartes, *Passions of the Soul*, in *Philosophical Writings*, 1:384.
[52] Descartes, *Passions of the Soul*, in *Philosophical Writings*, 1:384.
[53] Descartes, *Passions of the Soul*, in *Philosophical Writings*, 1:384.
[54] Descartes, *Passions of the Soul*, in *Philosophical Writings*, 1:387.
[55] Descartes, *Passions of the Soul*, in *Philosophical Writings*, 1:390–91.
[56] Descartes, *Passions of the Soul*, in *Philosophical Writings*, 1:391.

practice of generosity would seem to involve the same sort of elimination of regret and repentance that we find in Montaigne's account of human flourishing.[57] It would also alleviate anxiety in the soul over the incomplete mastery of nature.

Generosity is a self-regarding virtue, but it has salutary social and political consequences. For Descartes, pride is not, as it was for his Christian predecessors, a vice; instead, it is "a kind of joy based on the love we have for ourselves and resulting from the belief or hope we have of being praised by certain other persons."[58] Yet, as much as Descartes may concede that, perhaps in contrast to common sense, generosity is not evenly distributed, it has for him a decidedly egalitarian character. It engenders in its possessor the recognition that, unlike wealth, honor, or intelligence, generosity is "capable of being present in every other person."[59] Generosity also uproots the vices regarding others, such as jealousy and envy, "because everything they think sufficiently valuable to be worth pursuing is such that its acquisition depends solely on themselves."[60] Generosity thus serves the ends of both theory and practice; it has a direct impact upon our conduct in the pursuit of knowledge and in our comportment toward fellow human beings. Generosity calls to mind both pagan and Christian virtues. It resembles pagan virtues such as magnanimity, without its offensive aristocratic elements, and justice, without its degree of difficulty or seeming other-orientation. Moreover, it seems to do much of the work of Christian charity without its sacrificial character or its dependence on divine grace for its existence.

We have here a stage in the movement from the characteristically premodern porous self, in which the self is inexorably susceptible to external influences, to the dominantly modern buffered self, grounded in a clear sense of boundary between self and other. Generosity establishes proper attitudes toward others without having to know, serve, or judge them by their merits; it is dependent not on a divine gift but solely on oneself. This is yet another striking anti-Augustinian moment in Descartes' writings. The contrast between porous and buffered, which Charles Taylor develops in his book *A Secular Age*, can also be

---

[57] For an interesting study of the departure of both Montaigne and Descartes from Augustinian models of autobiography and of repentance, see Riley, *Character and Conversion in Autobiography*, 60–87.

[58] Descartes, *Passions of the Soul*, in *Philosophical Writings*, 1:401.

[59] Descartes, *Passions of the Soul*, in *Philosophical Writings*, 1:384.

[60] Descartes, *Passions of the Soul*, in *Philosophical Writings*, 1:385.

expressed in terms of the rise and demise of eros understood as longing for the whole.⁶¹ We have already detected a shift in this direction in Montaigne, but in his writings the self remains fluid, subject to vagrant passions and wayward thoughts and images. Of course, Descartes' own conception of reason may be seen as an extension of Montaigne's thesis that "reason plays its role apart." The distance between Montaigne and Descartes is perhaps nowhere more evident than in the complete absence in Descartes of any reflection on death, the event in which the buffered self suffers dissolution. Yet, here too, Descartes' position, his silence about death, may be a result of his having learned from Montaigne, from the insoluble conflict in his writings between, on the one hand, the proposal of strategies for overcoming the fear of death and, on the other, the concession that these strategies fail and our best hope consists in diversion. Better under such conditions, Pascal quips, to cease thinking about such matters.

The shift from fulfillment through proper pursuit of what is external to the self to contentment based on internal monitoring is evident in Descartes' redefinition of the virtues, indeed the passions themselves, as thoughts or perceptions or cognitive dispositions. The accent on cognitive awareness does not diminish the role of the will, which remains prominent because virtue is a firm resolve. It does diminish the older sense of the passion as a suffering or passive recipient of what comes from outside. That is not eliminated entirely; indeed, the receptive nature of passion is precisely the reason for its need of governance. But the accent is on the susceptibility of passion to rational control or, rather, upon the discovery of a master passion that can regulate the rest.⁶² What is also diminished, particularly from the Aristotelian perspective, is action itself. Descartes here sets up his argument in such a way that what is internal to the soul is the principal source of virtue and happiness. Resolute action is the natural result of the virtue of generosity. What recedes from view is the significance of the division of acts into diverse types, particularly the difference between the moral and the productive acts.⁶³ If on the classical understanding tragedy results

---

⁶¹ Charles Taylor, *A Secular Age* (Cambridge, Mass.: Harvard University Press, 2007).

⁶² On this and on the relationship of other virtues to generosity, see Kennington, "Rene Descartes," 398 and 407.

⁶³ The indifference to particular acts might well signal another parallel between the ethical and the geometrical. In both cases the exaltation of artistic

from a mysterious mixture of internal character traits and external circumstance, then Descartes can be seen as limiting the prospect, coming from outside, of tragedy. His very conception of virtue renders the individual less susceptible to tragedy and more capable of responding to it, if it should occur.

Despite his emphasis on mastery and rational control, Descartes does not exalt human nature entirely above the natural or bodily order. For example, he does not follow the Cynics in deeming the passions to be evil. On the contrary, he insists that the passions are "all by nature good."[64] Only their "misuse or excess" is bad, and for this Descartes' study of the passions provides a variety of remedies, chiefly the "foresight and diligence" that will enable us to "correct our natural faults by striving to separate within ourselves the movements of the blood and spirits from the thoughts to which they are usually joined."[65] We can limit the destructive influence of the passions and cultivate habits that will help us to experience ills in a tranquil way. In quite a different way from its original, Descartes incorporates Montaigne's strategy of accommodation to our condition.[66] In this, there is an unstated response to the accusation of angelism, the details of which are contained in *The Passions of the Soul*. At the end of that work, Descartes writes:

> The soul can have pleasures of its own. But the pleasures common to it and the body depend entirely on the passions, so that persons whom the passions can move most deeply are capable of enjoying the sweetest pleasures of this life. It is true that they may also experience the most bitterness when they do not know how to put these passions to good use and when fortune works against them. But the chief use of wisdom [*Mais la Sagesse est principalement utile en ce point*] lies in its teaching us to be masters of our passions and to control them with such skill that the evils which they cause are quite bearable, and even become a source of joy.[67]

---

creativity counsels flexibility in starting points and material conditions. What is most important is the resolve to bring to completion whatever is deemed most desirable.

[64] Descartes, *Passions of the Soul*, in *Philosophical Writings*, 1:403.

[65] Descartes, *Passions of the Soul*, in *Philosophical Writings*, 1:403.

[66] For Montaigne, see especially the concluding paragraphs of "On Experience," in *Complete Essays*, trans. M. A. Screech (New York: Penguin Classics, 2003), 1268–69.

[67] Descartes, *Passions of the Soul*, in *Philosophical Writings*, 1:404. Descartes, *Œuvres*, 11:488.

The passage is striking for a number of reasons, each of which counters a common assumption about Descartes. First, Descartes' emphasis here on the pleasures common to soul and body is apt to surprise those accustomed to thinking of his definition, early in the *Meditations*, of man as a thinking thing, to which the body seems to be only accidentally attached. By the end of the *Meditations*, he does come around to describing soul and body as intimately united. Still, the notion of Cartesian dualism has led most readers of Descartes to ignore what he has to say about the body and the passions. Second, the claim that the right use of the passions affords us "the sweetest pleasures of this life" is an unexpected claim for one whose greatest quest, as described in his somewhat autobiographical *Discourse on Method*, is to satisfy an intellectual craving for certitude and for the useful, productive arts. Here again, there is a potential link between the two discussions; when Descartes describes the chief benefits of his method, he cites bodily health, "the chief good and the foundation of all other goods in this life."[68] Third, the identification of the mastery of passion as the chief use of wisdom involves an exaltation, beyond what any reader might have expected from Descartes' better-known works, of the significance of the passions for the whole of human life.

§4. Theology, Philosophical Irony, and the Arts of (Re-)Writing

The original title for the *Discourse*, "The Project of a Universal Science Which Can Elevate Our Nature to Its Highest Degree of Perfection," raises an interesting theological puzzle. How can a believer propose to raise our nature to its highest degree of perfection and exclude theology, revelation, and grace from that process? Descartes here seems to deploy the same strategy as Montaigne with respect to theology: exaltation and separation. This allows him the freedom to investigate the most important human questions as if theology shed no significant light on them. In the *Discourse* itself, he mentions theology, only to set it aside as merely practical, as teaching "how to get to heaven." The reduction of theology to a merely practical discipline that has no direct bearing on the intellectual life here and now is telling.

---

[68] Descartes, *Discourse on Method*, in *Philosophical Writings*, 1:143. "*Le premier bien, & le fondement de tous les autres biens de cette vie.*" Descartes, *Œuvres*, 6:62.

Similarly, in the preface to the French edition of the *Principles*, in the course of talking about the source of knowledge, he excludes divine revelation because "it does not lead us on by degrees but raises us at a stroke to infallible faith."[69] Descartes is always careful to avoid direct contravention of religious doctrine and to rank the divine above the human. In the *Principles*, he states, "God alone is truly wise; men are more or less wise."[70] At the end of the first part of the *Principles*, after a summary of the rules constitutive of correct philosophical reasoning, he states:

> Above all else we must impress on our memory the overriding rule that whatever God has revealed to us must be accepted as more certain than anything else. And although the light of reason may, with the utmost clarity and evidence, appear to suggest something different, we must still put our entire faith in divine authority rather than in our own judgment. But on matters where we are not instructed by divine faith, it is quite unworthy of a philosopher to accept anything as true if he has never established its truth by thorough scrutiny.[71]

Thoughtful readers cannot help but pose pressing questions. What are we to make of the status and content of revelation in relation to the method and claims proposed in Descartes' philosophy? Is it possible that moral and theological matters could remain unaffected by this standard of human perfection? Can one hold to the veracity of the Christian faith and act, in one's investigation of the big questions, as if theology could shed no light on them?

The problem is perhaps most evident in Descartes' discussion of error and the will in Meditation 4. Having eliminated the prospect of the evil genius, Descartes turns to the mystery of error. He argues that error is due to the capacity of the will to move precipitately toward an object before the intellect has had adequate opportunity to examine the truth or falsity of the object. He ends the meditation by resolving to strive never to let his will run ahead of his intellect. Our chief perfection, he states, consists precisely in disciplining the will to be subordinate to the consideration of the intellect. Is there not an ethical aspiration at the base of the method, an aspiration for self-sufficiency and self-control,

---

[69] Descartes, preface to *Principles of Philosophy*, in *Philosophical Writings*, 1:181.
[70] Descartes, preface to *Principles of Philosophy*, in *Philosophical Writings*, 1:180.
[71] Descartes, *Principles of Philosophy*, in *Philosophical Writings*, 1:221–22.

more radical than anything known to antiquity? Indeed, the apparent intellectualism of Descartes appears elsewhere to be transformed into a voluntarism. Already in the *Meditations*, he states that the potential infinity of the will is the capacity in us that most resembles the divine. In his treatise *The Passions of the Soul*, he identifies freedom as that which provides "good reason to esteem ourselves."[72] Is it possible that practical or moral and theological matters could remain unaffected by this standard of human perfection? Furthermore, what is one to make of the act of faith, wherein the will assents to what the intellect considers to be uncertain? Of course, Descartes might return to his earlier claim to have bracketed questions of faith and practical matters. But if our chief perfection consists in keeping the will behind the intellect, then would not the act of faith be at best an anomaly?

In the dedicatory letter to the members of the theology faculty at the University of Paris, Descartes appeals to them to offer him their patronage for his work, a work that will be of benefit to the church because it establishes the existence of God and the immortality of the soul, basic truths undergirding the Catholic faith. He elaborates on this point:

> I have always thought that the two issues of God and the soul were the most important of those that should be resolved by philosophical rather than theological means. For although it is sufficient for us Christians to believe by faith . . . that God exists, yet it seems certain that unbelievers cannot be convinced of the truth of religion, and scarcely even of any moral values, unless these first two truths are proved to them by natural reason. And since often in this life there are greater rewards for the vices than for the virtues, few will prefer what is right to what is useful, if they neither fear God nor expect an afterlife.[73]

We can, he adds, believe in God because of authority, but there is "no point asserting this to unbelievers, because they would call it arguing in a circle."[74] Given the argument just made, there is a certain irony in Descartes proceeding to state that, without the authoritative and public

---

[72] Free will makes us "in a certain way comparable to God in making us masters of ourselves [*en nous faisant maistres de nous memes*]." Descartes, *Passions of the Soul*, in *Philosophical Writings*, 1:384.

[73] Descartes, letter of dedication, *Meditations on First Philosophy*, 3.

[74] Descartes, letter of dedication, *Meditations on First Philosophy*, 3.

support of the theology faculty, the arguments will have little impact. Did not Descartes just say that, to have any impact upon unbelievers, Christians must dispense with arguments from authority and provide rational demonstrations? Descartes proceeds to make another mystifying comment in the opening synopsis of the meditations: the method of doubt he will employ is not, he insists, applicable to questions of good and evil or of the "conduct of one's life." But that is precisely the method whereby he will arrive at truths that have direct bearing on how we are to live. Even more problematic is that Descartes argues in a number of other places that virtue is its own reward, that the proper cultivation of a rational approach to human life and to the passions of the soul will render the human soul content, tranquil, and happy.

One might suppose that faith and reason, theology and philosophy, could simply coexist, that they could constitute two separate, nonconflicting spheres. With the demise of ancient and medieval conceptions of hierarchy, a new arrangement of the relationship between faith and reason seems both possible and required. But this is the point at which Descartes' focus on the question of the best way of life puts such an arrangement in jeopardy. If a way of life has to do not simply with the intellectual assent to a set of principles but involves a set of practices, authoritative texts, and standards of what is best, then the both/and approach cannot be sustained. While a Christian can certainly engage in philosophical argument, a Christian cannot accept the claim that philosophy is the best way of life available to human persons, a way of life constitutive of human happiness and wisdom. The question of human excellence, of the sovereign good, arises here in an especially dramatic way. The previously quoted passage from Leo Strauss is pertinent:

> Man cannot live without light, guidance, knowledge; only through knowledge of the good can he find the good that he needs. The fundamental question, therefore, is whether men can acquire that knowledge of the good without which they cannot guide their lives individually or collectively by the unaided efforts of their natural powers, or whether they are dependent for that knowledge on Divine Revelation. No alternative is more fundamental than this: human guidance or divine guidance.[75]

---

[75] Leo Strauss, *Natural Right and History* (Chicago: University of Chicago Press, 1965), 74.

One begins to wonder whether Descartes' philosophical project is not essentially a defense of the autonomy and self-sufficiency of the philosophical life against an unstated theological challenge. This is to suggest, of course, that Montaigne and Descartes treat theology ironically, that they dissimulate on this matter, and that their writing reflects the gap between what they seem to hold and what they actually hold.

If both Montaigne and Descartes adopt an ironic stance toward theological discourse, their strategies for defending the philosophical life are distinct. Montaigne defends philosophy by reviving what he takes to be a proper understanding of Socrates and his way of life. Descartes defends it by accepting the standard set by Socrates and transcending it, by turning philosophy from a dubious pursuit of wisdom into a possession of wisdom.

Descartes' supplanting of the primacy of theological discourse can be seen in his order of proceeding. Descartes, the philosopher, is clearly influenced by a theological model of knowledge. In Thomistic terms, the theological order of proceeding is the inverse of that of philosophy. The latter begins from what is first in the order of experience, what is most obvious to us, that is, with sensible effects, and moves toward an apprehension of what is first in the order of being but secondary in our experience, namely, the highest principles and causes, especially God. By contrast, theology takes God the first cause as its object of study and begins from him, from what is absolutely first in the order of being and then descends from the first principle to his effects, to what is second in being but first in our experience. Theological wisdom, Thomas says, aims to participate in God's knowledge, which is knowledge of the world as an artifact, as something made by the divine artisan. Descartes wants to ground the study of nature in clear and distinct ideas about God, what is first in the order of being. If Descartes is always careful to acknowledge the superior status of theology, he does little to make us see the significance of its absence from philosophy.

Descartes' philosophical pedagogy underscores the notion that philosophy is a way of life, not merely an affirmation of a set of propositions. Instead, it is, as Hadot has put it, a set of practices to be enacted. The notion of texts as spiritual exercises, in Hadot's sense, is one of the boasts of Descartes' method. In the *Principles*, he describes a number of "fruits" of the study of his principles, each of which he depicts in terms of practices with palpable, practical results. The first fruit is the "satisfaction felt" in discovering "many truths which have been unknown up till now."⁷⁶ The second is to "accustom people little by little to form better judgments about all the things they come across."⁷⁷ The third is that its certitude will "eliminate all ground for dispute" and thus dispose minds to "gentleness and harmony," the opposite effect of the intellectual vices that plague debates in the Schools. The fourth and greatest of the fruits is the enabling of individuals to move "from one truth to the next" toward an acquisition of a "perfect knowledge of all philosophy" and rise to the "highest level of wisdom."⁷⁸

The role of text as spiritual exercise is nowhere more prominent than in Descartes' most influential book, *The Meditations on First Philosophy*. Numerous features of the *Meditations* call to mind the *Spiritual Exercises* of St. Ignatius of Loyola. The famous text from the founder of the Jesuits, with whose members Descartes studied, is designed to lead a Christian, over a series of four weeks, to discern his calling and elect a way of life. Ignatius aims to free the exercitant from all attachments, except to God and his will. Indifference is not resignation but a liberating detachment. The meditations strive first to induce in the sinner a deep sense of his own ignorance and evil, an unsettling confusion and regret over his waywardness and disorder. From this state, the one making the retreat encounters Christ, the redeemer from sin, in the scriptures and begins a process of transformation through grace and a retraining of one's imagination and habits of thought and action. At each stage, one comes to a deeper self-knowledge and a greater awareness of God. The retreat ends by returning the individual to the world, to perform praise, love, and serve the Lord in a particular calling. The regime of the exercises is a series of daily meditations and a regular review of one's progress at each stage and an awareness of the next step. The meditations involve what Ignatius calls a composition of place. On the basis of this acute awareness, the exercitant mulls over the lessons to be derived from the scene and then makes an effort of will for the purpose of amendment.

Anyone familiar with the *Exercises* can detect a number of echoes in Descartes' *Meditations*. Indeed, Descartes' text is a kind of ironic rewriting of that seminal text of Catholic Counter-Reformation thought.

---

⁷⁶ Preface to *Principles of Philosophy* in *Philosophical Writings*, 1:188.
⁷⁷ Preface to *Principles of Philosophy* in *Philosophical Writings*, 1:188.
⁷⁸ Preface to *Principles of Philosophy* in *Philosophical Writings*, 1:188–89. "Monter au plus haut degré de la Sagesse." Descartes, *Œuvres*, 9b:18.

Early in the first meditation, in the course of putting into question the information we receive from the senses, Descartes makes a concrete application, involving a composition of place, of what we think we know from the senses: "for instance, that I am now here, sitting by the fire, wrapped in a warm winter gown, handling this paper."[79] To doubt such obvious truths would seem the role of a lunatic. But then he immediately appeals to another concrete experience, namely, that of dreaming and being unable, in such a state, to determine whether what we experience is anything more than a "painted image." Having gone so far as to postulate the possibility of a powerful, cunning, and evil being, capable of deceiving us about an array of matters, Descartes resolves to take care not to give assent to anything false.[80]

In the same mood of apprehension, he begins the second meditation by recalling the first, the result of which is the feeling of having "slipped into a deep whirlpool."[81] Having found that point in the *cogito*, he reaches the conclusion that what he is essentially is a "thinking thing" and adds that he is "beginning to know rather better" what he is.[82] Still, his mind "enjoys wandering off the track" and needs to be tugged "back to obedience."[83] He ends the meditation by repeating a basic criterion of thought, namely, that "nothing can be perceived . . . more clearly than my own mind" and pauses there "to fix this newly acquired knowledge more deeply in my memory by long meditation."[84] The formal similarities to the method of the *Spiritual Exercises* are palpable.

Meditation 3 begins quite dramatically:

> I shall now close my eyes, I shall block up my ears, I shall divert all my senses, and I shall even delete all bodily images from my thought or, since this is virtually impossible to achieve, at least count them as empty and worthless; and I shall try, by conversing only with myself and looking deep within myself, to make myself gradually better known and more familiar to myself.[85]

---

[79] Descartes, *Meditations on First Philosophy*, 13.
[80] He worries that "indolence" may drag him "back to his customary way of life" and its "soothing illusions." Descartes, *Meditations on First Philosophy*, 17 and 3.
[81] Descartes, *Meditations on First Philosophy*, 21.
[82] Descartes, *Meditations on First Philosophy*, 21.
[83] Descartes, *Meditations on First Philosophy*, 21.
[84] Descartes, *Meditations on First Philosophy*, 24.
[85] Descartes, *Meditations on First Philosophy*, 25.

The conclusions reached in this pivotal meditation are no less startling than is its opening sequence. Descartes vanquishes the prospect of the evil genius, demonstrates (on the basis of the innate idea of infinite perfection) the existence of a benevolent deity, and realizes that he is "not alone in the world."[86]

The philosophical practice of meditation has borne fruit. Descartes announces at the start of Meditation 4 he is now so "accustomed to withdrawing his mind from the senses" that he glimpses "a path by which, from this contemplation of the true God, in whom indeed all the treasures of the sciences and wisdom lie hidden, we can pass to the knowledge of other things."[87] The proof of an omnipotent and benevolent God eliminates the hypothesis of the evil genius and allows Descartes to move from the isolated *ego cogito* to the existence of other things. The achievement of a number of fundamental truths confirms the value of his method. The God-given faculty of judging is "such that I shall never go astray, as long as I use it correctly."[88]

Turning from God to his creation, Descartes wonders at the source of imperfection in the universe, particularly the imperfection in human judgment that caused him to stray so far from clear and distinct truths. He notes that he has faculties both of acquiring knowledge and of choosing. In contrast to the limited capacity of the former, the latter is "unbounded by any limits."[89] Incomparably greater in God than in us, the power of the will in its essential capacity of being able "to do or not to do a given thing" is the same. To the disparity between intellect and will, Descartes traces the origin of error. The greater capacity of the will enables it to outstrip the intellect, to lurch ahead and affirm or deny, seek or flee, matters that the intellect has not yet had the opportunity to scrutinize fully. That is how we come to "be deceived and to sin."[90] From this realization, Descartes vows by "careful and frequently repeated meditation" to "acquire a certain habit of not making mistakes."[91] He resolves to "take particular care . . . in future" to "keep my will under control" in making judgments.

---

[86] Descartes, *Meditations on First Philosophy*, 23.
[87] Descartes, *Meditations on First Philosophy*, 38.
[88] Descartes, *Meditations on First Philosophy*, 38.
[89] Descartes, *Meditations on First Philosophy*, 41.
[90] Descartes, *Meditations on First Philosophy*, 42.
[91] Descartes, *Meditations on First Philosophy*, 44.

It is interesting that, after having asserted at the outset that his method applies only to speculative, not to practical, matters, Descartes applies his diagnosis of error to sin as well. The account of the origin of error and the commitment to amendment by limiting the will to what the intellect knows to be clear and distinct raise questions about the status of the act of faith, an act that consists in the will's moving the intellect to affirm matters that by definition exceed the intellect's power of judgment. Having come to know himself and God, he can return to the world less susceptible to its snares and deceptions. The broad structure of the *Meditations* is thus isomorphic to that of the *Spiritual Exercises*. Yet there are also telling disparities. Descartes makes no mention of the ravages of sin, redemption, or the role of grace as a necessary remedy for error and sin. Moreover, Ignatius' meditation commences with a meditation on death, a topic never mentioned in Descartes' work.

Also unmentioned is the chief Christian author whose presence can be felt throughout the *Meditations*, St. Augustine.[92] Descartes thus mimics Montaigne, who engages Plato and Aristotle directly but Augustine only indirectly. Augustine's retreat from the body to the intellectual soul, his insistence that his own doubting is confirmation of his existence, and his claims concerning the immediate intelligibility of the intellect to itself—all these themes are prominent in Descartes. But the differences are equally striking. Augustine moves from the body to the soul to God, who beckons alluringly to the erotic soul, the soul awakened from its sinful slumbers not by methodic doubt and the quest for indubitable certitude but by a transcendent and intoxicating beauty. For Augustine as for Descartes, a return to the material world, a descent to time and space, follows the ascent to the divine. But the goal for Augustine is teaching and works of charity, not the mapping of nature in mathematical terms and its mastery through technology.

The language Descartes deploys to describe the activities of the reformed intellect at the end of the *Meditations* mirrors the depiction of wisdom in the dedicatory letter of the *Principles*. The practice of wisdom consists in the resolve to reason rigorously and act decisively. Descartes' focus in the dedicatory letter is on the virtues. He distinguishes true

---

[92] The influence is, of course, much wider and more complicated than these brief remarks allow. For a recent study making the case for a much more positive embrace of Augustine by Descartes, see Stephen Menn, *Descartes and Augustine* (New York: Cambridge University Press, 2002).

from apparent virtue and notes, in classical fashion, that some vices, such as rashness, can be taken for virtue, in this case courage. He also distinguishes, with regard to true virtue, that which is based in exact knowledge and what includes some measure of ignorance. He then moves rapidly from the discussion of multiple, imperfect instantiations of the virtues to a unified account of the "pure and genuine virtues, which proceed solely from knowledge of what is right," which have "one and the same nature" and which "are included under the single term 'wisdom.'"[93]

The *Meditations* are crucial to the foundations of a new physical science and to the articulation and realization of the best way of life. The last point has been unduly neglected in the reading of Descartes. As was true for Plato, so for Descartes philosophical texts are themselves spiritual exercises, fields for the recognition and exercise of the very virtues propounded, often only indirectly, in them. Like Plato, Descartes sought a way of writing that would foster the practice of reading as dramatic re-enactment. As much as Descartes might deploy irony as a figure of speech that dissembles on the question of theology in order to protect philosophy from authorities who might find its teachings threatening, he also makes use of pedagogical irony to initiate capable readers into the life of intellectual and moral virtue.

The new account of nature renders it more susceptible to the probing and manipulation of human intelligence and will, even as it suits a novel articulation of the sovereign good. Before Descartes, Montaigne had downplayed the role of teleology, the ordination of nature to a transcendent cause, a final cause that draws all things to itself by appealing to the erotic inclination to the good built into the very structure of natural things. The ancients, of course, sought sufficiency, but for them certitude and control—in a phrase, modern autonomy—were less important than the longing, or eros, for the good and the beautiful. Aristotle and, after him, Aquinas urge that, where there is a conflict between the nobility of the object known and certitude, we should prefer a dim and partial apprehension of the more noble object to an exhaustive and sure knowledge of a less noble object.[94]

Montaigne's repudiation of teleology puts him at odds with Socrates. Montaigne's understanding of the complacency of the philosopher

---

[93] Descartes, preface to *Principles of Philosophy*, in *Philosophical Writings*, 1:191.
[94] *De Anima* 1.1.402^{a}1–20; *Ethics* 10.7.1177b26–1178^{a}5.

in the face of his own ignorance is void of the erotic longing for the whole that characterizes Socrates—what Montaigne dismisses as flights of transcendent fantasy, his "ecstasies and daemonizings."[95] Descartes goes much further and supplies a comprehensive rival account of nature, an account that not only supplants Aristotle and overcomes Socrates but also renders otiose the dialogue between philosophy and theology, reason and faith. In this way, Descartes' overcoming of Socrates, his new science of virtue, is simultaneously a strategy for bypassing the debate between Athens and Jerusalem.

The downplaying of that debate is a commonplace of early modern philosophy and may help explain why early modern philosophers did not continue the Renaissance revival of pagan philosophy, that is, why they did not revive the classical understanding of nature, as found in Plato and Aristotle. One reason is certainly that the methods of the new sciences required a decisive break from the methods of ancient philosophy. Pierre Manent detects another source for the attack on pagan philosophy:

> In order to liberate himself from the "supernatural," modern man cannot rest content with becoming "pagan" again. It is not enough to affirm or reaffirm nature. This latter is henceforth exposed to being outbid or trumped by the supernatural. If nature is good, even very good, the supernatural is necessarily better, because it is infinitely good. If the earthly city provides natural goods, the heavenly city, which the church prefigures, dispenses supernatural goods that are incomparably superior to the former. . . . If the critique of the supernatural is going to achieve its political ends . . . it must entail a critique of nature. The critique of Christian revelation implies the critique of pagan politics and philosophy.[96]

Manent underscores the modern antagonism toward a specific form of Christianity, namely, the catholic form, whose proclamation of an authoritative, public, and universal church is vehemently opposed by Machiavelli, Hobbes, and Locke, the founders of modern political thought. One of the peculiar, and often unremarked, features of the

---

[95] Montaigne, "On Experience," in *Essays*, 1268.

[96] Pierre Manent, "Christianity and Democracy," in *Modern Liberty and Its Discontents* (Lanham, Md.: Rowman & Littlefield, 1998), 111. For Manent's comprehensive treatment of modern political thought, see *The City of Man* (Princeton, N.J.: Princeton University Press, 1998).

attack on the church is the accompanying repudiation of pagan philosophers such as Plato and Aristotle. We need not enter here into the debates over whether and to what extent the West was Christianized during the Middle Ages. It suffices to note that the church had penetrated the crucial and sovereign institutions of political and intellectual life. The result, according to Locke, of this strange and unnatural mixture of "things remote and opposite" is religious war and a debilitating confusion in the allegiance of citizens. Early modern political theorists, from Machiavelli and Hobbes through Locke and Rousseau, engaged in a sustained battle against the church, lord of the Dark Ages.[97] Manent explains, "To stop it [the church] from immediately reconstituting itself, one must invalidate or at least decisively weaken many other ideas that appear to be unconnected with it, or that even seem to rival it rather than support it. I have in mind, for example, the idea of nature," which in Greek philosophy "had worked to deliver men from the fear of punitive gods."[98] Descartes performs that exorcism in his defeat of the evil genius in the *Meditations*. Of course, it is another sort of divinity that replaces the arbitrary deities of pre-Christian pagan myth and of late medieval voluntarism. But it is not obviously the Christian deity that Descartes revives. Indeed, Pascal objects that Descartes had established

[97] Like Strauss, Manent is operating here with a selective conception of the Enlightenment. Perhaps the most important corrective to our understanding of the Enlightenment is found in the writings of Knud Haakonssen. In *Natural Law and Moral Philosophy from Grotius to the Scottish Enlightenment* (New York: Cambridge University Press, 1996), Haakonssen argues that in eighteenth-century Scotland Enlightenment political theory was neither radically individualistic nor dominated by the language of individual rights (5–7). He speaks instead of a "conservative" Enlightenment, to which the thought of Hobbes is alien, which subordinated rights to duties and the latter to "historically given offices," all of which was derived from a "teleological and providentialist norm" (311–27). Making "rights the primary feature" of a moral theory via autonomy and self-legislation marks the "death of natural law thinking" (62). Haakonssen cautions that the necessary opposition between religious natural law thinking and modernity is an invention of nineteenth-century liberalism and should not be read back into the eighteenth century (326). And yet Haakonssen ends his book with the development in America of subjective rights (330ff.). Also of interest is Knud Haakonssen, ed., *Enlightenment and Religion: Rational Dissent in Eighteenth-Century Britain* (New York: Cambridge University Press, 1996). While it is certainly the case that nature and human nature retain their normative status for many writers in the modern period, Manent still captures both the roots and the ultimate trajectory of the distinctively modern flight from freedom.

[98] Manent, "The Truth, Perhaps," in *Modern Liberty and Its Discontents*, 41.

the existence of the God of deism, a divinity closer to atheism than to the Christian God who is active in history.

Descartes' new science would prove unpersuasive to another Frenchman whose obsession with Montaigne exceeds that of Descartes. Pascal counters the new science and its ironic stance toward Christianity by a twofold reversal. First, he argues that mature reflection on nature and the human condition does not minimize but in fact exacerbates wonder. The proper response is precisely what Descartes identifies as the vice of amazement.[99] Second, he counters the philosopher's ironic stance toward theology with an account of divine irony, which he articulates in terms of a proportion: as the philosopher stands in relation to the ordinary run of mankind, so does the believer stand in relation to the philosopher.[100] That irony exceeds in power the virtues of the new science even as it exceeds in wisdom the new science of virtue. Pascal's account of the sovereign good differs from that of Montaigne and Descartes and provides another distinctively modern perspective. Yet, here again Socrates is prominent. However much these early modern French philosophers might want to move beyond antiquity, they remain haunted by the founding figure of philosophy.

---

[99] For example, in the famous meditation on the twin infinities of large and small, Pascal thinks we should "tremble at these marvels [*il tremblera dans la vue de ces merveilles*]." Pascal, *Pensées*, trans. Krailsheimer, 199; Blaise Pascal, *Pensées*, ed. Dominique Descotes and Léon Brunschvicg (Paris: Flammarion, 1976), 72.

[100] "Philosophers: they surprise the ordinary run of men. Christians: they surprise the philosophers. [*Les philosophes. Ils étonnent le commun des hommes. Les chrétiens, ils étonnent les philosophes*]." Pascal, *Pensées*, trans. Krailsheimer, 613; Pascal, *Pensées*, ed. Brunschvicg, 443. The Socratic preference for the study of man to the inquiry into the exact sciences—an affirmation of the primacy of the intuitive over the mathematical mind—underscores Pascal's greater proximity to Montaigne than to Descartes. Jean-Luc Marion, who takes Descartes rather than Montaigne as Pascal's chief interlocutor, speaks of Pascal's overcoming of metaphysics and philosophy. Because Marion takes Descartes to be an exemplar of philosophy, he overstates Pascal's victory over philosophy. On the level of direct polemic, it is much easier for Pascal to combat Descartes' claims on behalf of the sufficiency of reason. But Descartes' is neither the only nor the most cogent defense of the philosophical life. See the final chapter of Marion, *On Descartes' Metaphysical Prism* (Chicago: University of Chicago Press, 1999); and, for a more detailed reading of Pascal on both Descartes and Montaigne that develops Marion's thesis, Vincent Carraud, *Pascal et la philosophie* (Paris: Presses universitaires de France, 1992).

Four

THE QUEST FOR WISDOM
Pascal and Philosophy

"Knowledge has two extremes that meet; one is the pure and natural ignorance of every man at birth; the other is the extreme reached by great minds who run through the whole range of human knowledge, only to find that they know nothing and come back to the same ignorance from which they set out, but it is a wise ignorance which knows itself" (83).[1]

The passage from the *Pensées* makes clear that, in the debate between Montaigne and Descartes over the possibility of philosophy moving from a love of wisdom to its actual possession, Pascal aligns himself with Montaigne, and—through him—with Socrates and his learned ignorance. As was true of Montaigne and Descartes, so too for Pascal the figure of Socrates is decisive concerning the nature, scope, and telos of philosophy. Now, this Socratic option puts Pascal most obviously at odds with Descartes and his claim to have achieved

---

[1] Blaise Pascal, *Pensées*, trans. A. J. Krailsheimer, rev. ed. (New York: Penguin Classics, 1995). "*Les sciences ont deux extrémités qui se touchent. La première est la pure ignorance naturelle où se trouvent tous les hommes en naissant. L'autre extrémité est celle où arrivent les grandes âmes, qui, ayant parcouru tout ce que les hommes peuvent savoir, trouvent qu'ils ne savent rien et se rencontrent en cette même ignorance d'où ils étaient partis; mais c'est une ignorance savante qui se connaît.*" Blaise Pascal, *Pensées*, ed. Dominique Descotes and Léon Brunschvicg (Paris: Flammarion, 1976), 327. I will cite the Krailsheimer numbering parenthetically at the end of each English quotation and the Brunschvicg, where necessary, in notes.

indisputable answers to some of the most important philosophical questions. Yet, even in the case of his criticisms of Descartes, Pascal shares much with the target of his attack. As Jean-Luc Marion has argued, the critic ends up weaving so much of his opponent's language into his own that he may almost be called a disciple as much as a critic.[2] Not just in his preoccupation with the infinite or with skepticism but also in his pervasive attention to "method" and "order," Pascal reflects Descartes, even as he departs decisively from him. Indeed, Pascal, himself a mathematician and inventor of some note, could not help but be impressed by the power, explanatory and practical, of the developments in the fields of math and science. As we shall see, Pascal's own innovations in the field of projective geometry provide a model for what it would mean to unite various phenomena under one explanation.[3] Of course, another Cartesian feature of Pascal's writing is its preoccupation with Montaigne.

§1. Socrates and the Quest for the Good Life

In this chapter, we will consider Pascal's engagement of Montaigne and Descartes and his own take on the figure of Socrates. Pascal repeats Socrates' turn from physics to the study of human things, a study he finds oddly neglected. It is not just the untutored many who avoid the pursuit of self-knowledge but the greatest intellects as well, the sort of intellects that are drawn to the mathematical sciences. In a passage reminiscent of Socrates' explanation of his early conversion, Pascal writes:

> I had spent a long time studying the abstract sciences, and I was put off them by seeing how little one could communicate about them. When I began the study of man I saw that these abstract sciences are not proper to man, and that I was straying further from my true condition by going into them than were others by being ignorant of them.... I thought I should ... find many companions in my study of man, since it is his true and proper study. I was wrong. Even fewer people study man than

---

[2] Jean-Luc Marion, *On Descartes' Metaphysical Prism: The Constitution and the Limits of Onto-theo-logy in Cartesian Thought* (Chicago: University of Chicago Press, 1999). See also the more expansive treatment of Pascal along these lines in Vincent Carraud, *Pascal et la philosophie* (Paris: Presses universitaires de France, 1992).

[3] See Jean Khalfa, "Pascal's Theory of Knowledge," in *The Cambridge Companion to Pascal*, ed. Nicholas Hammond (Cambridge: Cambridge University Press, 2003), 122–43.

mathematics. It is only because they do not know how to study man that people look into all the rest. (687)[4]

Pascal echoes Socrates' claims that the proper study of the human intellect is the question of the good life for human beings and that this sort of knowledge is not susceptible to treatment in the way scientific matters are. Thus Pascal hints at the need for something other than a mathematical method in the pursuit of knowledge about human things, however much he may deploy analogies to the mathematical order.

Pascal's own way of following the Socratic turn to human things does not simply leave science or nature behind. Instead, objective reflection about a question or subject matter turns out to provoke an inquiry about the inquirer, about the strange part of the whole that seeks both to know and to be oriented with respect to that whole. Pascal's ethics of thought aims to pierce our own self-understanding as it deprives us of any center of gravity, any fixed perspective from which we might assess the universe and our place within it. However much the whole might defy comprehension, awareness of the whole is a mark of the dignity of the human person: "Even if the universe were to crush him, man would still be nobler than his slayer, because he knows that he is dying and the advantage the universe has over him. The universe knows none of this" (200).[5] In relation to the infinite universe, the human being, vacillating between humiliation and exaltation, becomes a riddle to himself. He is "to himself the greatest prodigy in nature" (199).[6] Pascal's approach to the human being as something in and of the natural order belies the interpretive assumption that he abandons natural philosophy or repudiates inquiry into nature. Pascal's natural philosophy has as its goal a kind of self-knowledge, a knowing that is an unknowing, a recognition of the disproportion between the human intellect and the whole of which it is a part. Pascal asks, "How could a part possibly know

---

[4] *J'avais passé longtemps dans l'étude des sciences abstraites; et le peu de communication qu'on en peut avoir m'en avait dégoûté. Quand j'ai commencé l'étude de l'homme, j'ai vu que ces sciences abstraites ne sont pas propres à l'homme, et que je m'égarais plus de ma condition en y pénétrant que les autres en les ignorant. J'ai pardonné aux autres d'y peu savoir. Mais j'ai cru trouver au moins bien des compagnons en l'étude de l'homme et que c'est la vraie étude qui lui est propre. J'ai été trompé; il y en a encore moins qui l'étudient que la géométrie. Ce n'est que manque de savoir étudier cela qu'on cherche le reste* (144).

[5] *Mais, quand l'univers l'écraserait, l'homme serait encore plus noble que ce qui le tue, puisqu'il sait qu'il meurt, et l'avantage que l'univers a sur lui; l'univers n'en sait rien* (347).

[6] *L'homme est à lui même le plus prodigieux objet de la nature* (72).

the whole?"[7] The reflection deepens the sense of mystery concerning human nature with its precarious status in the middle of things. Pascal tantalizes the mind and heart of human beings by underscoring our natural desire for a knowledge that exceeds our grasp.

Against Descartes, Pascal repeats Montaigne's point concerning the subordination of thought to life. One of Pascal's fragments is entitled "Vanity of Science." It runs thus: "Knowledge of physical science will not console me for ignorance of morality in time of affliction, but knowledge of morality will always console me for ignorance of physical science" (23).[8] Now, this objection might seem to countenance anti-intellectualism, a reactionary exaltation of the practical above the theoretical. We ought to notice, however, that Pascal objects not to science itself but to the subordination of morality to science. And morality here should be taken in the broadest possible sense, that is, in the classical sense, as concerning the best way of life for human beings: "Man's true nature, his true good and true virtue, and true religion are things which cannot be known separately" (393).[9] Unlike the scientific disciplines that treat a limited segment of the real, religion, virtue, and the true good concern matters coextensive with human life. They concern the shape of one's entire life, its end and all its parts. In this, Pascal affirms a decidedly premodern thesis, a Socratic thesis about the inescapable priority of the question of the good life.

That we can and should raise questions about the shape of the whole of human life and that, once we do, the answers are not obvious, means that human life has the structure of a quest. Inquiry about our ultimate destiny is the defining feature of human life, something evident to the "least enlightened," apart from grace. "Our chief interest and chief duty is to seek enlightenment on this subject, on which all our conduct depends" (427).[10] The quest befits beings situated between presumption and despair, between certitude and doubt. In his articulation of the quest, we can discern the features of what we might call Pascal's

---

[7] *Comment se pourrait-il qu'une partie connût le tout?* (72).

[8] *La science des choses extérieures ne me consolera pas de l'ignorance de la morale, au temps d'affliction; mais la science des moeurs me consolera toujours de l'ignorance des sciences extérieures* (67).

[9] *La vraie nature de l'homme, son vraie bien, et la vraie vertu, et la vraie religion, sont choses dont la connaissance est inséparable* (442).

[10] *Ainsi que notre premier intérêt et notre premier devoir est de nous éclaircir sur ce sujet, d'où dépend toute notre conduit* (194).

ethics of thought. The necessity for a reorientation of habit is thus a key stage in the search: "I should like to arouse in man the desire to find the truth, to be ready, free from passions, to follow it wherever he may find it, realizing how far his knowledge is clouded by passion. I should like him to hate his concupiscence which automatically makes his decisions for him" (119).[11] In contrast to Montaigne and Descartes, Pascal stresses the gap between desire and achievement, between the ultimate end of human life and the current condition of human persons. For Pascal, the question of how well or ill equipped an inquirer is to pursue a particular line of inquiry, especially inquiry about the good, is fundamental. Thus Pascal counsels an ironic retreat in the quest for knowledge, a stepping back to put the inquirer in question.

According to Pascal, the best life available to unaided human reason is a quest to discern, and live in accord with, the truth about the human condition, but the life of the quest does not itself constitute happiness; only the successful conclusion of the quest does. This, we shall argue below, is the proper context for understanding the wager argument. Given that we are situated somewhere between certitude and invincible doubt, risk cannot be eliminated from human reasoning, deliberation, and choice: "If we must never take any chances, . . . we should have to do nothing at all, for nothing is certain" (577).[12] But which chances ought to be taken and why?

That question calls to mind Pascal's wager, to an examination of which the next chapter is devoted. For now, we will turn to the following topics. First, we will consider Pascal's ironic engagement of Descartes' methodic doubt, an engagement that reverses the Cartesian

---

[11] "*Je voudrais donc porter l'homme à désirer d'en trouver, à être prêt, et dégagé des passions, pour la suivre où il la trouvera, sachant combien sa connaissance s'est obscurcie par les passions; je voudrais bien qu'il haït en soi la concupiscence qui le determine d'elle-même*" (423). On the "machine" or the "automaton," as Pascal also calls it, see Georges Desgrippes, *Études sur Pascal de l'automatisme a la foi* (Paris: Pierre Téqui, 1933); and Dominique Descotes, *L'argumentation chez Pascal* (Paris: Presses Universitaires de France, 1993). Also see Carraud's discussion of the machine (*Pascal et la philosophie*, 401), in which he takes Pascal's deployment of the language of Cartesian mechanism far too literally and thus concludes that Pascal's goal is to render the human subject void of all feeling. That runs afoul of the passage just cited, in which Pascal states that he wants to arouse a desire for truth: "*Je voudrais donc porter l'homme à désirer d'en trouver.*"

[12] *S'il ne fallait rien faire que pour le certain, on ne devrait rien faire pour la religion; car elle n'est pas certaine. Mais combien de choses fait-on pour l'incertain, les voyages sur mer, les batailles! Je dis donc qu'il ne faudrait rien faire du tout, car rien n'est certain* (234).

attempt through mathematics and science to overcome wonder with scientific knowledge. Here Cartesian certitude is reduced to Socratic amazement. Pascal's critique of Cartesian philosophy, along with his apparent skepticism and relativism, has led many to assume that he aims to deconstruct philosophy. Sophisticated readers of his texts have proposed that such a deconstructive strategy can be aimed at Pascal's own project, depriving him of the basis for affirming any truth, philosophical or theological. We will take up this instructive objection. If Pascal sees Descartes' project as excessive in its optimism about the prospects for human knowledge and mastery, he deems Montaigne's account of human desire deficient. Pascal will argue that Montaigne's account of the human condition domesticates it and minimizes its deeply unsettling implications. Pascal detects an ulterior motive at work, that of curtailing the human aspiration toward transcendence. In this way and against both Montaigne and Descartes, Pascal insists that philosophical eros aspires to what exceeds the grasp of philosophy. We will attend finally to the issue raised at the outset of this chapter concerning method and Pascal's indebtedness and resistance to Descartes. Pascal certainly finds a place for mathematical method, but he repudiates the paradigmatically Cartesian attempt to reduce all intelligible subject matters to one method. Pascal's methodic pluralism does not, however, mean that there cannot be a unified inquiry into the human good. Pascal seeks a synoptic vision, a way of seeing and living within the whole.

§2. Ironic Reversal: The Reduction of Cartesian Certitude to Socratic Amazement

As Matthew Jones observes, whereas "Descartes hoped to delimit astonishment... and to replace it with more controlled forms of appreciation," Pascal "praised mathematical reason in no small part because it could generate affective wonder that forced human beings to acknowledge their limits, to recognize that at appropriate moments they ought to cease their investigative quest and simply gawk." Pascal fittingly develops a conception of mathematical practice as spiritual exercise: "Mathematical practice can move, can transform a human being into a state of reasonable abasement, into a different relationship with his own epistemic and affective capacities."[13] Also in contrast

---

[13] Matthew L. Jones, *The Good Life in the Scientific Revolution: Descartes, Pascal, Leibniz, and the Cultivation of Virtue* (Chicago: University of Chicago Press, 2006), 124.

to Descartes, Pascal urges that "wonder should be a permanent affective state," not a transitory condition on the way to the achievement of philosophical certitude.[14] Pascal thus brings about an ironic reversal of scientific inquiry, which aims to know the whole, or at least its principles, with peremptory certitude. This is the "extreme reached by great minds who . . . come back to the same ignorance from which they set out, but it is a wise ignorance which knows itself" (83).[15] Pascal's task in responding to Descartes is to show that his methodical attempt to transcend knowing ignorance is unsuccessful.

Among the fragments that constitute the *Pensées*, a few memorable aphorisms refer to Descartes by name. Some of the statements are terse and polemical, even mocking. One, "Descartes: useless and uncertain" (887),[16] turns inside out the chief boasts of Descartes' method. In the *Discourse on Method*, as we have seen, he seeks to replace the fruitless and dubious pedagogy of his day with a method that would produce clear and distinct ideas and render us masters and possessors of nature. Descartes' method subjects everything to reason, to a standard of absolute certitude. Pascal deploys the notion of the infinite, so central to Descartes' own thinking about God and about mathematics, to lay bare the "disproportion" between the human intellect and nature, the latter of which is distended between the two infinites, the infinitely small and the infinitely large (199). In his treatment of nature, Pascal makes certain audacious claims. Pascal invokes a traditional medieval image, that of the infinite sphere, in a revolutionary manner. "Nature," he writes, "is an infinite sphere whose centre is everywhere and circumference nowhere" (199).[17]

In the meditation on the "disproportion of man," Pascal first invites the reader to consider the "whole of nature in her full and lofty majesty (199)."[18] We are invited to contemplate visually the limitless heavens above; but our imagination is capable of conceiving worlds beyond what we can see. "The whole visible world is only an imperceptible dot in nature's ample bosom" (199).[19] Nature escapes not only vision and

---

[14] Jones, *Good Life in the Scientific Revolution*, 162.
[15] *Extrémité est celle où arrivent les grandes âmes, qui . . . se rencontrent en cette même ignorance d'où ils étaient partis; mais c'est une ignorance savante qui se connaît* (327).
[16] *Descartes inutile et incertain* (78).
[17] *C'est une sphère infinie dont le centre est partout, la circonférence nulle part* (72).
[18] *La nature entière dans sa haute et pleine majesté* (72).
[19] *Tout le monde visible n'est qu'un trait imperceptible dans l'ample sein de la nature* (72).

imagination but understanding as well. Having pondered the infinitely large through vision, imagination, and thought, Pascal urges man to "return to himself" and consider "what he is in comparison with what exists.... What is a man in the infinite?" (199).[20] We should notice here the way Pascal gives a novel twist to the classic path of self-knowledge, which in the Platonic and Christian tradition begins with the external world, turns within, and then ascends to higher realities.[21] Pascal uses the language of returning to oneself. But the pattern his meditation follows is not that of a straightforward ascent from the external through the internal to the superior. There is no possibility of an ordered ascent through a series of proportionately related orders; there is no hierarchy of disciplines, no great chain of being.

Following the return from whole to part and from the universe to the self, Pascal does not allow the inquirer to rest but urges the reader to consider the "tiniest things he knows" (199).[22] By a process of analytical division—through the parts of a mite, its veins, blood, humors, and vapors—we are advised to continue to divide until we "exhaust the powers of imagination." Just when we suppose we have reached the limit of division, Pascal presents a "new abyss." He proposes, within a "miniature atom," an "infinity of universes, each with its firmament, its planets, its earth" (199).[23] Pascal then rapidly shifts back to us, to our bodies, which just a moment before we had envisioned as a vanishing dot within the scope of the universe. Now, the human body appears as a "colossus, a world, or rather a whole, compared to the nothingness beyond our reach" (199).[24]

The meditation on infinity and nothing is not customary or easy for us. Large and small do not ordinarily unsettle us, but that is only because we do not direct our attention to either in its extreme. We exist in the middle, but it is a precarious balance: "Nature has set us so exactly in the middle that if we alter one side of the scales we alter

---

[20] *Que l'homme, étant revenu à soi, considère ce qu'il est au prix de ce qui est.... Qu'est-ce qu'un homme dans l'infini?* (72).

[21] See, for example, Augustine, *On Free Choice of the Will* and *Confessions*; Bonaventure, *The Journey of the Mind to God*; and Petrarch, "The Ascent of Mount Ventoux to Dionisio da Borgo San Sepolcro."

[22] *Dans ce qu'il connaît les choses les plus délicates* (72).

[23] *Une infinité d'univers, dont chacun a son firmament, ses planètes, sa terre* (72).

[24] *Un colosse, un monde, ou plutôt un tout, à l'égard du néant où l'on ne peut arriver* (72).

the other as well" (519).²⁵ Befitting the focus on quantity and size, the meditation requires that we turn our heads away from what is immediately before us; in this, the meditation on the "disproportion of man" involves a movement from what is immediately evident to us in concrete experience, corresponding to the way of reasoning that Pascal calls *finesse*, prominent in Montaigne, toward a more abstract analysis, which corresponds to the Cartesian method that Pascal calls the way of *geometrie*. But this is not a simple shift from Montaigne to Descartes, *finesse* to *geometrie*. Instead, it is a critique of both. To Montaigne, Pascal suggests that immediate experience is interconnected with the extremes of which we are only dimly aware. Yet such reflection is necessary if we are to see man clearly. "What," he queries, "is man in nature? A nothing compared to the infinite, a whole compared to the nothing, a middle point between all and nothing, infinitely remote from an understanding of the extremes; the end of things and their principles are unattainably hidden from him in impenetrable secrecy" (199).²⁶ Yet the shift to geometry fails to yield mathematical lucidity, and the implications indicate the subordination of science to ethics. The inference that Pascal wishes us to draw from the meditation is not geometrical or scientific but ethical, a humbling of reason.²⁷

So long as we remain in the sphere that is proper to us, our "intermediate state," we can to some extent think and act without disruption. Of course, philosophers and scientists are not content with a partial,

---

²⁵ *La nature nous a si bien mis au milieu que si nous changeons un coté de la balance, nous changeons aussi l'autre* (70).

²⁶ *Car enfin, qu'est-ce que l'homme dans la nature? Un néant à l'égard de l'infini, un tout à l'égard du néant, un milieu entre rien et tout. Infiniment éloigné de comprendre les extrêmes, la fin des choses et leur principe sont pour lui invinciblement cachés dans un secret impénétrable* (72).

²⁷ Perhaps even more pertinent than the humbling of reason is the humiliation of imagination, which Pascal describes as a "proud power" (*superbe puissance*). As Amos Funkenstein points out in his magisterial study of early modern science, the new, constructive theory of knowledge makes possible the notion of science as productive, rather than contemplative. The flourishing of that constructive conception of knowledge rests upon an exaltation of the capacity of the imagination as a freely creative faculty, no longer merely a receptacle for what Hobbes calls "decaying sense." The new conception of the imagination invites human beings to reimagine their relations to God, the world, and other persons. As Funkenstein writes, "applying knowledge-through-construction to the whole was as inevitable as it was dangerous. It was dangerous because it makes mankind be 'like God knowing good and evil.'" Funkenstein, *Theology and the Scientific Imagination* (Princeton, N.J.: Princeton University Press, 1986), 327.

middle view of things; they go beyond this to the foundations; they compose treatises on the "principles of things."

To conceive of the infinite, whether the infinitely small or the infinitely large, requires removing oneself from the order of ordinary experience and common language; it requires a point of departure characteristic of the mathematical mind. In this respect, Pascal shares much with the most influential advocates of the modern sciences, for whom ordinary sense-experience is at best inadequate and at worst misleading when it comes to understanding nature as it is in itself. Moving from the world as it appears to us to the world as it actually is puts into question many of the assumptions operative in ordinary experience. And yet Pascal is more concerned than are his contemporaries to trace a path not only from ordinary experience to the scientific account of nature but also back to its implication for ordinary agents. Pascal's famous aphorism concerning the dread provoked by the silence of infinite space (201) is but one way in which he expresses a link between cosmology and human alienation. But he also sees a positive result: the humbling of reason.[28]

The meditation on the twin infinites alters our disposition toward nature and knowledge, transforming our curiosity into wonder and prompting contemplative silence rather than investigative presumption: "These extremes touch and join by going in opposite directions, and they meet in God and God alone" (199).[29] Only God, the transcendent source of the whole, can fathom the inconceivable lower and upper limits of the universe. "It is the greatest perceptible mark of God's omnipotence that our imagination should lose itself in that thought" (199).[30] The meditation on nature and infinity chastens the imagination, which is prone to disordered judgments, reversing the large and the small, the grand and the petty. We should "tremble at these marvels" (199). The result is a direct contravention of Descartes' stipulation that wonder ought to be merely an initial and brief state of the human intellect and that excessive wonder is characteristic of those with limited intelligence.

---

[28] That is the goal of what Vincent Carraud has called the rhetorical use of the infinite. See Carraud, *Pascal et la philosophie*, 395–452. Also see Pierre Magnard, "L'infini pascalien," *Revue de l'Enseignement philosophique* 31, no. 1 (1980): 2–16.

[29] *Ces extrêmités se touchent et se réunissent [à force de s'être éloignées et se retrouvent] en Dieu, et en Dieu seulement* (72).

[30] *Enfin c'est le plus grand caractère sensible de la toute-puissance de Dieu, que notre imagination se perde dans cette pensée* (72).

Pascal, by contrast, insists, "Wisdom has two ends that meet" (83). Philosophical reflection on nature can serve a vital goal, that of transforming impassive curiosity about the universe into wonder at the limits of human knowledge.

Ironic reversal is Pascal's dominant strategy in his engagement of Descartes. Precisely in the mathematical arena, in which Descartes is most confident, he can reach clear and distinct ideas and thus reduce wonder to certitude, Pascal engenders bafflement. We can detect a similar strategy in Pascal's engagement of Descartes' account of doubt and his grounding of certitude in the transparent intelligibility of the *ego cogito*. The self is, as Pascal proclaims at one point, a "monster," unintelligible by natural reason.

According to Pascal, Descartes' method is uncertain; once the method of doubt is unleashed, it cannot be controlled. It undermines everything. Descartes pursues a method of hyperbolic doubt as a means of clearing away partial and dubious truths in order to reach a certitude invulnerable to doubt. Pascal counters that doubt here is never radical; it is instead a methodically controlled doubt. If complete doubt were unleashed, it would undermine everything: "What . . . is man to do in this state of affairs? Is he to doubt everything . . . ? Is he to doubt whether he is doubting, to doubt whether he exists?" (131).[31] Descartes, for example, never doubts the significance of his language, of the transparency of terms such as "think," "doubt," "exist," or "I." If we put these into question, we shall be reduced to silence or the gibberish of a madman. We shall lose confidence in our ability not just to assert the truth but also to put anything into question in a meaningful way. Radical doubt engenders horror, not the comforts of Enlightenment reason.

In a famous passage in his *Meditations*, Descartes poses the question of whether we can with certainty determine that we are now not dreaming. What is the basis for our confident assumption that we can separate waking from sleeping states? Descartes comes around to answering this question only toward the end of the work, after he has established the certainty of the *cogito* and of the existence of an all-perfect God who thus cannot be conceived as a deceiver. On that basis, Descartes thinks that our ordinary way of distinguishing sleeping from waking

---

[31] *Que fera donc l'homme en cet état? Doutera-t-il de tout? . . . Doutera-t-il s'il doute? [D]outera-t-il s'il est?* (434).

states is sufficient. Descartes' initial suggestion, not his tidy resolution, intrigues Pascal:

> Who knows whether the other half of our lives, when we think we are awake, is not another sleep slightly different from the first, on to which our dreams are grafted as our sleep appears, and from which we awake when we think we are sleeping? And who can doubt that, if we dreamed in the company of others and our dreams happened to agree, which is common enough, and if we were alone when awake, we should think things had been turned upside-down? (131)[32]

Pascal doubts that the puzzles Descartes formulates can be so easily resolved. There is a further point here. Whereas Descartes simply wants to eliminate doubt, Pascal thinks we have much to learn from the sort of doubts to which we are inevitably prone. Our difficulty getting a quick and peremptory hold on the difference between appearance and reality is instructive about our condition, which is characterized by seemingly irresolvable paradox. Our tentative uncertainty about reality opens up the possibility of seeing this life as but a partial realization of a more complete reality. But it goes further than that, as it creates the suspicion that we may not easily be able to distinguish true from false images. Once again, Pascal insists that the imagination is not as readily susceptible to the control of reason as Descartes supposes.

Crucial to the *Meditations* is Descartes' resolution of questions about human nature. Unlike Descartes, he offers no sustained argument on behalf of the distinction of soul and body. Instead, he poses certain dilemmas for those who would reduce human nature to matter. One pithy aphorism runs thus: "Instinct and reason, signs of two natures" (112).[33] Another, on the topic of the immateriality of the soul, wonders, "When philosophers have subdued their passions, what material substance has managed to achieve this?" (115).[34] Or again, "What part of us feels pleasure? Is it our hand, our arm, our flesh, or our blood? It

---

[32] *Qui sait si cette autre moitié de la vie où nous pensons veiller n'est pas un autre sommeil un peu différent du premier dont nous nous éveillons quand nous pensons dormir? Et qui doute que, si on rêvait en compagnie, et que par hasard les songes s'accordassent, ce qui est assez ordinaire, et qu'on veillât en solitude, on ne crût les choses renversées?* (434).

[33] *Instinct et raison, marques de deux natures* (344).

[34] *Les philosophes qui ont dompté leurs passions, quelle matière l'a pu faire?* (349).

must obviously be something immaterial" (108).³⁵ As Pascal puts it in the fragment on the "disproportion of man," there is "nothing so inconceivable as the idea that matter knows itself" (199).³⁶

Pascal's approach to the distinction between the material and the immaterial is indirect and by negation. Against Descartes, he holds that there is no direct, unmediated access to self-thinking thought. He assumes that the body is, and will remain, more obvious to us than what is not body. The existence of some nonmaterial power is suggested by the limited explanatory power of the body with regard to certain human capacities or activities. Human nature is a strange composition of seemingly opposed things: mind and matter, the immaterial and the material. Yet Pascal does not follow Descartes' demarcation of the realms of mind and matter or his insistence that man is essentially a "thinking thing [*res cogitans*]." In direct contrast to Descartes, Pascal states that "man is properly speaking wholly animal" (664).³⁷ Also in contrast to Descartes, who holds that thinking operates best when it is freed from all bodily conditions, Pascal observes that "memory is necessary for all the operations of reason" (651).³⁸ The severing of mind from matter is as damaging to human nature and our understanding of it as is the reduction of the former to the latter. That is why we must think of ourselves as neither angels nor beasts but we must be aware of both. If Descartes is tempted by what Jacques Maritain would later call the heresy of angelism, Montaigne's attempt to curb human desire for transcendence means that he promotes forgetfulness of the angel in favor of the beast.³⁹ Pascal refuses reductionism of either sort.

§3. Philosophy Deconstructed? Pascal Deconstructed?

Pascal's own antireductionism in certain areas has appeared to some readers to be incongruous with his seeming reductionism in other areas. Pascal's seeming deconstruction of any type of affirmative philosophy, of any claims on the part of philosophy to knowledge, rests upon his

---

[35] *Qu'est-ce qui sent du plaisir en nous? Est-ce la main, est-ce le bras, est-ce la chair, est-ce le sang? On verra qu'il faut que ce soit quelque chose d'immatériel* (966).

[36] *N'y ayant rien de si inconcevable que de dire que la matière se connaît soi-même* (72).

[37] *L'homme est proprement omne animal* (94).

[38] *La mémoire est nécessaire pour toutes les opérations de la raison* (369).

[39] Jacques Maritain, *Three Reformers: Luther, Descartes, Rousseau* (New York: Charles Scribner's Sons, 1929).

account of the human condition, a condition that Pascal often depicts in quite dramatic terms as void of standards or order. Thus, charges of reductionism and irrationalism have been leveled against Pascal, both in his time and by contemporary critics. Sara Melzer argues that Pascal's account of the fall reduces to an irresolvable aporia. How so? There is, on the one hand, the "lost truth" as "the origin and goal of our desire. The story of the Fall and Redemption implies that its narrator has transcended language to acquire, through faith, the object of his desire: the certainty of a transcendent truth, of God." But, paradoxically, the historical fall puts us in a state of uncertainty, so that we are unable to say whether a fall, in fact, even occurred. "Trapped as we are in signs, we cannot escape the hermeneutic circle to gain knowledge of an origin from which we have fallen. Within the hermeneutic circle, all that humans can experience is a fall from the illusion of truth."[40] Thus, Pascal's own text affords no basis for deciding between the doctrinal truth of the fall and the fall as mere myth, indicating nothing more than our perpetual and irreversible alienation from truth. She puts the point more tersely toward the end of the book: "As the language in which we are trapped is a fallen language, the meta-language with which we represent to ourselves our attempts to transcend language is also fallen."[41] The grounds of Pascal's deconstruction of Cartesian philosophy suggests that any positive Pascalian project could itself be subject to deconstruction.

Melzer's deconstruction of Pascal's text restates in a particularly concise form a set of objections to Pascal raised by philosophers such as Nietzsche and J. L. Mackie.[42] Pervading Pascal's discussion of nature and instinct is the doctrine of original sin. Some of his statements about the fall are striking and severe. Man, he writes, "is nothing but a subject full of error, natural and ineffaceable without grace."[43] Pascal also suggests that we are unable to distinguish nature from habit: "Nature itself

---

[40] Sara E. Melzer, *Discourses of the Fall: A Study of Pascal's "Pensées"* (Berkeley: University of California Press, 1986), 76.

[41] Melzer, *Discourses of the Fall*, 142.

[42] In *Beyond Good and Evil*, trans. Walter Kaufmann (New York: Random House, 1966), Nietzsche describes the faith of Pascal as a "continual suicide of reason—a tough, long-lived, wormlike reason that cannot be killed all at once and with a single stroke" (46). J. L. Mackie, *The Miracle of Theism: Arguments for and against the Existence of God* (Oxford: Clarendon, 1982), 200–204.

[43] *L'homme n'est qu'un sujet plein d'erreur, naturelle et ineffaçable sans la grâce* (83).

is nothing other than first custom and custom is but second nature."[44] It seems that reason can be bent in any direction and thus cannot be a trustworthy guide in any sense. The fideist interpretation of Pascal seizes on this strain of his thought. If nature is utterly depraved, then an account of the movement from what human nature is to what it might become under the influence of grace seems undercut at the outset.

Precisely at this point does the charge of incoherence arise. The corruption of human nature threatens to undermine Pascal's project, as it renders human beings incapable of seeing any truth apart from grace. How could the proofs be instruments of grace? To what could Pascal be appealing in his audience? What use would the giving of reasons be? Some critics have asserted that the passages on the depravity of nature belie Pascal's positive appraisal of reason and conceal his actual intent, which is to undercut reason and to force the unbeliever into a situation where fear engenders an irrational leap of faith. J. L. Mackie, for example, has argued that the wager demands the denial of reason, while Nietzsche excoriated Pascal's faith as a continual sacrifice of reason. If these passages are taken as Pascal's peremptory statement on human nature, then he risks reducing religion to terror, conflating it with superstition, and undermining his own project. On this view, Pascal's project is tyrannical and vulnerable to an ethical critique. All that would remain of Pascal's apology is the crass appeal to calculative self-interest. In the course of his defense of Pascal's wager, Nicholas Rescher compares Pascal's approach to Thomas Hobbes' appeal to "personal advantage."[45] There are indeed similarities between the two approaches, but these are mainly superficial. Yet the surface resemblance makes a comparison useful.

To see what is at stake in Pascal's emphasis on the corruption of nature, it helps to consider Hobbes' account of the origin of religious belief, a position that renders religion indistinguishable from superstition. In *Leviathan*, Hobbes denies that there is any natural end to human life; instead, the "general inclination of mankind" is a "perpetual and restless desire of power after power, that ceaseth only in death."[46] Pascal nearly concurs when he writes, "Our nature consists in movement;

---

[44] *Cette nature ne soit elle-même qu'une première coutume, comme la coutume est une seconde nature* (93).

[45] Nicholas Rescher, *Pascal's Wager: A Study of Practical Reasoning in Philosophical Theology* (Notre Dame, Ind.: University of Notre Dame Press, 1985).

[46] Thomas Hobbes, *Leviathan* (Indianapolis: Hackett, 1994), 1:11.

absolute rest is death" (641).[47] For Hobbes, nature is mute concerning good and evil. Hobbes traces the origin of religious belief to two features of the human condition: "ignorance of causes," which "disposes or constrains men to rely on the advice and authority of others," and anxiety or fear over the future, which disposes human beings to posit, and then seek to appease, invisible causes controlling the future. As he puts it, "The perpetual fear, always accompanying mankind in the ignorance of causes, as it were in the dark, must needs have for an object something."[48] How does this compare with Pascal's approach to religion? One of the obstacles to answering this question is that, for all his preoccupation with method, Pascal is not a systematic thinker. His thought is mobile, discursive, and dialectical, with initial formulations being open to refinement or alteration in light of further evidence and additional reflections. Moreover, Pascal's aim is not simply to lay out a position in a linear, deductive fashion but to induce self-knowledge, a self-knowledge to which he thinks we are especially averse. He thus deploys hyperbole to shock his audience into a knowing recognition of itself and its condition. This much is clear. The complete denigration of reason would lead human beings to despair, which is one of two great evils of human life. The other, opposed evil is presumption. Neither angel nor beast, the human person is neither totally depraved nor capable of achieving the good by its own powers. Pascal's study of nature focuses on the wretchedness or corruption of human nature. Pascal adduces a plethora of examples of our wretchedness, three of which help illustrate the connection between wretchedness and greatness, the conceptual dependence of the former on the latter. The apprehension of human nature as wretched presupposes a grasp of what it means for human beings to possess integrity and health.

First, Pascal observes that we rarely live in the present; in fact, we find the present painful. We spend most of our time relishing or regretting the past and fearing or anticipating the future. Still, we incessantly and indefatigably pursue happiness as if it were somehow within our reach—as if it were inexplicable that we should not possess it. Thus, we never live but only hope to live, and our inveterate tendency to plot ways to achieve happiness is the surest sign that we will never attain

---

[47] *Notre nature est dans le mouvement; le repos entier est la mort* (129).
[48] Hobbes, *Leviathan*, 1:13.

it (47).[49] Alienation is a prominent motif. Pascal highlights the way we lead imaginary lives, concerned more about how we appear to others than about how we actually live. The result is that our lives are more fictional than real. To counter this tendency, Pascal offers a series of scenes designed to jolt us into recognizing our true condition. Pascal's theatrical depiction of the human condition offers a corrective to the imagination's tendency toward falsification.

Vincent Carraud describes Pascal's account of the human condition as "a spectacle, a theater."[50] Pascal's pedagogy is designed to remind human persons continually, in an ever deepening and expanding manner, of this duality, of the paradoxes of the human condition. Descartes writes in such a way as to inculcate in appropriately able readers the precise capacities needed to make progress in the reading of his texts. Skeptical of the claims of philosophical and spiritual exercises, Montaigne constructs essays, trials or tests of the self, which can provide points of departure for his readers to begin testing themselves. More fragmentary than either of these sets of texts, Pascal's writing seems to offer only piecemeal, isolated bits of insight, but the cumulative effect is to foster a sense of the extremes between which human life is pitched. Neither a series of ordered meditations nor an essay, Pascal's text is, for Carraud, a theatrical presentation of the human condition that affords a vision of only one thing: our inability to see. Pascal supplies exclusively "a theater of blindness."[51] But this is to overlook Pascal's paradoxical depiction of the human condition. If Pascal's drama confronts us with our blindness, it confronts us with a strange fact, a contradiction to our nature. Indeed, we could not recognize blindness as blindness, as a horrifying state, unless we also apprehended another state that is proper to us.

Second, unable to live in the present and averse to self-knowledge, we have given our lives over to diversion. Our inconstancy reflects the need to be diverted from the present, from ourselves. The cause of the state of "inconstancy, boredom, and anxiety" is the "realization that present pleasures are false, together with the failure to realize that

---

[49] *Ainsi nous ne vivons jamais, mais nous espérons de vivre; et, nous disposant toujours à être heureux, il est inévitable que nous ne le soyons jamais* (172).

[50] "*Une mise en scène, un théâtre.*" Carraud, *Pascal et la philosophie*, 398 (transl. mine).

[51] "*Un théâtre de l'égarement. L'égarement est fondamentalement ce qui, de l'homme, se donne à voir.*" Carraud, *Pascal et la philosophie*, 398 (transl. mine).

absent pleasures are vain" (73).[52] Part of the explanation has to do with the infinite variety of experience—a motif Pascal inherits from Montaigne. The lengthy historical "test" of the human pursuit of happiness should have convinced us "that we are incapable of attaining the good by our own efforts."[53] Yet we fail to learn from example precisely because "no two examples are exactly alike." We are deceived by the variety of experience into supposing "our expectations will not be disappointed this time as they were last time" (148).[54] To counter these tendencies, Pascal underscores the vastness of eternity in relation to time and the imminent possibility of death.[55]

Third, what typifies our condition is the apparently systematic subversion of higher, properly human capacities by lower, subhuman powers and drives. Imagination overpowers reason, truth and virtue are no match for charm and novelty, and concupiscence renders human freedom otiose. For Pascal, all these features of the human condition are signs of the wretchedness of human nature. But does not our ability to apprehend the various sorts of disorder in ourselves presuppose some apprehension of what is natural, normative, and good? In the course of discussing the obvious wrongness of homicide, Pascal states, "We know very well what is evil and false" (905).[56] To lament our inconstancy and inability to live in the present, must we not recognize, at least dimly, that our natural end is happiness? Our indomitable longing for happiness, even in the face of repeated failure, is a sign that we think happiness is proper to us. The very fact that we deem our condition wretched indicates that we think some better condition would be more appropriate to our nature. Similarly, to appreciate the subversion of higher by lower, must we not have some hold on what is natural, on the proper ordering and functioning of human capacities? Does not Pascal concede all this when he states that our greatness consists in our ability to understand our wretchedness? To make depravity the whole picture is to grasp only one part of our duality, to exaggerate our wretchedness

---

[52] *Le sentiment de la fausseté des plaisirs présents, et l'ignorance de la vanité des plaisirs absents causent l'inconstance* (110).

[53] *Nous convaincre de notre impuissance d'arriver au bien par nos efforts* (425).

[54] *C'est de là que nous attendons que notre attente ne sera pas deçue en cette occasion comme en l'autre* (425).

[55] *Entre nous et l'enfer ou le ciel, il n'y a que la vie entre deux, qui est la chose du monde la plus fragile* (425).

[56] *Car nous connaissons bien le mal et le faux* (385).

and to neglect entirely our greatness. Without a residue of greatness, we would not recognize our condition as wretched. Pascal makes this point explicitly: "All these examples of wretchedness prove his greatness. It is the wretchedness . . . of a dispossessed king" (116).[57]

Hobbes holds that there is no natural end to human desire and that desire cannot be understood except serially, as an insatiable urge for one thing after another. Pascal concedes something to Hobbes' description of our present state. On account of our failure to realize "the insatiable nature of cupidity," we think we "genuinely want rest when all we really want is activity."[58] For Pascal, the evidence is more complex than Hobbes allows. He observes of human beings that they exhibit contradictory impulses toward rest and activity. Pascal states that this reveals a confused plan in the depths of the human soul. Once again, and here in direct contrast with Hobbes, Pascal highlights the duality of the human condition. Hobbes refuses to make any judgment on the state of nature; he calls it "inconvenient" and yet "natural," and this evinces his distance from Pascal, who perceives that something is deeply awry in the human condition, something for which there is no extant explanation or remedy.

Moving from one experience, one pleasure, to another in an endless search for fulfillment, Hobbesian calculative reason fails to learn from its failures. The longing for happiness is one of the reasons of the heart that reason does not know or at least that reason is apt to forget or suppress. One of the difficulties with interpreting Pascal's account of the heart is that it is often rendered into English as "feeling" or "instinct." But *sentiment* or *sent* has in French, as in the Latin roots, cognitive dimensions as well as emotional elements. The Latin *sentire*, for example, means "sense" or "perceive." Pascal is to be taken seriously when he states the "heart has its reasons"; the heart is a faculty of perception, of awareness, and thus a vehicle of knowledge about the world.

Both reason and the heart are cognitive. Thus, Pascal describes those who have received the gift of faith as "judging by their heart" (382).[59] *Coeur* is, as Hans Urs von Balthasar observes, "the sensorium of

---

[57] *Toutes ces misères-là même prouvent sa grandeur. Ce sont misères de grand seigneur, misères d'un roi dépossédé* (398).

[58] *La nature insatiable de leur cupidité. Ils croient chercher sincèrement le repos, et ne cherchent en effet que l'agitation* (139).

[59] *Ils en jugent par le coeur* (287).

the whole."⁶⁰ The heart involves an immediate apprehension of complex wholes, rather than a discursive movement from one principle or assumption to others and through these to conclusions. By contrast to reason, the heart is more receptive than active. Pascal insists that reason is dependent on the heart precisely because reason must assume its starting points, must be given the materials upon which it works, to reject, to doubt, or to affirm.

In certain respects, Pascal should be seen as reformulating Augustine's argument on behalf of the priority of faith over knowledge. Without trust, we could know very little indeed. There is a link between the primacy of trust and the view of human life as a quest. There is no Archimedean point from which to initiate a quest; every quest begins in the middle of things and is partly determined by contingencies beyond the control of the seeker. If the confidence afforded by trust cannot refute skepticism, it is nonetheless a sufficient starting point in the quest for the good.

Pascal indicates that something more than passion or feeling is capable of informing human reasoning and action. He presupposes that we can recognize the way that disordered passion infects not just our desires but our perceptions and the activities of our reason. He also assumes that, in light of this recognition, we can make some effort in the direction of reforming our passions, of redirecting them toward truth, even if these efforts inevitably fall short of anything approaching complete reform. "We must resort to habit," he writes, "once the mind has seen where the truth lies. . . . With no violence, art or argument it makes us believe things, and so inclines all our faculties to this belief that our soul falls naturally into it" (821).⁶¹ He concludes, "We must . . . make both parts of us believe: the mind by reasons . . . and the

---

⁶⁰ Hans Urs von Balthasar, "Pascal," in *Studies in Theological Styles: Lay Styles*, vol. 3 of *The Glory of the Lord: A Theological Aesthetics*, by Hans Urs von Balthasar, trans. Andrew Louth et al., ed. John Riches (San Francisco: Ignatius, 1986), 184. Also see Jennifer Yhap, "Pascal and Descartes on First Ideas," *American Catholic Philosophical Quarterly* 69, no. 1 (1995): 39–50, which stresses the role of the heart as the basis of "dispositional acts of understanding"; and Jan Miel, *Pascal and Theology* (Baltimore: Johns Hopkins University Press, 1969), which underscores the biblical roots of the heart, as the center or core of the human person, uniting volitional, cognitive, and affective capacities.

⁶¹ *Il faut avoir recours à elle quand une fois l'esprit a vu où est la vérité. . . . Sans violence, sans art, sans argument, nous fait croire les choses et incline toutes nos puissances à cette croyance, en sorte que notre âme y tombe naturellement* (252).

automaton by habit.... *Incline my heart*" (821).⁶² But this way of putting things—in terms of an opposition between reason and passion or imagination—gives us only a partial and inadequate picture of the human condition as Pascal depicts it. For he wants to insist not just on the limits to reason and the corruption of the passions but on a more complicated account of our access to truth than what is allowed in the nascent rationalism of early modern philosophy. About the apparently inconclusive arguments over whether we can determine with certainty that we are not dreaming, Pascal concludes:

> We know that we are not dreaming, but, however unable we may be to prove it rationally, our inability proves nothing but the weakness of OUR reason, and not the uncertainty of all our knowledge.... For knowledge of first principles ... is as solid as any derived through reason, and it is on such knowledge, coming from the heart and instinct, that reason has to depend and base all its argument. (110)⁶³

Argument cannot silence the objections of the skeptics. On its own, reason is helpless to resist the onslaught of doubt, but skepticism remains a practical impossibility. A "perfectly genuine skeptic has never existed. Nature backs up helpless reason and stops it going so wildly astray" (131).⁶⁴ Pascal does concede something to the dogmatists, the opponents of skepticism: "We cannot doubt natural principles if we speak sincerely and in all good faith" (131).⁶⁵ What does this mean? Although reason is capable of mounting irresolvable objections to dogmatic claims concerning the certitude of natural principles, no one honestly doubts them. There is a gap, and potentially an opposition, between reason and instinct, between reason and nature.

---

⁶² *Il faut donc faire croire nos deux pièces: l'esprit, par les raisons ... et l'automate, par la coutume.... Inclina cor meum Deus* (252).

⁶³ *Nous savons que nous ne rêvons point; quelque impuissance où nous soyons de le prouver par raison, cette impuissance ne conclut autre chose que la faiblesse de notre raison, mais non par l'incertitude de toutes nos connaissances, comme ils le prétendent. Car la connaissance des premier principles ... est aussi ferme qu'aucune de celles que nos raisonnements nous donnent. Et c'est sur ces connaissances du coeur et de l'instinct qu'il faut que la raison s'appuie, et qu'elle y fonde tout son discours* (282).

⁶⁴ *On n'en peut venir là et je mets en fait qu'il n'y a jamais eu de pyrrhonien effectif parfait. La nature soutient la raison impuissante, et l'empêche d'extravaguer jusqu'à ce point* (434).

⁶⁵ *Qu'en parlant de bonne foi et sincèrement, on ne peut douter des principes naturels* (434).

There is then a sort of performative refutation of skepticism. The refutation is not internal to reason itself but rather to the whole of human nature, of which reason is a part. It is a part that is strangely able to put itself at odds with the whole. Nature, understood in terms of instinct or the heart, is always already involved in living a certain kind of life and hence cannot dispense with the assumptions constitutive of that life. Reason has no such mooring and can operate in an utterly disengaged fashion, so long as it attends solely to theoretical questions.

Pascal's ethics of thought counsels reason to check its desire to be autonomous and instead consult, and acknowledge its dependence on, nature, instinct, and the heart. The failure to refute skepticism thus has a positive corollary, the possibility of another avenue to the truth, the avenue of nature, instinct, or the heart: "We know the truth not only through our reason but also through our heart. It is through the latter that we know first principles, and reason, which has nothing to do with it, tries in vain to refute them. . . . Principles are felt, propositions proved, and both with certainty though by different means" (110).[66]

One might suppose that the heart, as a repository of first principles, was a faculty capable of supplying certain foundations for knowledge, provided, of course, we are willing to concede that our starting points themselves cannot be proved but must be taken on faith. Yet the disorder of our inclinations means that we will have difficulty with absolute confidence distinguishing authentic from deceptive deliverances of the heart. Moreover, unless we know that the source of the heart, indeed of human nature itself—whether these are the result of mere chance or of some sort of ordering principle—we will have lingering reasons to doubt its deliverances.

§4. The Restless Heart: Pascal's Residual Teleology

Even more important than the heart's curbing of the excesses and distortions of reason is the heart's locus as the core of the human person. The heart is the source of love, the weight, as Augustine would put it, of the self. It is precisely in the universal affirmation of the desire for happiness that Pascal discovers the starting point for a conversation

---

[66] *Nous connaissons la vérité, non seulement par la raison, mais encore par le coeur; c'est de cette dernière sorte que nous connaissons les premiers principes, et c'est en vain que le raisonnement qui n'y a point de part essaye de les combattre. . . . Les principes se sentent, les propositions se concluent et le tout avec certitude, quoique par différentes voies* (282).

with the philosophers, as with all human beings. "All men seek happiness. There are no exceptions. However different the means they may employ, they all strive towards this goal.... This is the motive of every act of every man, including those who go and hang themselves" (148).[67] As profoundly struck by this universal pursuit as was nearly every ancient philosopher, Pascal is equally struck by the glaring gap between aspiration and achievement, between reach and grasp: "All men complain: princes, subjects, nobles, commoners, old, young, strong, weak, learned, ignorant, healthy, sick, in every country, at every time, of all ages, and all conditions" (148).[68]

If Pascal repudiates the classical account of natural teleology, he nonetheless retains an element of that classical account, the ordering of the human person to happiness as its ultimate end. Pascal thinks this is one of the things we can learn from the failures, both our own and those of our entire species, to achieve happiness in any finite activity or state. The longing for an infinite good is what explains both our repeated dissatisfaction and why we keep pursuing happiness. It is also a clue to the duality of our condition. There is, as Jonathan Lear might put it, a pretense-transcending thrust to our desire for happiness, an erotic openness to the transcendent. The examination of the claimants to happiness, central to the classical discussion of the good life but suppressed in the modern period, even in the texts of Descartes and Montaigne, lies at the center of Pascal's analysis of the human condition. As is true for his chief interlocutors, Pascal examines themes and questions concerning happiness that arise in the classical tradition of pagan philosophy and in the thought of early Christians, especially Augustine.

As Augustine notes early in the Christian era, the ancient philosophers knew something about happiness. They knew enough to see that it was the ultimate end of human life, that it constituted the deepest and most ineradicable longing of the human soul. They also correctly identified happiness as something desired for its own sake, not as a means to some other good; were this not so, it could not be the ultimate end. Happiness is an end not just in the sense that other things contribute to it but also in the sense that it constitutes what is highest and best,

---

[67] *Tous les hommes recherchent d'être heureux; cela est sans exception; quelques différents moyens qu'ils y emploient, ils tendent tous à ce but.... C'est le motif de toutes les actions de tous les hommes, jusqu'à ceux qui vont se pendre* (425).

[68] *Tous se plaignent: princes, sujets; nobles, roturiers; vieux, jeunes; forts, faibles; savants, ignorants; sains, malades; de tous pays, de tous les temps, de tous âges, et de toutes conditions* (425).

most desirable, and lacking in nothing. Such a good must satisfy all desire, including the desire not to lose it. The philosophers also knew enough to recognize those activities or ways of life that could not fulfill the criteria for happiness or the ultimate end. So the life of money making, which supplies means to the possession of other things, could not provide happiness. Nor could sensual pleasure, as it satisfies only what is lowest in us and it does so only intermittently and often with an admixture of pain. Honor, sought in battle or in the arena of politics, depends too much on the opinion of others and hence could not constitute a self-sufficient good.[69] In a fragment entitled "Seeking the True Good," Pascal observes, "For the ordinary run of men their good consists in fortune and external wealth or at least in diversion. The philosophers have shown how vain all this is and have defined it as best they could" (626).[70]

In classical philosophy, the chief contenders for the ultimate end are the active and the contemplative lives. On the dominant pagan view, the practice of virtue is intrinsically fulfilling; hence, virtue is desired for its own sake and not merely as a means to other goods. These activities are noble and perfective of our nature. Yet not even these virtues can fill the longing for happiness as that which is self-sufficient and lacking in nothing. Each human being tries to fulfill the desire for happiness "with everything around him, seeking in things that are not there the help he cannot find in those that are, though none can help, since this infinite abyss can be filled only with an infinite and immutable object; in other words by God himself" (148).[71] Beyond the individual desire for this or that good, beyond this or that activity, there are more extensive accounts of the good, embodied in a variety of ways of life. Accordingly, Pascal seeks to "show the vanity of all kinds of conditions, show the vanity of ordinary lives, and then the vanity of

---

[69] The clearest formulation of these arguments can be found in Aristotle's *Ethics*, book 1.

[70] *Le commun des hommes met le bien dans la fortune et dans les biens du dehors, ou au moins dans le divertissement. Les philosophes ont montré la vanité de tout cela et l'ont mis où ils ont pu* (462).

[71] *De tout ce qui l'environne, recherchant des choses absentes le secours qu'il n'obtient pas des présentes, mais qui en sont toutes incapables, parce que le gouffre* [Var. ed.: *ce gouffre*] *infini ne peut être rempli que par un objet infini et immuable, c'est-à-dire que par Dieu même?* (425).

philosophers' lives, whether sceptical or Stoic" (694).[72] Here Pascal's strategy mirrors that of Augustine in book 19 of the *City of God*, where he offers a lengthy investigation and critique of the various pagan claimants to have resolved the problem of the ultimate end of human life.

In his critique of the philosophical path to happiness, Pascal begins with an appeal not to the revealed claims of Christianity but to standards internal to philosophy itself, to its definition of happiness and the human good. Thus, Pascal's famous critique of the philosophers reposes upon an affirmation of their achievement, of what they got right. Indeed, he speaks in terms of gradations of recognition concerning the supreme good. Pascal's universalist account of the good insists that if there is truly such an ultimate good, it must be available to all human persons, not just to the philosophers. The following passage is pertinent:

> Others again, who have indeed come closer to it, have found it impossible that this universal good, desired by all men, should lie in any of the particular objects which can only be possessed by one individual and which, once shared, cause their possessors more grief over the part they lack than satisfaction over the part they enjoy as their own. They have realized that the true good must be such that it may be possessed by all men at once without diminution or envy, and that no one should be able to lose it against his will. Their reason is that this desire is natural to man, since all men inevitably feel it, and man cannot be without it, and they therefore conclude. . . . (148)[73]

One of the most sustained pieces of reasoning in the entire *Pensées* comes to an abrupt halt in midsentence. The syntactical inconclusiveness reflects the way in which natural reason itself is caught up short in its inquiry into the highest good. In recognizing the human aspiration

---

[72] *Pour montrer la vanité* [Var., ed.: *des vies*] *de toutes sortes de conditions, montrer la vanité des vies communes, et puis la vanité des vies philosophiques, pyrrhoniennes, stoïques* (61).

[73] *D'autres, qui en ont en effet plus approché, ont considéré qu'il est nécessaire que le bien universel, que tous les hommes désirent, ne soit dans aucune des choses particulières qui ne peuvent être possédées que par un seul, et qui, étant partagées, affligent plus leur possesseur, par le manque de la partie qu'il n'a pas* [Var. ed.: *qu'ils n'ont pas*], *qu'elles ne le contentent par la jouissance de celle qui lui appartient. Ils ont compris que le vrai bien devait être tel que tous pussent le posséder à la fois, sans diminution et sans envie, et que personne ne le dût* [Var. ed.: *pût*] *perdre contre son gré. Et leur raison est que ce désir étant naturel à l'homme puisqu'il est nécessairement dans tous, et qu'il ne peut pas ne le pas avoir, ils en concluent* . . . (425).

for transcendence and the failure of reason to fulfill it, philosophy achieves an unstable and unsettling insight. Moreover, the more deeply the philosopher investigates the human condition, the more perplexing it becomes. Philosophy is no more than a laudable protreptic, an initiation of the quest. Yet this is not without merit. It raises legitimate questions, indeed the most important questions, and it aids in the refinement of those questions and in the analysis of the possible answers. However, when it goes beyond initiation and clarification and promises to deliver answers to the questions that afflict the human heart, it exceeds its capacity. Even as a protreptic, philosophy is not, for Pascal, an initiation into a life of contemplative happiness or virtuous equanimity. It begins a quest whose resolution is fraught with uncertainty and danger, with the prospect of failure and the possibility that misery may be increased rather than assuaged.

The succinct assessment of Epictetus encapsulates Pascal's view of philosophy: "Epictetus . . . only told men: 'you are on the wrong track.' He shows that there is another, but he does not lead us there" (140).[74] This calls to mind Pascal's terse description of the philosopher as the one "who will worry the man who seeks." Epictetus illicitly concludes from our capacity, on some occasions, to resist passion that we are always capable of resisting. As for Seneca's advice ("Be content with yourself and the good things innate in you"), Pascal finds it odd that the Stoics would end up recommending suicide when life becomes burdensome: "How happy is a life we throw off like the plague" (147).[75]

The attempt to reach God by natural reason can engender in the human intellect a proud celebration of his own intellect. The glory goes not to God but to the philosopher who claims to have reached God. But such a disposition in fact creates an obstacle to knowing who God really is. The philosopher risks simultaneously losing both knowledge of God and self-knowledge. Pascal quotes Augustine: "What they gained by curiosity they lost through pride" (190).[76] The allusion to Augustine is instructive. Aside from the question of philosophical pride, there is the deeper issue of mediation between human and divine. Indeed, this might be said to be the crucial question of the pagan world. The

---

[74] *Epictète . . . il dit aux hommes: "Vous en suivez un faux"; il montre que c'en est un autre, mais il n'y mène pas* (466).

[75] *Oh! quelle vie heureuse, dont on se délivre comme de la peste!* (361).

[76] "*Quod curiositate cognoverunt* [Var. ed.: *cognoverint*] *superbia amiserunt*" [Augustin/Augustine, *Sermons*, 141] (543).

recognition of the human as an intermediate realm, between the divine and the bestial, was common to poets and philosophers. Both the poets and the philosophers make claims to mediation, to be able to provide a path, an avenue of communication, between the human and the divine. The poems of Homer and the dialogues of Plato, most notably the famous ascent passage in the *Symposium*, aim to do precisely this. As Pierre Manent puts it, "All men, one way or another, experience the desire for immortality, in every case a desire for commerce with immortals."[77]

It might seem that Pascal should side, against philosophy, with common opinion, with the unreflective judgments of the common man. Yet, Pascal's own method resembles the counsel of the philosophers. He urges man to begin "with himself, with his author and his end." Montaigne, of course, begins and ends with himself, while Descartes includes both the *ego* and God; yet it is not clear that he treats God as an end of his inquiry but perhaps merely as a function, providing a foundation for the intelligibility of mathematical physics, within a system whose telos lies elsewhere.

The argument that human life has the structure of a quest involves a critique of the way most human beings live; it also involves an implicit affirmation of the lives of the philosophers, who attempt to live in accord with reason or nature. Following Augustine's line of argument in *The City of God*, Pascal notes the utter lack of consensus among the philosophers concerning the nature of the sovereign good. Conflicting and incommensurable, the opinions of the philosophers are isomorphic to those of the many. The many seek happiness in external activity, whereas the philosophers counsel a return to ourselves, the cultivation of an interior life of thought and virtue. They say, "Withdraw into yourselves and there you will find your good." But the counsel runs counter to powerful forces in human nature and is futile as a cure for what ails us: "We are full of things that impel us outwards. Our instinct makes us feel that our happiness must be sought outside ourselves. Our passions drive us outwards, even without objects to excite them" (143).[78]

---

[77] "*Tous les homes sans doute, d'une façon ou d'une autre, éprouvent le désir de l'immortalité, en tout cas le désir de nouer commerce avec immortels.*" Pierre Manent, *Les métamorphoses de la cité: Essai sur la dynamique de l'Occident* (Paris: Flammarion, 2010), 346 (transl. mine).

[78] *Nous sommes pleins de choses qui nous jettent au dehors. Notre instinct nous fait sentir qu'il faut chercher notre bonheur hors de nous. Nos passions nous poussent au dehors, quand même les objets ne s'offriraient pas pour les exciter* (464).

The Pascalian dialectic between the philosophers and the many mirrors the double irony we noted earlier in Montaigne's criticism of the ordinary and the wise. Yet Pascal's irony does not seek simply to humble the presumption of the wise; it seeks to underscore the gap between desire and achievement and to urge both the many and the few to continue to seek. The impotence of philosophy is not without effect; it leaves us with a set of aporias, questions on which one can argue equally persuasively on either side. Echoing Montaigne's embrace of skepticism and mimicking his very language, Pascal urges, "Let us . . . concede to the sceptics what they have so often proclaimed, that truth lies beyond our scope . . . , that it is no earthly denizen, but at home in heaven, lying in the lap of God, to be known only in so far as it pleases him to reveal it" (131).[79] Recall the passage from Montaigne, "There is no end to our investigations; our end is in the other world."[80] The influence on Pascal is palpable, as is the distance between them. Pascal derives from Montaigne the insight that experience is too diverse and varied to be brought under systematic unity, or at least that this cannot be done without leaving behind much of what is most interesting in experience. He also concurs with Montaigne's assertion that our quest for answers cannot be completed in this life. Montaigne's attitude toward endless ambiguity, however, is one of equanimity, while Pascal finds the contradictions and paradoxes of our condition a cause for alarm.

Pascal embraces the thesis of the skeptics about the limitations to human knowledge but deduces from it quite a different conclusion. Their view is that truth is beyond us, not proper to us, and should be left to God; we should remain agnostic on the big questions. For Montaigne, this is an ethical imperative: be aware of, and obedient to, human limitations. To try to reach beyond the scope of human reason and grasp absolute truth distorts and does harm to the human condition. That is the insight behind Montaigne's remark, dear to Pascal, that he who tries to make himself an angel becomes a beast. Yet, as we have seen, Montaigne is less worried about the human proclivity toward the beast. If this sort of skepticism defers answers to the big questions,

---

[79] *Qu'on accorde donc aux pyrrhoniens ce qu'ils ont tant crié: que la vérité n'est pas de notre portée . . . qu'elle ne demeure pas en terre, qu'elle est domestique du ciel, qu'elle loge dans le sein de Dieu, et que l'on ne la peut connaître qu'à mesure qu'il lui plaît de la révéler* (434).

[80] Michel de Montaigne, *The Complete Essays*, translated by M. A. Screech (New York: Penguin Classics, 2003), 348.

it nonetheless proffers a specific wisdom about the human condition, what Montaigne calls a "merry and companionable wisdom."[81]

Pascal articulates and affirms Montaigne's thesis: "It is deserting humanity to desert the middle way. The greatness of the human soul lies in knowing how to keep this course; greatness does not mean going outside it, but rather keeping within it" (518).[82] Pascal concurs with Montaigne's judgment that we cannot on the basis of reason or will alter our condition; indeed, the desire to do so by our own efforts is bound to lead us to desert the middle way. But this leaves us not at peace but with an unsettling insight concerning the duality of the human condition: "Unhappy as we are, we have an idea of happiness but we cannot attain it. We perceive an image of the truth and possess nothing but falsehood, being equally incapable of absolute ignorance and certain knowledge."[83] In the face of such perversion and of our repeated and universal failure to achieve happiness, another mystery emerges: the conundrum of why we continue to pursue and hope for happiness, despite the evidence.

According to Pascal, at the root of our alienation, our flight from self-knowledge, is fear of death, a resistance to our own mortality: "It is easier to bear death when one is not thinking about it than the idea of death when there is no danger" (138).[84] Even as we expend enormous effort, time, and money in an attempt to control nature, to alleviate pain and suffering, and to postpone death, we realize at some level that we can never fully succeed in this quixotic project. "Being unable to cure death, wretchedness and ignorance, men have decided, in order to be happy, not to think about such things" (133).[85] On the topic of death there is a striking disparity between Montaigne and Descartes; whereas the former makes the art of dying the centerpiece of his philosophy, the latter occludes it from view. It is as if Descartes' reading of Montaigne made him aware of the philosophical failure to respond to the fear of death and thus he decides precisely "not to think about such things."

---

[81] Montaigne, *Essays*, 1269.

[82] *C'est sortir de l'humanité que de sortir du milieu. La grandeur de l'âme humaine consiste à savoir s'y tenir; tant s'en faut que la grandeur soit à en sortir, qu'elle est à n'en point sortir* (378).

[83] *Malheureux que nous sommes, et plus que s'il n'y avait point de grandeur dans notre condition, nous avons une idée du bonheur, et ne pouvons y arriver; nous sentons une image de la vérité, et ne possédons que le mensonge: incapables d'ignorer absolument et de savoir certainement* (434).

[84] *La mort est plus aisée à supporter sans y penser, que la pensée de la mort sans peril* (166).

[85] *Les hommes n'ayant pu guérir la mort, la misère, l'ignorance, ils se sont avisés, pour se rendre heureux, de n'y point penser* (168).

Yet, Descartes does talk about illness with the expectation that fear of bodily pain will teach us to place our hope in scientific and technological progress. For Pascal, neither the neglect of death nor its purported treatment by philosophical therapy is satisfactory. As we have seen, Montaigne initially adopts an ancient view of philosophy as preparation for dying. The strategies Montaigne deploys to defuse the horror of death cannot eradicate our fear of what is in fact a great taunt to our rational nature. Pascal goes so far as to accuse Montaigne of cowardice in the face of death:

> Montaigne's faults are great. . . . His views on deliberate homicide, on death. He inspires indifference regarding salvation: "without fear or repentance." . . . His completely pagan views on death are inexcusable; for all hope of piety must be abandoned if we are not at least willing to die as Christians. Now, throughout his book he thinks only of dying a death of cowardly ease. (680)[86]

Indeed, as we have seen, Montaigne rejects the notion of repentance not only in the face of death but throughout the whole of life and in all circumstances.

Now, the accusation of cowardice might seem an odd objection, since Montaigne, at least in his initial reflection on death, counsels overcoming fear of death. But Montaigne's therapy for the mortal soul in fact eliminates the need for courage, as it attempts to strip death of every malignity. His later reflections, which exhibit skepticism about the viability of philosophical therapies for the fear of death, take an entirely different tack on courage, as the counsel of diversion indicates that courage in the face of death is impossible. For Pascal, this is not confrontation but avoidance. Deploying the sort of dramatic language familiar from Montaigne's reflection on the significance of our final act, Pascal writes bluntly, "The last act is bloody, however fine the rest of the play. They throw earth over your head and it is finished for ever" (165).[87] Death endures as a taunt and something rightly to be feared, at

---

[86] *Montaigne.—Les défauts de Montaigne sont grands . . . sur la mort. Il inspire une nonchalance du salut, sans crainte et sans repentir. . . . On ne peut excuser ses sentiments tout païens sur la mort; car il faut renoncer à toute piété, si on ne veut au moins mourir chrétiennement; or, il ne pense qu'à mourir lâchement et mollement par tout son livre* (63).

[87] *Le dernier acte est sanglant, quelque belle que soit la comédie en tout le reste: on jette enfin de la terre sur la tête, et en voilà pour jamais* (210).

least from the perspective of natural reason. Montaigne and Descartes suppress Augustine's insight into the human condition: the weight of our desires is rooted in an ineradicable and unquenchable desire for the infinite, for a happiness that cannot be lost and that fulfills all our longings.

Of course, Montaigne's considered views on death concede the impotence of philosophical therapy. Instead, Montaigne credits ordinary folks who have the good sense to divert themselves from such unsettling thoughts. In a series of fragments responding to Montaigne on diversion, Pascal writes, "Diversion. Being unable to cure death, wretchedness and ignorance, men have decided, in order to be happy, not to think about such things" (133).[88] Instead of fostering self-knowledge, such diversion enervates and causes forgetfulness of self. Thus, for Pascal, there is a positive thrust underlying the obsession with self-deceiving illusion: "Despite these afflictions man wants to be happy, only wants to be happy, and cannot help wanting to be happy" (134).[89]

Pascal defends a kind of residual teleology, but he does so mainly through negation and indirection. It is the persistent and universal failure of any finite good or set of goods that suggests only an infinite object could satisfy human longing. In his discussions of happiness and death, Pascal's target is mainly Montaigne, whereas in the critique of the ambitions of scientific knowledge, he takes aim at Descartes.[90] In the case of Descartes, the worry is about excess; with Montaigne, the concern is about a deficiency, an attempted policy of tempering the insatiable longing of the human heart.

---

[88] *Divertissement.—Les hommes n'ayant pu guérir la mort, la misère, l'ignorance, ils se sont avisés, pour se rendre heureux, de n'y point penser* (168).

[89] *Nonobstant ces misères, il veut être heureux, et ne veut être qu'heureux, et ne peut ne vouloir pas l'être* (169).

[90] "Since all things are both caused and causing, assisted and assisting, mediate and immediate, providing mutual support in a chain linking together naturally and imperceptibly the most distant and different things, I consider it as impossible to know the parts without knowing the whole as to know the whole without knowing the individual parts [*Donc toutes choses étant causées et causantes, aidées et aidantes, médiates et immédiates, et toutes s'entretenant par un lien naturel et insensible qui lie les plus éloignées et les plus différentes, je tiens impossible de connaître les parties sans connaître le tout, non plus que de connaître le tout sans connaître particulièrement les parties*]" (199; 72).

§5. Pascal's Methods and the Quest for a Synoptic Vision

Against Descartes' attempt to treat the human subject in a scientific and transparent manner, Pascal opts for the digressive style of Montaigne. Some have supposed that a polished version of Pascal's apology, had he lived to complete it, would have brought the scattered fragments into a clear order. Yet, Pascal denies this: "I will write down my thoughts here as they come and in a perhaps not aimless confusion. This is the true order and it will always show my true order by its very disorder. I should be honouring my subject too much if I treated it in order, since I am trying to show that it is incapable of it" (532).[91] Pascal's own writing is more fragmentary and more oblique than is that of Montaigne.[92] Given these comments and his penchant for stylistic fragmentation, it might seem that Pascal could not have set ambitious explanatory goals. It would seem further that any conception of method would have to be minimal indeed. Yet, Pascal is nearly as obsessed with the question of method as is Descartes. As we shall see, he shares with the philosophical tradition the quest for knowledge about the whole. Unlike Descartes, he resists the temptation to reduce the variegated means of pursuing truth to one overarching method. Moreover, Pascal matches method to subject matter rather than insisting that subject matters be measured by their susceptibility to manipulation by a single, rational method.

Pascal's insistence that the abstract, mathematical sciences be situated within the framework of a whole that cannot be reduced to any particular science reposes upon assumptions about the interconnection of parts and whole, both in the real order and in the order of knowing. The assumption here is that wherever one thing depends upon or is intimately related to another, the relations must be known in order for

---

[91] *Pyrrhonisme.—J'écrirai ici mes pensées sans ordre, et non pas peutêtre dans une confusion sans dessein: c'est le véritable ordre, et qui marquera toujours mon objet par le désordre même. Je ferais trop d'honneur à mon sujet si je le traitais avec ordre, puisque je veux montrer qu'il en est incapable* (373).

[92] Pascal objects, furthermore, to Montaigne's endless and deeply un-Socratic penchant for self-display and for talking about himself. Just as much as Descartes, Montaigne is a philosopher of the ego or self. Carraud comments, "In so far as he is a philosopher of the subject, Montaigne can be assimilated to Descartes. Montaigne and Descartes are philosophers who too often say 'I' [*En tant que philosophe du sujet, Montaigne peut être assimilé à Descartes. Montaigne et Descartes sont des philosophes qui disent (trop) je*]." Carraud, *Pascal et la philosophie*, 299–300.

the thing to be known. Only by isolation, abstraction, and reduction can we know anything about anything. Of course, these are precisely the strategies that modern science deploys to gain a rigorous and certain knowledge of things. Pascal is willing to grant much to the power of the mathematical sciences, but he also wants to stress the limitations to such knowledge. Without such an acknowledgement, modern science exemplifies tyranny, the attempt to extend one's authority beyond the limited sphere in which one can justifiably claim it: "Tyranny consists in the desire to dominate everything regardless of order. . . . Tyranny is wanting to have by one means what can only be had by another" (58).[93]

In his broad-based inquiry into the human good, no one method of proceeding suffices. Pascal resists the modern tendency to reduce the operation of reason to a univocal language or a homogeneous method.[94] This does not mean that he fails to see the power of mathematical reasoning; instead, he argues for a plurality of methods of inquiry, with distinctive types of evidence and divergent cognitive stances, corresponding to different subject matters. Pascal combines the means of investigation deployed by Montaigne and Descartes in his reflections on *finesse* and *geometrie*.

The great attraction of mathematics is precisely its clarity, rigor, and order. Pascal observes that, once the principles are apprehended, conclusions follow readily. The difficulty is in reaching the principles, which requires a turning of the mind not natural to us. Conversely, those who are inclined to mathematical thinking are often incapable of handling the "intricate and numerous principles" right in front of them. Such principles are "perceived instinctively rather than seen" (512).[95] Although the principles of *finesse* are there "for all to see," it is not the case that everyone apprehends them equally well. Most persons are incapable of quickly seeing either type of principle: "Unsound minds are never either intuitive or mathematical." In *finesse*, the principles "are so delicate and numerous that it takes a sense of great delicacy and precision to perceive them and judge correctly and accurately from this perception. . . . Things must be seen all at once, at a glance, and not

---

[93] *La tyrannie consiste au désir de domination, universel et hors de son ordre. . . . La tyrannie est de vouloir avoir par une voie ce qu'on ne peut avoir par une autre* (332).

[94] See Funkenstein, *Theology and the Scientific Imagination*.

[95] *On les voit à peine, on les sent plutôt qu'on ne les voit* (1).

as a result of progressive reasoning" (512).⁹⁶ If the spirit of geometry is evident in the ability to apprehend the principles of mathematics and demonstrate truths from these starting points, the spirit of *finesse* may be seen in the ability to read a poem by tracing the supple use of metaphor and by grasping complex relationships of meter, rhyme, and mood. The former reduces and abstracts in order to reach clear and distinct principles, whereas the latter grasps complex wholes and perceives the implicit connections between parts.

Pascal never denies the certitude and power of mathematics in its own order. In the mathematical order, "principles are obvious, but remote from ordinary usage, so that from want of practice we have difficulty turning our heads that way; but once we do turn our heads the principles can be fully seen" (512).⁹⁷ The most important truths of human life, those that aid us in conducting ourselves as human beings in the world, depend not on the order of mathematics but on the order that falls to *finesse*. When mathematicians attempt to apply the one rule of geometry to the whole of human life, they "make themselves ridiculous." With the spirit of *finesse*, the "principles are in ordinary usage and there for all to see. There is no need to turn our heads, or strain ourselves; it is only a question of good sight, but it must be good; for the principles are so intricate and numerous that it is almost impossible not to miss some" (512).⁹⁸ The juxtaposition of the spirit of *finesse* with the spirit of geometry is intended to circumscribe the scope and function of the mathematical model of reasoning and to make room for an alternative conception of human inquiry. Martin Warner suggests that the judgment called for in differentiating true from false authority is of a piece with that of *finesse*, which sorts veridical from deceptive sentiments. So long as reason is construed in terms of *geometrie*, philosophy

---

⁹⁶ *Ce sont choses tellement délicates et si nombreuses, qu'il faut un sens bien délicat et bien net pour les sentir, et juger droit et juste selon ce sentiment. . . . Il faut tout d'un coup voir la chose d'un seul regard et non pas par progrès de raisonnement* (1).

⁹⁷ *Les principes sont palpables, mais éloignés de l'usage commun; de sorte qu'on a peine à tourner la tête de ce côté-là, manque d'habitude: mais pour peu qu'on l'y tourne, on voit les principes à plein* (1).

⁹⁸ "*Les principes sont dans l'usage commun et devant les yeux de tout le monde. On n'a que faire de tourner la tête, ni de se faire violence; il n'est question que d'avoir bonne vue, mais il faut l'avoir bonne: car les principes sont si déliés et en si grand nombre, qu'il est presque impossible qu'il n'en échappe*" (1). These principles cannot be set out in a deductive fashion; they must be "seen all at once, at a glance [*Il faut tout d'un coup voir la chose d'un seul regard*]" (512; 1).

is deadlocked; the vicious circle of dogmatist and skeptic can be broken only by enlarging our conception of rationality to include *finesse*, thus making possible an appeal to the reasons of the heart, about which we will have more to say below.[99]

Problems arise when those skilled in one operation of the mind apply that method to a subject matter not amenable to it. "Mathematicians try to treat intuitive matters mathematically, and make themselves ridiculous," whereas "intuitive minds . . . are taken aback when presented with propositions of which they understand nothing . . . and consequently feel repelled and disgusted" (512).[100] Put more positively, Pascal writes, "Mathematicians would be intuitive if they had good sight . . . and intuitive minds would be mathematical if they could adapt their sight to unfamiliar principles" (512).[101] Pascal's point here recalls one made by Aristotle in *Metaphysics*, book 2, chapter 3:

> The effect which lectures produce on a hearer depends on his habits; for we demand the language we are accustomed to, and that which is different from this seems not in keeping but somewhat unintelligible and foreign because of its unwontedness. For it is the customary that is intelligible. The force of habit is shown by the laws, in which the legendary and childish elements prevail over our knowledge about them, owing to habit. Thus some people do not listen to a speaker unless he speaks mathematically, others unless he gives instances, while others expect him to cite a poet as witness. And some want to have everything done accurately, while others are annoyed by accuracy. . . . Hence one must be already trained to know how to take each sort of argument, since it is absurd to seek at the same time knowledge and the way of attaining knowledge; and it is not easy to get even one of the two.[102]

---

[99] Martin Warner, *Philosophical Finesse: Studies in the Art of Rational Persuasion* (Oxford: Clarendon, 1989). See also Hugh Davidson, *Pascal and the Arts of the Mind* (Cambridge: Cambridge University Press, 1993).

[100] *Les géomètres veulent traiter géométriquement ces choses fines, et se rendent ridicules. . . . Et les esprits fins, au contraire, ayant ainsi accoutumé à juger d'une seule vue, sont si étonnés . . . qu'ils s'en rebutent et s'en dégoûtent* (1).

[101] *Tous les géomètres seraient donc fins s'ils avaient la vue bonne . . . et les esprits fins seraient géomètres, s'ils pouvaient plier leur vue vers les principes inaccoutumés de géométrie* (1).

[102] Aristotle, *Metaphysics*, in *The Complete Works of Aristotle*, ed. Jonathan Barnes, vol. 2 (Princeton, N.J.: Princeton University Press, 1984).

One of the marks of an educated intellect, for both Plato and Aristotle, is a capacity to discern which questions, what degree of certitude, and which methods are appropriate to which fields of inquiry. There is, it should be noted, ample opportunity for irony here, as inquirers apply the standards and methods appropriate to one sphere of inquiry to a foreign sphere or assume that a specific mode of investigation, one method, is applicable always and everywhere. From the perspective of the one who possesses the virtue of discerning the proper and variegated paths of inquiry, the result is comic. "Ironists," as Brad Frazier points out, "are especially perceptive of incongruities of various sorts, gaps between what is and what ought to be or between what is said to be and what is."[103]

One of the advances in Pascal scholarship in recent years has been greater attention to the role of dialectic and rhetoric. Martin Warner argues that Pascal's approach echoes Aristotle's conception of dialectical inquiry, which sorts through received opinions (*endoxa*), paradigmatic examples, and reasoned theories in an effort to arrive at the most adequate account of the subject matter in question.[104] The more attentively and minutely we observe the phenomena, the less coherent they seem and the less persuasive seem the rival accounts. What Pascal counsels about the interpretation of scripture is pertinent: A good portrait can be made only by reconciling all our contradictory features, and it is not enough to follow through a series of mutually compatible qualities without reconciling their opposites; to understand an author's meaning all contradictory passages must be reconciled (257).[105]

The attempt to account for complex and seemingly contradictory phenomena, which is the goal of Aristotelian dialectic, is precisely the method Pascal follows in his inquiry into the human condition. But this is not a method that can be captured in rules or reduced to a single insight. Linda Zagzebski takes a similar approach in her account of intellectual virtue, which she illustrates by analogy to the "way a good detective solves a mystery." She writes, "He will exhibit such virtues as the ability to think up explanations of complex sets of data. . . . No

---

[103] Brad Frazier, *Rorty and Kierkegaard on Irony and Moral Commitment* (New York: Palgrave Macmillan, 2006), 201.

[104] Warner, *Philosophical Finesse*, 158.

[105] *On ne peut faire une bonne physionomie qu'en accordant toutes nos contrariétés, et il ne suffit pas de suivre une suite de qualités accordantes sans accorder les contraires. Pour entendre le sens d'un auteur, il faut accorder tous les passages contraires* (684).

specifiable procedure tells a person how to recognize the salient facts, how to get insight, or how to think up good explanations, much less how to use all three to get to a single end." Solving the mystery is a matter of "putting the evidence together in a certain order that permits him to 'see' a pattern that points to a certain culprit."[106] In the practical order and in the order of the discovery of contingent truths such as the identification of a culprit of a crime, the dispositions of the agent—the complex set of moral and intellectual virtues—are crucial. To quote Aristotle again, as a man is, so does the good appear to him. Here we come up against the greatest of obstacles, our own multiple aversions to truth, especially to the truth about ourselves, self-knowledge: "We hide and disguise ourselves from ourselves" (655).[107] The first stage in self-knowledge is negative and painful; it involves recognizing the many ways in which we frustrate our own desire for truth, perhaps the strongest sign of the duality of our condition. We are, as Pascal insists, prey to illusions, gullible, and easily derailed by images, fantasies, and the passions of vain self-love.[108]

Mesnard proposed that Pascalian reasoning involves a dialectic of opposites; it unveils a series of antinomies, which reason itself is unable to resolve.[109] The synthesis comes from outside, from God. As Erec Koch has pointed out, Mesnard's conception of Pascalian dialectic is too static; instead, Pascalian dialectic involves an "infinitely productive" and "sequential movement," in which each opposite reverses itself into the other. For Koch, the process draws the opposites "into an underlying unity" that is not so much a synthesis as a dissolution of the original problem.[110] Going beyond the classic interpretations of

---

[106] See Linda Zagzebski, *Virtues of the Mind* (Cambridge: Cambridge University Press, 2002), 226; on *phronesis*, see 219–31.

[107] *Nous cachons et nous déguisons à nousmêmes* (377).

[108] Pascal would concur with Zagzebski's list of intellectual vices: "Intellectual pride, negligence, idleness, cowardice, conformity, carelessness, rigidity, prejudice, wishful thinking, closed-mindedness, insensitivity to detail, obtuseness, and a lack of thoroughness" (*Virtues of the Mind*, 152).

[109] Jean Mesnard, *Pascal*, trans. Claude and Marcia Abraham (Tuscaloosa: University of Alabama Press, 1969), 38.

[110] Erec Koch, *Pascal and Rhetoric: Figural and Persuasive Language in the Scientific Treatises, "The Provinciales," and the "Pensées"* (Charlottesville, Va.: Rookwood Press, 1997), 114–20. Essays by Paul de Man and Jacques Derrida inform Koch's study, *Pascal and Rhetoric*, the argument of which is that Pascal's dialectical method ends up dissolving, rather than resolving, the very questions he thinks are most pressing.

Goldmann and Melzer, both of whom see Pascal's dialectic as trapped in a tragic choice between contradictory and insuperable opposites, Koch argues that the dialectic leaves us not with "absence of meaning as opposed to presence," but with "non-meaning," not "absence of truth as opposed to its presence," but "non-truth."[111] Koch goes beyond those who see Pascal's apologetic project as a failure, as somehow faulty in this or that argument or as containing contradictions for which Pascal cannot account. He thinks that Pascal's central dialectical method dissolves the very possibility of framing the questions in the first place.

Fortunately for Pascal, there are two reasons not to adopt Koch's interpretation, which has the odd effect of depicting dialectic as both motion without rest and rest without the possibility of motion. Pascal intends for philosophical dialectic not to resolve or come to rest but to stay in motion. First, the result of Koch's analysis would be that religion could enter the mind only through an irrational and violent seduction of the soul. To support his view, he attends exclusively to the passages in which Pascal speaks of God as moving the will and concludes

---

Also Paul de Man, "Pascal's Allegories of Persuasion," *Allegory and Representation*, ed. Stephen Greenblatt (Baltimore: Johns Hopkins University Press, 1981); and Jacques Derrida, "Force of Law: The Mystical Foundations of Authority," *Cardozo Law Review* 11, no. 5 (1990): 920–1045.

[111] Koch, *Pascal and Rhetoric*, 137. See Lucien Goldmann, *Le Dieu caché: Étude sur la vision tragique dans les "Pensées" de Pascal et dans le théâtre de Racine* (Paris: Gallimard, 1959). Also see Leszek Kołakowski, *God Owes Us Nothing: A Brief Remark on Pascal's Religion and on the Spirit of Jansenism* (Chicago: University of Chicago Press, 1998); and Lucien Goldmann, *The Hidden God: A Study of Tragic Vision in the "Pensées" of Pascal and the Tragedies of Racine* (London: Routledge & Kegan Paul, 1964). Although Goldmann's interpretation of Pascal and tragedy contains many insights, the exegesis of Pascal is not adequate to the whole of Pascal's thought. First, Goldmann reads Pascal not on his own terms but as one moment, an early and immature moment, in the development of modern philosophy. Pascal thus appears as an incomplete modern, who discovered the rudiments of dialectical thought but was unable to achieve the historical synthesis of Hegel or Marx. Second, Goldmann distorts the proper role of the heart in Pascal's conception of human nature (*Hidden God*, 195, 200). Goldmann's tragic Pascal is a Pascal stripped of his cogent religious response to the impasse at which the uncertain but searching human being arrives on the basis of a purely rational quest. But this is only part of Pascal's integral vision of the human condition. For theologically informed interpretations of Pascal, see Marion, *Descartes' Metaphysical Prism*; and Balthasar, "Pascal," in *Studies in Theological Styles*, 184. Also see my "Habits of the Heart: Pascal and the Ethics of Thought," *International Philosophical Quarterly* 45, no. 2 (2005): 203–20.

that Pascal's Christianity is a rhetoric of force. Yet Pascal explicitly denounces the introduction of religion through force:

> The conduct of God, who disposes all things kindly, is to put religion into the mind by reason, and into the heart by grace. But to will to put it into the mind and heart by force and threats is not to put religion there, but terror, *terorrem potius quam religionem*. (172)[112]

In the section entitled "Submission and Use of Reason," from which the passage on terror is taken, Pascal distinguishes true religion from both superstition and rationalism: "Two excesses: to exclude reason, to admit nothing but reason" (183).[113] Pascal does not argue, as proponents of natural theology might, that reason can demonstrate a portion of what is revealed, but he does argue that reason and faith cannot conflict. He affirms Augustine's claim that "reason . . . judges that there are occasions when it ought to submit" (174).[114]

As we have already noted, there is a long tradition of reading Pascal as hostile to reason itself, as engaging exclusively in a rhetoric of destruction that would force his interlocutor to adopt the Christian faith in ignorance and out of fear.[115] Pascal does indeed think that a healthy dose of fear is appropriate to our experience of being lost in a seemingly indifferent and silent universe. But, as we have seen, reason is also prominent in his writings. Indeed, for all his observations about the impotence of reason, Pascal at times seems a protorationalist, multiplying proofs and urging ways to prepare reason for the search.[116]

---

[112] *La conduite de Dieu, qui dispose toutes choses avec douceur, est de mettre la religion dans l'esprit par les raisons, et dans le coeur par la grâce. Mais de la vouloir mettre dans l'esprit et dans le coeur par la force et par les menaces, ce n'est pas y mettre la religion, mais la terreur, terrorem potius quam religionem* (185).

[113] *Deux excès: exclure la raison, n'admettre que la raison* (253).

[114] *Il est donc juste qu'elle se soumette quand elle juge qu'elle se doit soumettre* (270).

[115] Alasdair MacIntyre, *After Virtue: A Study in Moral Theory* (Notre Dame, Ind.: University of Notre Dame Press, 1981), 51–52. The brief remarks about Pascal in *After Virtue* should not be taken as the complete word on MacIntyre's view of Pascal. For an alternative approach to Pascal, see his book review "Pascal and Marx: Lucien Goldmann's *The Hidden God*," in *Against the Self-Images of the Age*, by Alasdair MacIntyre (Notre Dame, Ind.: University of Notre Dame Press, 1978), 76–87. In the course of his defense of Pascal's wager, Nicholas Rescher compares Pascal's approach to Hobbes' appeal to "personal advantage." See Rescher, *Pascal's Wager*.

[116] On this topic, I have learned a great deal from Pierre Manent's unpublished essay "Pascal's Paradoxical Rationalism," delivered at Boston College in the 1990s.

Following Pierre Manent, we would do well to speak of Pascal's "paradoxical rationalism." As Hugh Davidson notes, Pascal repudiates a "procedure that would address arguments to someone with the aim of producing conviction, apart from a logic of demonstrative sequences," "nor will he espouse the notion of strictly contextual truths and goods, determined apart from a comprehensive scheme."[117] Throughout his apology, Pascal's goal is "integrative, synoptic thinking."[118]

Pascal's explanatory goal is ambitious indeed. He seeks nothing less than a comprehensive account of the whole that would both render the whole intelligible and inform us how we are to live in it. In his response to the quest for wisdom, the hypothesis he finds most compelling is theological; the question is properly theological. Commentators have observed that Pascal's work in science and mathematics provides him with an ideal of what a complete explanation would look like. In an essay entitled "Pascal's Theory of Knowledge," Jean Khalfa argues for the centrality to Pascal's method of his novel treatment of conic sections, projective geometry. Instead of defining and constructing each of the conic sections independently, Pascal treats the "different features of curves . . . as variations of a singular point of view, not as the inner properties of ideal forms."[119] The problem of the apology is this: "Find a particular point of view from which all the effects (*divertissement*, or the irrationality of political and ethical systems, or the survival of the Jewish people, or the power of imagination and custom over reason, etc.) make sense, and demonstrate its superiority over all other possible ones." Pascal has an ambitious explanatory goal in mind. Pascal's argumentation works "not by planned stages" or by "axioms and consequences" but "by relations that are seen immediately, in a light radiating from a central source."[120] Thus does mathematics enter into the heart of Pascal's apology, which encompasses both *finesse* and *geometrie*.

The second reason to resist Koch's interpretation is that it runs afoul of Pascal's insistence that the dialectic cannot come to rest. Pascal's account here fits well with Lear's account of Socratic irony, the chief effect of which is to render the most important matters full of wonder. As we have already noted, one consequence of Lear's view is

---

[117] Davidson, *Pascal and the Arts of the Mind*, 219.
[118] Davidson, *Pascal and the Arts of the Mind*, 252.
[119] Khalfa, "Pascal's Theory of Knowledge," 128.
[120] Davidson, *Pascal and the Arts of the Mind*, 255.

that the paradigmatic case of irony is not as a figure of speech deployed by someone in a position of superior knowledge in order to block the access, or mock the misunderstanding, of someone in an inferior position. It is rather something that happens to superior types. So, Socrates is not so much a perpetrator of irony as he is its willing victim. This is evident in Plato's dialogues, especially *Hippias Major* and *Hippias Minor*, in which Socrates confesses that he suffers from a kind of seizure, called *polytropia*, according to which what at first seemed one way suddenly strikes him as not that way. David Corey provides a helpful explanation of *polytropia*:

> Once we see this philosophical quality of Socrates' polytropic arguments, I think we are in a good position to appreciate Socrates' description of himself (372d–e, 376c, cf. *Hippias Major* 304c) as someone who "vacillates" (*planōmai*). According to Socrates, a certain "seizure" befalls him while he is talking to Hippias. He is suddenly struck by the notion that "those who voluntarily go wrong . . . seem better than those who do so involuntarily." However, Socrates says, the opposite view seems to strike him at others [sic] times. Thus he is forced to vacillate or wander back and forth.
>
> Socrates makes it sound as if he is the special victim of some epistemic seizure he cannot control. Is he? The answer is yes and no. He is indeed the victim of a kind of intellectual seizure, but this he has in common with all of mankind (376c). We all have opposing ideas in our minds, which shift uncontrollably back and forth as we move from context to context. We are all polytropic in this (Hippian) sense. But is Socrates really the victim of this seizure in the same way that we are? Not at all. For one thing, we do not tend to notice the contradictory ideas floating around in our heads. Socrates is unique in noticing them. Second, Socrates is able to *induce* the seizure in a way that few others can. In other words, he uses his polytropic skills as a philosophical tool to invoke puzzles and thus wonder.[121]

What Corey calls Socrates' "polytropic skills" matches nicely with Lear's notion of the capacity for irony. In his various criticisms of philosophical schools for their tendency to reduce paradoxes to simplified one-sided answers to the big questions, Pascal restores to philosophy its polytropic or ironic character. Although he does not develop it, there

---

[121] David D. Corey, *The Sophists in Plato's Dialogues* (Albany: State University of New York Press, 2015); emphasis in original.

are grounds for establishing a kind of hierarchy among natural intellects, a ranking based on the ability to articulate the contradictions, the dialectic of opposites, without either abandoning the quest or resting in half truths. For Pascal, this presents the prospect of a dreadful vision of the truth about the human condition, a repulsion arising not from our passions—our tyrannical pride or murderous envy—but from the very operation of the intellect in its pursuit of truth.

We might wonder, finally, whether the task of enduring irony entails an agnosticism that would be, in practical terms, a form of atheism, something Pascal rejects. Indeed, the quotation with which we began this chapter, Pascal's echoing of the late medieval version of the Socratic description of wisdom as learned ignorance, might seem to support such a view. The notion that atheism might display a greater strength of mind than do certain kinds of belief is suggested in the aphorism "Atheism indicates strength of mind, but only up to a certain point" (157).[122] Pascal certainly admires the polytropic capacity, even as he appreciates the *force d'esprit* of atheism. Two things keep him from resting there. The first is the impending fact of death and the uncertainty about the state of soul beyond this life. In such a circumstance, an examination of the relevant hypotheses is in order and indeed urgent. The second concerns the peculiarity of the Christian hypothesis, which is neither reducible to myth or reason nor susceptible to easy defeat by reason's objection. "Christians astonish philosophers."

---

[122] *Athéisme marque de force d'esprit, mais jusqu'à un certain degré seulement* (225).

Five

WAGERING ON AN IRONIC GOD

The following two passages—one from Goldmann on the role of risk, contingency, and the situatedness of the human agent and the other from Pascal himself on ciphers and double meanings—highlight distinctive and often neglected features of Pascal's vision of the human condition and his account of human inquiry. The emphasis upon contingency and personal engagement and upon different levels of meaning (veiled on one level, manifest on another) points to an important role for ironic discourse.

> From Hegel and Marx onwards, both the finite goods and even the evil of terrestrial life—Goethe's Devil—will receive a meaning inside the framework of faith and of hope in the future.
>
> But however important these differences may be, the idea that man is embarked and that he must wager becomes, after Pascal, the central idea in any philosophical system which recognises that man is not a self-sufficient and isolated monad but a partial element inside a whole which transcends him and to which he is linked by his aspirations, his actions and his faith. . . .

Risk, possibility of failure, hope of success and the synthesis of these three in the form of a faith which is a wager are the essential constituent elements in the human condition.[1]

A cipher has two meanings. When we come upon an important letter, whose meaning is clear but where we are told that the meaning is veiled and obscure, that bqit is hidden so that seeing we shall not see and hearing we shall not hear, what else are we to think but that this is a cipher with a double meaning? (260)[2]

Our contention is that Pascal construes the relationship of revelation to reason, of faith to philosophy, in ironic terms. In this chapter, we will turn our attention to revelation's ironic mode of discourse. We will begin with the famous wager argument, which we will argue is best read as a piece of ironic pedagogy. Of course, this is not a common interpretation. Pascal is seen as forcing upon unbelievers a tragic path, one that involves playing tricks upon themselves in an effort to bring about belief. The standard picture of the wager would seem to undermine rather than support a reading of Pascal's apology as a form of ironic discourse. We will begin then with the wager and show that in it can be found the leitmotifs of ironic pedagogy: that one must first retreat rather than march forward, confident of one's own capacity for determining the truth; that the inquiry puts into question the inquirer even as it seeks to investigate the truth of the matter about God; that knowledge is self-implicating; that rationality is not so much a matter of discerning clear and distinct first principles as it is a matter of retrospective justification through the writing of compelling narratives; that the Christian narrative involves ironic, specifically comic, reversal; and that divine irony befits the Christian God, rather than either of the two conceptions of God invoked early in Descartes' *Meditations*, the evil

---

[1] Lucien Goldmann, *The Hidden God: A Study of Tragic Vision in the "Pensées" of Pascal and the Tragedies of Racine* (London: Routledge & Kegan Paul, 1964), 302.

[2] Blaise Pascal, *Pensées*, trans. A. J. Krailsheimer, rev. ed. (New York: Penguin Classics, 1995). "*Le chiffre a deux sens. Quand on surprend une lettre importante où l'on trouve un sens clair, et où il est dit néanmoins que le sens en est voilé et obscurci, qu'il est caché, en sorte qu'on verra cette lettre sans la voir et qu'on l'entendra sans l'entendre; que doiton penser, sinon que c'est un chiffre à double.*" Blaise Pascal, *Pensées*, ed. Dominique Descotes and Léon Brunschvicg (Paris: Flammarion, 1976), 678. I will cite the Krailsheimer numbering parenthetically at the end of each English quotation and the Brunschvicg, where necessary, in notes.

demon divinity of voluntarism and the deistic divinity that undergirds Descartes' system.

§1. Rereading the Wager

Pascal's wager is typically read the way Dostoevsky's "Grand Inquisitor" in the *Brothers Karamazov* is read—as if it were not part of a larger book, as if it could be understood in isolation from the author's other statements or depictions in the same work. It does have the look of a self-contained argument; as such, it fits nicely in the contemporary tendency in philosophy to look for brief proofs, which philosophers and their students can then proceed to dismantle in one or two classes. However, from Pascal's other statements in the *Pensées*, we can see that he could not have intended it to stand alone, that it is embedded within the larger project of the apology. More important for our purposes is that the rhetoric of the wager exhibits a number of ironic strategies.

Pascal begins with a series of negations. We can know, he states, the existence and nature of the finite because we are finite and extended. We can know the infinite without knowing its nature because it has extension, but, unlike us, it has no limits. God, by contrast, has neither extension nor limits. He has "no relation to us." The wager assumes speculative uncertainty about the existence of God. Pascal begins with a meditation on the infinite: "If there is a God, he is infinitely beyond our comprehension, since, being indivisible and without limits, he bears no relation to us. We are therefore incapable of knowing either what he is or whether he is" (418).[3] So, we can know neither his existence nor his nature. In language that mimics Descartes' discussion of the light of nature, Pascal invites us to speak according to our natural lights.

The allusion to Descartes calls to mind his grounding of certitude in the natural light of human reason, which reveals the fundamental truths concerning the *cogito* and the existence of God. For Descartes, we begin in a position of confusion and uncertainty, which is rooted in a naïve faith in the knowledge we have received from external sources: custom, education, religion, and a panoply of sense experiences. Once put to serious questioning, none of these sources of knowledge proves stable. They are all dubitable. Descartes' method of radical doubt begins with an inventory of the various claimants to knowledge in order

---

[3] *S'il y a un Dieu, il est infiniment incompréhensible, puisque, n'ayant ni parties ni bornes, il n'a nul rapport à nous. Nous sommes donc incapables de connaître ni ce qu'il est, ni s'il est* (233).

to clear away what is truly natural and reliable from what is merely conventional and untrustworthy. The truths regarding the *cogito* and the existence of God are clear and distinct ideas, whose veracity, once properly understood, is invulnerable to skeptical attack. Pascal treats Descartes' foundationalism ironically. Not clear and distinct ideas but a confused awareness of what we desire is the motivating force behind the wager.

Our starting point is not what we possess with certitude but what we know that we do not know and what we know we lack. "You have two things to lose: the true and the good; and two things at stake: your reason and your will, your knowledge and your happiness; and your nature has two things to avoid: error and wretchedness" (418).[4] Our inescapable desire for truth and goodness, veracity and happiness, constitutes the assumed teleology of the wager. But we must pursue the ends or goals of truth and happiness without recourse to a purified foundational moment; we begin in medias res, in the midst of life, already under the influence of various passions and habits. The setting of the wager is the drama of the human pursuit of happiness in the here and now, in contingent and temporal circumstances.

In the practical order, where we must act and where the choice of one act excludes a host of other possible acts, we implicitly follow laws of probability. As Pascal puts it, "If we must never take any chances ... we should have to do nothing at all, for nothing is certain. And there is more certainty in religion than that we shall live to see tomorrow" (577).[5] Pascal claims to have discovered a "rule of probability" (577).[6] That rule or logic informs the wager, but it is important to see that it is a general rule applicable across the entire order of practice. It is not constructed as an ad hoc principle for thinking about God.

The background to Pascal's consideration of the existence of God is his critique of the traditions of natural theology. I speak here of

---

[4] *Vous avez deux choses à perdre: le vrai et le bien, et deux choses à engager: votre raison et votre volonté, votre connaissance et votre béatitude; et votre nature a deux choses à fuir: l'erreur et la misère* (233).

[5] *S'il ne fallait rien faire que pour le certain, on ne devrait rien faire pour la religion; car elle n'est pas certaine. Mais combien de choses faiton pour l'incertain, les voyages sur mer, les batailles! Je dis donc qu'il ne faudrait rien faire du tout, car rien n'est certain; et qu'il y a plus de certitude à la religion que non pas que nous voyions le jour de demain: car il n'est pas certain que nous voyions demain, mais il est certainement possible que* (234).

[6] *La règle des partis* (234).

traditions because there are quite different approaches to the topic, say, in Thomas Aquinas and Descartes.[7] There are significant differences in the nature and origins of the proofs offered, in what they claim to conclude about God, and in what way they see the proofs in relation to religious faith—that is, in how they construe the relationship of the God of the philosophers to the God of Abraham, Isaac, and Jacob. Pascal seems to lump all of these together as attempts to reach God from nature or by natural reason. One of Pascal's concerns is whether, even if the proofs were valid, they would have the desired effect on the lives of those who receive them as true. Pascal seems to admit at one point that, even in our fallen condition, "metaphysical proofs" might be valid, but they remain "so remote from human reasoning and so involved that they make little impact, and, even if they did help some people, it would only be for the moment during which they watched the demonstration, because an hour later they would be afraid they had made a mistake" (190).[8] One might say the same for any complex mathematical proof, but in that case the corrective would simply be to return to the proof and clear up any doubts about its validity. Why is this not sufficient in the case of the metaphysical proofs for the existence of God? Pascal sees the question of God's existence ultimately as a practical question, whereas that question surfaces in pagan philosophy and then in Christian natural theology as a speculative or theoretical question, a question about the truth of the proposition "God exists." Pascal worries that, although the proof may persuade for a moment, its complexity and distance from immediate experience render it a feeble foundation upon which to rest living a certain way of life. Pascal shifts the reader's attention from the theoretical to the practical. God has provided evidence to convince not the detached inquirer but rather the one "who seeks with groans" (427), who longs from the depths of his soul to find a truth that will order his entire life. Nature everywhere proclaims the human loss of an infinite good, an inexplicable and ineradicable longing in the human soul that nothing finite can satisfy.

---

[7] I have examined the connections among natural theology, metaphysics, and revelation in Thomas Aquinas in my *Aquinas, Ethics, and Philosophy of Religion: Metaphysics and Practice* (Bloomington: University of Indiana Press, 2007).

[8] *Les preuves de Dieu métaphysiques sont si éloignées du raisonnement des hommes, et si impliquées, qu'elles frappent peu; et quand cela servirait à quelquesuns, cela ne servirait que pendant l'instant qu'ils voient cette démonstration, mais une heure après* [Var. ed.: *parès*] *ils craignent de s'être trompés* (543).

If Pascal repudiates both traditional and contemporary forms of natural theology, he does not entirely repudiate the intelligibility of nature or the manifestation of God in and through it. Instead, he offers an alternative account of the intelligibility of nature, one that locates the intelligibility of nature within the order of divine providence. As he puts it, "Nature . . . points at every turn to a God who has been lost, both within man and without" (471).[9] He expands, "If the world existed in order to teach man about God, his divinity would shine . . . in a way that could not be gainsaid: but as it only exists through Christ, for Christ, and to teach men about their corruption and redemption, everything in it blazes with proofs of these two truths" (449).[10]

There is, then, a path from nature to God in Pascal, but it is not the direct path of the natural theology that was becoming dominant in Pascal's day. Instead, Pascal offers what von Balthasar calls an "*anthropologia ancilla theologiae christianae* [an anthropological aid or servant of Christian theology]."[11] As we noted above, Pascal made the transition from an investigation of physics to an inquiry into human nature. His description of man as "*monstre, chimère, chaos, prodige*" underscores not so much the "depravity of man" as "his indecipherability."[12] His question is this: "From what perspective must man be seen so that the deformed is integrated into a true form, the disproportionate into a true proportion?"[13] The hypothesis, known only through revelation, that "reconciles contradictory" evidence is the incarnation of God in the person of Christ, a hypothesis offensive to both Jews and Greeks. There is an instructive overlap here between Balthasar's theological reading of Pascal and that offered by Khalfa and Davidson on Pascal's mathematics and philosophy of science.

---

[9] *Car la nature est telle, qu'elle marque partout un Dieu perdu, et dans l'homme, et hors de l'homme, et une nature corrompue* (441).

[10] *Si le monde subsistait pour instruire l'homme de Dieu, sa divinité y reluirait de toutes parts d'une manière incontestable; mais comme il ne subsiste que par JésusChrist et pour JésusChrist et pour instruire les hommes et de leur corruption et de leur rédemption, tout y éclate des preuves de ces deux vérités* (556).

[11] Hans Urs von Balthasar, "Pascal," in *Studies in Theological Styles: Lay Styles*, vol. 3 of *The Glory of the Lord: A Theological Aesthetics*, by Hans Urs von Balthasar, trans. Andrew Louth, John Saward, Martin Simon, and Rowan Williams, ed. John Riches (San Francisco: Ignatius, 1986), 190.

[12] Balthasar, "Pascal," in *Studies in Theological Styles*, 219.

[13] Balthasar, "Pascal," in *Studies in Theological Styles*, 210.

Christ is the true center, the mediator between the finite and the infinite, the mean that holds together and reconciles the extremes.[14] The problem of mediation is resolved not by the construction of elaborate myths or by the intervention of the godlike philosopher but by the descent of God to us. That descent, the way in which God generously configures himself to our humanity, explains how we can attain transcendence without deserting the middle way. Through Christ we gain proper self-knowledge; the religion of the humiliated God who teaches ascent through descent, union with the divine through the embrace of suffering and death, counters simultaneously the vices of presumption and despair by offering both hope and humility. In Christ, God continues to teach indirectly since he does not come in power and majesty but in vulnerable weakness and as a suffering servant. Hence, hiddenness is maintained, as is the ironic mode of communication.

Pascal speaks of the "boldness" of those who attempt to appeal to "works of nature" in an effort to move unbelievers from doubt to belief. Underlying his concern here is the difference between appropriate rhetorical starting points for divergent audiences. Regarding the advocates of natural theology, Pascal writes:

> I marvel at the boldness with which these people presume to speak of God.
>
> In addressing their arguments to unbelievers, their first chapter is the proof of the existence of God from the works of nature. Their enterprise would cause me no surprise if they were addressing their arguments to the faithful, for those with living faith in their hearts can certainly see at once that everything which exists is entirely the work of the God they worship. But for those in whom this light has gone out and in whom we are trying to rekindle it, people deprived of faith and grace, examining with such light as they have everything they see in nature that might lead them to this knowledge, but finding only obscurity and darkness; to tell them, I say, that they have only to look at the least thing around them and they will see in it God plainly revealed; . . . this is giving them cause to think that the proofs of our religion are indeed feeble, and . . . nothing is more likely to bring it into contempt in their eyes. (781)[15]

---

[14] *Qu'on examine l'ordre du monde sur cela, et qu'on voie si toutes choses ne tendent pas à l'établissement des deux chefs de cette religion: JésusChrist est l'objet de tout, et le centre où tout tend. Qui le connaît la raison de toutes choses* (556).

[15] *J'admire avec quelle hardiesse ces personnes entreprennent de parler de Dieu. En adressant leurs discours aux impies, leur premier chapitre est de prouver la Divinité pas les ouvrages de la nature. Je ne m'étonnerais pas de leur entreprise s'ils adressaient leurs discours aux fidèles, car il est*

The problem is not in nature but in us: "those in whom this light has gone out and in whom we are trying to rekindle it, people deprived of faith and grace, examining with such light as they have everything they see in nature that might lead them to this knowledge, but finding only obscurity and darkness." For Pascal, natural theology assumes that everyone is equally well equipped to profit from proofs or at least that all those who have the intellectual ability to follow the arguments are similarly situated with respect to the truth. But the question of God is equally a question about the inquirer, not just about how he will live but also about the ways in which he is disposed or ill disposed to pursue, recognize, and live out the truth about God. In addition to assuming that the logical force of the proofs is obvious, the advocates of natural theology ignore the subjective conditions of belief. Such an approach gives unbelievers "cause to think that the proofs of our religion are indeed feeble." Pascal prefers to use the language of scripture, which states that "God is a hidden God, and that since nature was corrupted he has left men to their blindness, from which they can escape only through Jesus Christ" (781).[16] Pascal does not deny that the evidence is there in nature but only that, without grace, we lack the requisite capacity to see it. By comparison, "those living with faith in their hearts can certainly see at once that everything which exists is entirely the work of the God they worship" (781).

Given that "reason cannot decide" whether God is or is not, it might seem that the most reasonable course would be to suspend belief, to remain agnostic on the question. It should be clear from the introductory remarks about God that Pascal thinks atheism is not a rational

---

certain que ceux qui ont la foi vive dedans le Coeur voient incontinent que tout ce qui est n'est autre chose que l'ouvrage du Dieu qu'ils adorent. Mais pour ceux en qui cette lumière s'est éteinte, et dans lesquels on a dessein de la faire revivre, ces personnes destituées de foi et de grâce, qui recherchant de toute leur lumière tout ce qu'ils voient dans la nature qui les peut mener à cette connaissance, ne trouvent qu'obscurité et ténèbres; dire à ceuxlà qu'ils n'ont qu'à voir la moindre des choses qui les environnent, et qu'ils y verront Dieu à découvert, et leur donner, pour toute preuve de ce grand et important sujet, le cours de la lune et des planètes, et pretender avoir achevé sa preuve avec un tel discours, c'est leur donner sujet de croire que les preuves de notre religion sont bien faibles; et je vois par raison et par expérience que rienn'est plus propre à leur en faire naître le mépris (242).

[16] *Ce n'est pas de cette sorte que l'Ecriture, qui connaît mieux les choses qui sont de Dieu, en parle. Elle dit au contraire que Dieu est un Dieu caché; et que, depuis la corruption de la nature, il les a laissés dans un aveuglement dont ils ne peuvent sortir que par Jésus-Christ, hors duquel toute communication avec Dieu est ôtée: Nemo novit Patrem nisi Filius, et cui voluerit Filius revelare* [Matt 11:27] (242).

option. We do not know enough about God to know that he does not exist. What about agnosticism? Pascal responds, "You are already committed [*Vous êtes embarqué*]." But that is precisely what the agnostic refuses. Pascal departs from both the rationalist believer and the agnostic unbeliever in thinking of the existence of God as a practical question, one having to do with living in a certain way or not. From this perspective, agnosticism is indistinguishable from atheism; both entail not living in a way that is faithful to God. Still, there is a sense in which, even on Pascal's terms, agnosticism should not necessarily be assimilated to atheism. Pascal holds that two classes of people are reasonable: "Those who serve God with all their heart because they know him and those who seek him with all their heart because they do not know him" (427). The latter group could plausibly be classified as agnostics who remain actively open to belief. Indeed, this seems to be precisely the sort of person for whom the wager is likely to have the most chance of success. Yet, the interlocutor whom Pascal imagines in the discourse on the wager is at least initially someone who resists the idea of wagering at all.

The key question for the inquiring intellect usually shows up in the form of a skeptical doubt or taunt voiced by the agnostic or atheist. If God is the sort of being religious believers claim he is and if he wanted us to believe in him, he could certainly have done a better job of making his presence known. To respond by insisting that God is hidden would seem to invite scorn. But Pascal asks further questions: How do you know that God does not have good reasons to remain hidden? Might there be a purpose in God's remaining seemingly aloof from the sort of inquirer you currently are? Once again, the inquirer, who supposes he is adequately equipped and well positioned to inquire about God, finds himself put into question. An irony of concealment rather than deception aims to draw the inquirer out of himself and into a quest.

If the irony of the philosopher confounds and unsettles ordinary folks, divine irony perplexes the philosopher. Philosophic inquiry involves a retreat from the comfortable certitudes of conventional assumptions, a retreat that asks one to adopt a critical stance not just toward common opinion but also toward oneself as an inquirer. This comes as a surprise, indeed an offensive taunt, to those ordinarily praised for wisdom who until this point have seen no good reason to doubt the efficacy of their resources. But as is clear from Plato's dialogue *Meno*, the first step is not a straightforward enumeration of what one knows but the acknowledgment that one does not know. As is clear from other Platonic dialogues and especially in the Augustinian/Platonic tradition, the question about an individual's knowledge is also a question about the whole, our place within it, and the transcendent ground of the whole. Adopting Augustinian language, Pascal proposes that we must begin with self-knowledge and with a knowledge of our author and end. The question about God is a question about me, about the capacities, dispositions, and desires of the one seeking. Kierkegaard is germane: "The objective problem consists of an inquiry into the truth of Christianity. The subjective problem concerns the relationship of the individual to Christianity."[17] Much of the apology attends to the evidence concerning the objective problem, but never without regard to the subjective problem. The subjective problem comes dramatically to the fore in the wager.

Few commentators have noticed the role of ironic reversal in Pascal's presentation of the wager to the self-interested gambler. Pascal begins matter-of-factly, "Every gambler takes a certain risk for an uncertain gain" (418).[18] In this case, the finite risk or cost is living in the way one wants, with no regard for God and perhaps for others either. But the possible gain here is an infinite good; as Pascal puts it, an infinity of infinitely happy lives. What is to be gained if God exists and we live faithfully in accord with that belief is an eternal life of happiness in union with him who is himself infinitely good and eternally blessed. When one weighs the finite risk against the infinite potential gain, the conclusion that one should wager becomes incontrovertible. So far, so good.

Nonetheless, there is something problematic here, puzzling, about the line of argument Pascal puts forth. In every other wager, one holds back something for future wagers at least in this sense. One holds back the capacity to attain something in the future that one could wager on some later bet. One holds back, at a minimum, oneself. Here, as Pascal

---

[17] Søren Kierkegaard, *Concluding Unscientific Postscript to Philosophical Fragments*, vol. 12.1 of *Kierkegaard's Writings*, trans. and ed. H. V. Hong and E. H. Hong (Princeton, N.J.: Princeton University Press, 1992), 18–20. The wager shifts from a purely self-interested calculation to something more akin to that offered by Kierkegaard's pseudonymous Climacus: "An objective uncertainty held fast in an appropriation-process of the most passionate inwardness is the truth, the highest truth attainable for an existing individual" (182).

[18] *Tout joueur hasarde avec certitude pour gagner avec incertitude* (233).

puts it, you must "wager all you have" (418).[19] One might say, you must wager "all you are." The common interpretation of the wager assumes that the target of the argument is the purely self-interested individual who acts or at least tries act on the basis of calculative reason. For that person, the logic is, or should be, compelling. Yet, the interlocutor here resists, fails to be convinced. From Pascal's account of the way the passions and the imagination can tyrannically hold sway over reason, it seems clear that he would be skeptical of any agent's boast to act on the basis of reason alone. Indeed, this point is implicit in the wager itself; if human beings acted on the basis of self-interest rightly understood, the wager would be obvious to them. They would not need an elaborate argument or the sort of cajoling in which Pascal engages with his imaginary interlocutor. Pascal's manner of appealing to self-interest, by means of an argument whose logic requires an alteration in the current desires of the interlocutor, indicates that the wager aims not just to address but also to transform desire.

The resistance of desire to the compelling logic of the wager, that is, the refusal to obey the calculations of self-interest, is itself revelatory. In a fragment that begins "self-interest," Pascal observes, "nothing else matters, and nothing is so neglected." He amplifies, "Our imagination so magnifies the present, because we are continually thinking about it, and so reduces eternity, because we do not think about it, that we turn eternity into nothing and nothing into eternity, and all this is so strongly rooted within us that all our reason cannot save us from it and ..." (432). Contrary to those who object to the wager as a crude appeal to self-interest, we hold that the wager itself contains an ironic reflection on the incapacity of calculative self-interest to guide us in these matters: "I should ask them if it is not true that they confirm in themselves the foundation of the faith they are attacking, which is that man's nature lies in corruption" (432). In the wager itself, he concludes, "you must be renouncing reason if you hoard your life rather risk it for an infinite gain, just as likely to occur as a loss amounting to nothing" (418).[20] The language of "hoarding" and "risking," along with the earlier injunction to "wager all you have," indicates that the wager is hardly a matter of

---

[19] *Il faut tout donner* (233).
[20] *Il faut renoncer à la raison pour garder la vie, plutôt que de la hasarder pour le gain infini aussi prêt à arriver que la perte du néant. Car il ne sert de rien de dire qu'il est incertain si on gagnera et qu'il est certain qu'on* (233).

detached calculation or of merely intellectual assent. As Pascal puts it, this is an issue in which "your all is at stake."

That, of course, is precisely what provokes resistance in the gambler. Overwhelmed by the relentless logic of the wager, the frightened interlocutor responds, "I confess, I admit it, but is there really no way of seeing what the cards are?" The response? "Yes, but my hands are tied and my lips are sealed; I am being forced to wager and I am not free.... I am so made that I cannot believe" (418).[21] The interlocutor proceeds to make reference to "Scripture and the rest," an indication that the wager is both part of a larger argument and a specific risk, the risk of believing in the Christian God. The passage eliminates one of the chief objections to the wager, the so-called many claimants objection. The objection is that, even were the wager logically valid, it would be ineffectual because it leaves us with too many possible options, too many ways of living in accordance with belief in God. Which God? Whose faith? Of course the determination of which religion is the most viable candidate for such a wager is the burden of the rest of the *Pensées*. Pascal is not defending a generic wager on God but a wager on the Christian God. Another reason that Pascal could not mean to include the option in the wager of belief in a generic God has to do with his focus on self-knowledge and self-transformation. As he bluntly puts it, "It is not only impossible but useless to know God without Christ.... The better one is, the worse one becomes if one ascribes this excellence to oneself" (191).[22] Pascal is here concerned about the existential situation of the knower.

That God is hidden does not mean that there is no evidence supporting God's existence. However much reason might remain in suspense about that matter, the evidence is not weighted against existence:

> The prophecies, even the miracles and proofs of our religion, are not of such a kind that they can be said to be absolutely convincing, but they are at the same time such that it cannot be said to be unreasonable to

---

[21] *Oui; mais j'ai les mains liées et la bouche muette; on me force à parier, et je ne suis pas en liberté; on ne me relâche pas, et je suis fait de telle sorte que je ne puis croire. Que voulez-vous donc que je fasse?* (233).

[22] *Il est non seulement impossible, mais inutile de connaître Dieu sans Jésus-Christ. Ils ne s'en sont pas éloignés, mais approchés; ils ne se sont pas abaissés, mais.... Quo quisque optimus eo pessimus, si hoc ipsum, quod optimus sit, abscribat sibi* [St. Bernard, *In Cantica Sermones/Sermons on the Canticle*, 84] (549).

believe in them. . . . The evidence is such as to exceed, or at least equal, the evidence to the contrary [*Mais l'évidence est telle, qu'elle surpasse, ou égale pour les moins, l'évidence du contraire*], so that it cannot be reason that decides us against following it. (835)

Because the evidence from nature itself is mixed and the case for specifically theological claims is inconclusive, Pascal states, "reason is not affronted either way." The seeming neutrality of the evidence befits not so much deism as the Christian God, since there is both "evidence and obscurity to enlighten some and obfuscate others" (835).[23] Precisely because the issue here involves more than an abstract, theoretical matter, Pascal insists that we cannot simply leave it at this. There are two sorts of things at stake: true and good, reason and will, knowledge and happiness, error and wretchedness. The question shifts decisively from knowledge, truth, and reason to happiness, good, and will.

Bereft of any reasonable objection against the wager, the interlocutor nonetheless finds himself paralyzed, unable to move forward. Apparently, Pascal's appeal to happiness and the good, even to an eternal happiness with an infinite good, has not worked as an incentive. He feels himself being pushed or forced rather than drawn and invited. He experiences compulsion rather than attraction. The next step in the conversation is complex and not entirely satisfactory. Pascal urges self-knowledge and a strategy of self-transformation. He urges that the unbeliever's problem has to do with his passions rather than his reason; the task is to "diminish the passions." There is something certainly right about this. The passions, particularly for the sort of sensible goods one would have to sacrifice in a life of faith, can be obstacles to the act of believing. When the good and happiness are at issue, however, we also need more than just the tempering of disordered desire. We need different, positive desires. We need to experience an attraction to that which we are to embrace.

Pascal urges his interlocutor to bridge the gap between what reason recognizes in the logic of the wager and his unruly passions by actively combatting the passions and beginning to act in accord with the judgment of reason. He urges behaving as if one already had faith. Follow the path of others, he suggests:

---

[23] *Il y a de l'évidence et de l'obscurité, pour éclairer les uns et obscurcir les autres* (564).

> You want to find faith and you do not know the road. You want to be cured of unbelief and you ask for the remedy: learn from those who were once bound like you and who now wager all they have. These are people who know the road you wish to follow, who have been cured of the affliction of which you wish to be cured: follow the way by which they began. They behaved as if they did believe, taking holy water, having masses said, and so on. That will make you believe quite naturally, and will make you more docile. (418)[24]

The French word *abêtira*, which Krailsheimer translates as "docile," has a more pejorative sense, something like "stupefy." This highlights a problem with Pascal's strategy. There is first the difficult question of whether one can, in any case, make oneself have certain beliefs; beyond that, there is the question whether one can or should attempt to generate beliefs by playing tricks on oneself. As Simone Weil observes, Pascal seems to confuse "faith and autosuggestion."[25] One way to read the passage is to construe the stupefying of the intellect through habituation as a means of subduing the endlessly calculative predilection of reason, the habit of incessantly measuring profit and loss, the sort of habit of soul that makes rest impossible and that engenders fearful uncertainty about every decision.

Part of what Pascal has hit upon here has to do with the mystery of moral transformation, the circularity involved in the movement in the direction of virtue. For we are formed by the customs and habits of those around us. To be able to judge which customs and habits are virtuous—indeed which persons are virtuous—requires some antecedent possession of virtue, as Aristotle argued many years ago. But we shall not have that unless we have already been fortunate or lucky. Pascal writes:

> Our minds and feelings are trained by the company we keep, and perverted by the company we keep. Thus good or bad company trains or

---

[24] *Vous voulez aller à la foi, et vous n'en savez pas le chemin; vous voulez vous guérir de l'infidélité, et vous en demandez le remède* [Var. ed.: *les remèdes*]: *apprenez de ceux qui ont été liés comme vous, et qui parient maintenant tout leur bien; ce sont gens qui savent ce chemin que vous voudriez suivre, et guéris d'un mal dont vous voulez guérir. Suivez la manière par où ils ont commencé: c'est en faisant tout comme s'ils croyaient, en prenant de l'eau bénite, en faisant dire des messes, etc. Naturellement même cela vous fera croire et vous abêtira* (233).

[25] Simone Weil, "Forms of the Implicit Love of God," in *Waiting for God*, trans. Emma Craufurd (New York: Harper, 2009), 126.

perverts respectively. It is therefore very important to be able to make the right choice so that we train rather than pervert. And we cannot make this choice unless it is already trained, and not perverted. This is thus a vicious circle from which anyone is lucky to escape. (814)[26]

How is this relevant to the wager? Although he does not develop the idea in the argument of the wager itself, his proposal that the gambler overcome a gap between the truth recognized by reason and unruly passion might well be seen as a suggestion that he involve himself with a more virtuous group of individuals.

The integral role of friendship in the quest for the human good runs through Pascal's discussion of human life as a quest, the most frightening observation concerning which has to do with the way we are insouciantly indifferent to the state of our souls. "This carelessness in a matter which concerns themselves, their eternity, their all, moves me more to anger than pity; it astonishes and shocks me; it is to me monstrous. I do not say this out of the pious zeal of a spiritual devotion. I expect, on the contrary, that we ought to have this feeling from principles of human interest and self-love; for this we need only see what the least enlightened persons see."[27] On the basis not of pious zeal but of mere human interest and self-esteem, Pascal calls such indifference "monstrous." He proceeds to wonder about those who practice indifference and recommend it to others: What sort of a friend would such a person be? What sort of confidante? What help in adversity?

The prominence of friendship and dialogue befits the pedagogical use of irony, which is a matter of deft rhetorical skill and prudential assessment. It is most fruitfully exhibited in the dialogue of two or three interlocutors, where the needs and capacities of each soul can be detected in the concrete flow of the conversation. It is thus a highly personal mode of communication, one that cannot be reduced to abstract principles or to a written text. Although Christian revelation takes

[26] *On se forme l'esprit et le sentiment par les conversations. On se gâte l'esprit et le sentiment par les conversations. Ainsi les bonnes ou les mauvaises le forment ou le gâtent. Il importe donc de tout de les savoir choisir pour se le former et ne le point gâter; et on ne peut faire ce choix, si on ne l'a déjà formé et point gâté. Ainsi cela fait un cercle, d'où sont bienheureux ceux qui sortent* (6).

[27] *Cette négligence en une affaire où il s'agit d'euxmêmes de leur éternité, de leur tout, m'irrite plus qu'elle m'attendrit; elle m'étonne et m'épouvante: c'est un monstre pour moi. Je ne dis pas ceci par zèle pieux d'une dévotion spirituelle. J'entends au contraire qu'on doit avoir ce sentiment par un principe d'intérêt humain et par un intérêt d'amourpropre: il ne faut pour cela que voir ce que voient les personnes les moins éclairées* (194).

shape in authoritative texts and doctrinal pronouncements, revelation itself is from, about, and to persons, as the wager itself indicates.

What are we to make of the proposal that friends might alter our affective dispositions and enhance our cognitive capacities? C. S. Lewis makes a compelling case for such a course of action in a chapter in *Mere Christianity*, entitled "Let's Pretend":

> What is the good of pretending to be what you are not? Well, even on the human level, you know, there are two kinds of pretending. There is a bad kind, where the pretence is there instead of the real thing; as when a man pretends he is going to help you instead of really helping you. But there is also a good kind, where the pretence leads up to the real thing. When you are not feeling particularly friendly but know you ought to be, the best thing you can do, very often, is to put on a friendly manner and behave as if you were a nicer person than you actually are. And in a few minutes, as we have all noticed, you will be really feeling friendlier than you were. Very often the only way to get a quality in reality is to start behaving as if you had it already. That is why children's games are so important. They are always pretending to be grown-ups—playing soldiers, playing shop. But all the time, they are hardening their muscles and sharpening their wits so that the pretence of being grown-up helps them to grow up in earnest.[28]

If one should find oneself suddenly and perhaps surprisingly in the midst of persons whom one judges to be happier and more virtuous than one currently is, one can strive to imitate them, to pretend that one possesses the relevant traits of character by acting accordingly. It is, after all, only by performing the acts of the virtues, before we are virtuous, that we come to possess the character traits of the virtues. Lewis' argument, however, presupposes something in the not yet virtuous that Pascal's gambler does not seem yet to possess, namely, a desire to be transformed. Concerning the notion that practice could generate belief, Terence Penelhum writes:

> From within the viewpoint of belief, such practices as religious services, association with other believers, and the like have as one of their purposes the removal of hindrances to the creation and maintenance of the religious vision and world view; they are not, from this viewpoint, persuasive devices, but aids to insight, much as careful concentration and

[28] C. S. Lewis, *Mere Christianity* (San Francisco: HarperCollins, 2001), 161.

a tidy workbench are aids to scientific discovery. If, then, someone who does not believe could be induced to go through these procedures, he would perhaps come to see what he now cannot see.[29]

As a general point about the role of habit in the cultivation of understanding, Penelhum's remark has much to offer. But, of course, in the case of redemptive religious faith no activity of reasoning or of practical habituation can produce what is essentially a freely bestowed divine gift. The wager, we need always to recall, is but a part of a much larger project. In other parts of the apology, Pascal indicates that habit can contribute to belief, but, particularly in the case of saving belief, this could not produce the desired result. He puts the point succinctly:

> There are three ways to believe: reason, habit, inspiration. Christianity, which alone has reason, does not admit as its true children those who believe without inspiration. It is not that it excludes reason and habit, quite the contrary, but we must open our minds to the proofs, confirm ourselves in it through habit, while offering ourselves through humiliations to inspiration, which alone can produce the real and salutary effect. *Lest the Cross of Christ be made of none effect.* (808)[30]

From this passage alone it should be clear that the wager could play only a limited and subordinate role in the movement of someone to faith. It can at best play the role of removing obstacles to the reception of faith, but even this role would have to be seen, retrospectively, as a result of the activity of grace in the soul of someone who does not yet know how to recognize that activity.

Commentators have often found objectionable Pascal's accentuation of the role of fear in the wager and in other passages in the *Pensées*. Not just the fear of the loss of an infinite good but of incurring eternal punishment would seem to be operative in the wager. In the argument against indifference, a discussion closely related to the wager, Pascal refers to individuals entering eternity not knowing whether they will fall

---

[29] Terence Penelhum, "Pascal's Wager," *Journal of Religion* 44, no. 3 (1964), 206.
[30] *Il y a trois moyens de croire: la raison, la coutume, l'inspiration. La religion chrétienne, qui seule a la raison, n'admet pas pour ses vrais enfants ceux qui croient sans inspiration; ce n'est pas qu'elle exclue la raison et la coutume, au contraire; mais il faut ouvrir son esprit aux preuves, s'y confirmer par la coutume, mais s'offrir par les humiliations aux inspirations, qui seules peuvent faire le vrai et salutaire effet: Ne evacuetur crux Christi* [1 Cor 1: 17] (245).

"into nothingness or into the hands of a wrathful God" (427).³¹ Despite his association with the quasi-Calvinist Catholic reform movement of Jansenism, Pascal explicitly resists the Calvinist teaching on damnation; indeed, he is worried even about the topic being debated: "My God, what stupid arguments! Would God have created the world in order to damn it? Would he ask so much of such feeble people?" (896).³² Moderate skepticism once again performs a salutary role in Pascal's thought. The recognition of the limits of our knowledge tempers the temptation to make certain grandiose claims about our knowledge of God's will: "Scepticism is the cure for this disease, and will put this vanity in its place" (896).³³ He applies a similar remedy to the claim that God does not offer his salvation to all human beings (912). In addition to undercutting the divine generosity and ignoring what we can know about God's intentions, such teachings have the opposite effect of what is desired. They foster despair. Such a method of fear and intimidation is contrary to the pedagogy of God. As we have already noted, Pascal insists, "The way of God, who disposes all things with gentleness, is to instill religion into our minds with reasoned arguments and into our hearts with grace, but attempting to instill it into hearts and minds with force and threats is to instill not religion but terror. *Terror rather than religion*" (172). We should note here not just the opposition of religion to terror but also the pairing of heart and mind, the insistence on the persuasion of the whole human person.

The persuasion of the whole person presupposes self-knowledge and moral transformation on the part of the inquirer. Yet, on Pascal's view, we flee such awareness; even when we attempt to know ourselves, we do not have the sort of immediate access to ourselves that Cartesian introspection promises to offer. Alasdair MacIntyre describes the problem with resorting to simple introspection "in search of self-knowledge." What we encounter through introspection is "the self's self-serving presentation of itself to itself, a presentation designed to sustain an image of the self as well-ordered, free from fundamental conflict, troubled

---

³¹ *Comme je ne sais d'où je viens, aussi je ne sais où je vais et je sais seulement qu'en sortant de ce monde je tombe pour jamais ou dans le néant, ou dans les mains d'un Dieu irrité, sans savoir à laquelle de ces deux conditions je dois être éternellement en partage. Voilà mon état, plein de faiblesse et de l'incertitude* (194).

³² *Mon Dieu! que ce sont des sots discours! Dieu auraitil fait le monde pour le damner? demanderaitil tant de gens si faibles?* (390).

³³ *Pyrrhonisme est le remède à ce mal, et rabattra cette vanité* (390).

perhaps by occasional akratic difficulties, but for the most part entitled to approval both by itself and by others." MacIntyre's account of the opacity of self-knowledge fits nicely Pascal's description of the way we "hide and disguise ourselves from ourselves." Because self-presentation is typically selective, we find ourselves trapped. "To break out of this circle," we need "some standard that initially appears to be external to the self, even alien to it, in such a way as to occasion a particular kind of pain, . . . the pain felt by a self when treated by the prospect of having to acknowledge a truth about itself that it has not yet been able to bear." Here it is not so much knowledge in conflict with passion, as two sorts of knowledge at odds, the knowledge of memory, which would confess one's evil deeds, and the knowledge of pride, which denies or revises what has been done.[34] Pascal puts the point this way concerning the difficulty or pain associated with the movement from unbelief to belief:

> It is true that there is something painful in beginning to practise piety, but this pain does not arise from the beginnings of piety within us, but from the impiety that is still there. . . . We only suffer in so far as our natural vice resists supernatural grace: our heart feels torn between these contrary forces, but it would be very wrong to impute this violence to God, who draws us to him, instead of attributing it to the world which holds us back. (924)[35]

Pascal's own style is designed to prompt us to see ourselves, to begin to experience the painful longing to be rescued from our alienation, and to engender in us hope for transformation. As Goldmann observes, one of the aims of the wager is to "change behavior in order to create the only conditions that will enable" one "genuinely to assimilate the truth which he has understood, and henceforth give an authentic meaning to his behavior."[36]

---

[34] Alasdair MacIntyre, "What Has Christianity to Say to the Moral Philosopher?" in *The Doctrine of God and Theological Ethics*, ed. Michael C. Banner and Alan J. Torrance (New York: T&T Clark, 2006), 17–32.

[35] *Il est vrai qu'il y a de la peine, en entrant dans la piété. Mais cette peine ne vient pas de la piété qui commence d'être en nous, mais de l'impiété qui y est encore. . . . Nous ne souffrons qu'à proportion que le vice, qui nous est naturel, résiste à la grâce surnaturelle; notre coeur se sent déchiré entre des efforts contraires; mais il serait bien injuste d'imputer cette violence à Dieu qui nous attire, au lieu de l'attribuer au monde qui nous retient* (498).

[36] Goldmann, *Hidden God*, 258.

Pascal does not conceive of the Christian way of life as a path of unremitting pain and self-abnegation. The note of hoped-for transformation comes to the fore in a profound and moving way in the final paragraphs of the wager. As if conceding the weakness of the preceding discussion, Pascal presents the way of life of a believer as an attractive alternative to the way of unbelief. "You will be faithful, honest, humble, grateful, full of good works, a sincere, true friend. . . . It is true you will not enjoy noxious pleasures and good living, but will you not have others?" (418).[37] Pascal appeals here to the desirability of living a certain way of life, a life characterized by the practice of the virtues, character traits that involve not merely sacrificial obedience to divine imperatives but an admirable and pleasant manner of living. The fear of annihilation has given way to the aspiration for transformation, an aspiration whose very presence is itself a sign that grace is already at work in the soul. In precisely these terms, he ends his appeal to the gambler: "I tell you that you will gain even in this life, and that at every step you take along this road you will see that your gain is so certain and your risk so negligible that in the end you will realize that you have wagered on something certain and infinite for which you have paid nothing" (418).[38]

The dialectic of nothingness and infinity reverses itself here, as does the dialectic of the empty and the full. From having been urged to sacrifice all things, to make oneself nothing, in the hope of gaining everything, the gambler now receives the promise that he will come to see that he has gained everything while losing nothing. The accent here is not upon an isolated act of will made in ignorance but upon a journey, the stages of which are marked by the growing intelligibility and increasing happiness of the life of faith. The change in Pascal's discourse prompts an alteration in his interlocutor, who exclaims: "How these words fill me with rapture and delight!" (418).[39]

---

[37] *Or, quel mal vous arriveratil en prenant ce parti? Vous serez fidèle, honnête, humble, reconnaissant, bienfaisant, ami sincère, véritable. A la vérité, vous ne serez point dans les plaisirs empestés, dans la gloire, dans les délices; mais n'en aurezvous point d'autres?* (233).

[38] *Je vous dis que vous y gagnerez en cette vie; et qu'à chaque pas que vous ferez dans ce chemin, vous verrez tant de certitude du gain, et tant de néant de ce que vous* [Var. ed.: *hasardez, que vous connaîtrez à la fin que vous*] *avez parié pour une chose certaine, infinie, pour laquelle vous n'avez rien donné* (233).

[39] *Oh! ce discours me transporte, me ravit* (233).

§2. Wagering as Self-Emptying

As is now palpable, the wager is much more than a self-interested, calculative device for attaining an infinite good. It is replete with ironic reversal. It moves the gambler from protection of self to willing relinquishing of self, from an isolated atom in a lonely universe to a participant in a community, a body, as Pascal puts it, of "thinking members." References to "nothing" surface repeatedly in the wager, as they do throughout the entire book. Indeed, it is easy to forget that title of the section containing the wager is not "The Wager," but rather "Infinite—Nothing [*Infini-rien*]." William Desmond's recent work, specifically the discussion of nihilism in *God and the Between*, illumines Pascal's varied use of "nothing." Desmond offers a cogent analysis of the different senses of "nothingness." Like "being," the term "nothing" signifies in many ways. There is, for example, the empty nothing of nihilism, the feared annihilation of death, the howling nothing of the damned, the nothing of forgiveness practiced by the merciful, and the kenotic nothing of sacrificial self-emptying. Desmond resists the univocity and reductionism that have plagued twentieth-century discussions of nihilism. He situates his own analysis of the phenomenon of nihilism, a perpetual possibility for philosophy and humanity, within modernity, whose cycle of ambition and despair belong together: Hegel's ascendant reason is followed by Schopenhauer's descendant reason. Both the insistence on multiple senses of nothingness and the prognosis concerning modernity's presumption to provide a comprehensive account of the whole giving way to nihilistic despair are anticipated in Pascal, who could have easily predicted the vacillation of modern philosophy between dogmatism and skepticism, presumption and despair.

Desmond does not focus exclusively on the Nietzschean theory of nihilism as the "devaluation of the highest values." Nietzsche, who called nihilism the unwelcome guest waiting at the door, wanted not to wallow in nihilism but to overcome it. The question is whether thoroughgoing nihilism, which would deprive of us of any standard, framework, or orientation, allows for the possibility of its overcoming. Because Desmond finds the case for thoroughgoing nihilism unpersuasive, indeed impossible, he turns nothingness into the welcome guest that opens up the possibility of a recovery of being, goodness, and God. That philosophy "comes to nothing, that our reasoning reduces to zero, can be seen as an end that is also a beginning." In Pascal, the failure of philosophy, its unfinished quest, serves to render the seeker receptive to revelation. Whereas Nietzsche detects the sources of nihilism in the theological tradition, Desmond sees nihilism as a prelude to a return to theology. In this, he replicates Pascal. Pavlovits writes, "Pascal's astonishment and admiration signal the end of philosophy because in them thinking faces its utmost limits, the incomprehensible it cannot rationalize any more by itself, so the only remaining possibility is to renounce understanding and to silently admire what remains incomprehensible."[40]

Desmond invites us to consider the common phrase "it is nothing." That can be used to indicate a dismissal of the significance of something, or it can signal forgiveness, a canceling of evil suffered. This could also be understood as a releasing from a burden. As Pascal consoles his imaginary interlocutor: "Be comforted: it is not from yourself that you must expect it, but on the contrary you must expect it by expecting nothing from yourself" (202).[41]

There is ironic reversal here. The earlier illusion of fullness, the preposterous assertion of autonomy, brought to nothing by Pascal's tragic theater, is prelude to the experience of fullness as gift. The possession of the highest good is not a matter of our achievement; it is the result of a gift. Receptivity to the gift involves an acknowledgment of our incapacity to achieve what we long for. Our response to the gift is gratitude. Goldmann speaks of a "true selfishness which laughs at selfishness," that allows one "to understand that it is by making a gift of himself that he can really love himself, and by going beyond man that he can really become a man."[42] The response to the self-emptying of God in Christ is the offering of self to God and others. It is instructive that Pascal includes among the desirable traits to be inculcated by a life of faith becoming a "sincere, true friend." That is precisely what motivates the author of the wager. The words, both pleasant and cogent, come "from a man who went down upon his knees . . . to pray . . . that

---

[40] Tamás Pavlovits, "Admiration, Fear, and Infinity in Pascal's Thinking," in *Philosophy Begins in Wonder: An Introduction to Early Modern Philosophy, Theology, and Science*, ed. Michael Funk Deckard and Péter Losonczi (Eugene, Ore.: Pickwick, 2010), 124.

[41] *Consolez-vous! ce n'est pas de vous que vous devez l'attendre, mais au contraire, en n'attendant rien de vous, que vous devez l'attendre* (517).

[42] Goldmann, *Hidden God*, 256.

he might bring your being also to submit to him for your own good and for his glory" (418).[43]

The going down and emptying of oneself on behalf of the other imitates the descent of Christ. Desmond speaks of the "agapeic servant who consents to the good by being willing to be as nothing." Latent in this insight is an account of the hiddenness of God. God is hidden not just in order to test us but because hiddenness befits the self-effacing activity of the loving creator. God's hiddenness can be an occasion for temptation to despair or to assert humanity's autonomy. For Pascal, the hiddenness of God is an invitation for us to abase ourselves, to be as naught, in the face of the infinite creator. God creates other things in order to let them exist in their otherness, not merely as means or instruments of his own ends. It also means that the motive for creation must itself be agapeic: "The good of being is for nothing, nothing but goodness itself."[44]

In this engagement, the accusation of pride is prominent. Those committed to modern, Kantian conceptions of autonomy may find unsettling the asymmetry between God and creatures inherent in the conception of creation as agapeic love. Indeed, in some cases the assertion of autonomy is rooted in a deliberate repudiation of divine agape. Following this project, we engage in a futile and self-defeating *imitatio Dei*. Radical claims to autonomy are subject to the law of diminishing returns. Attempting to make ourselves the whole, we lapse into nothingness. Existence itself, an enduring gift from the self-effacing God, undermines the bold affirmation of autonomy. It is "impossible to sustain the 'to be' outside an affirmation of its goodness," apart from receptive gratitude, that reconciles strength and lowliness (*la force s'accorde avec cette bassesse*) and results in rapture and delight (*ce discours me transporte, me ravit*) (418).[45]

The indictment of proud reason is a commonplace in religious discourse. But we must be careful to preserve Pascal's paradoxical account of reason, since alongside the accusation of the pride of reason stands his insistence on the sovereignty of reason. Indeed, without the sovereignty

---

[43] *Si ce discours vous plaît et vous semble fort, sachez qu'il est fait par un homme qui s'est mis à genoux auparavant et après pour prier cet Etre infini et sans parties, auquel il soumet tout le sien, de se soumettre aussi le vôtre pour votre propre bien et pour sa gloire; et qu'ainsi la force s'accorde avec cette bassesse* (233).

[44] William Desmond, *God and the Between* (Malden, Mass.: Blackwell, 2008), 335.

[45] Desmond, *God and the Between*, 326.

of reason, pride would not be such a temptation for us; it is precisely because, as Pascal puts it, our morality, the good life for human beings, consists in thinking well that we can be so easily seduced into thinking that our judgments, uninformed by truth and influenced by passion and vanity, are unimpeachable. Still, it remains the case that it is for reason to judge whether and when it ought to submit. The paradox is perhaps best captured thus. Abdication, the handing over of power, is itself an act of sovereignty.[46]

Charity frees us from our inveterate tendency to imagine ourselves to be "the center of the world." It corrects what Weil calls "the illusion of perspective" that leads us to locate ourselves at "the center of space" and the related illusion that "falsifies" our idea of time. Corresponding to the illusion of spatial perspective is an illusion of values that sees and ranks all things in relation to the individual ego. She explains, "We live in a world of unreality and dreams. To give up our imaginary position as the center, to renounce it, not only intellectually but in the imaginative part of our soul, that means to awaken to what is real and eternal, to see the true light and hear the true silence."[47] Weil goes on to make explicit the connection between such decentering of the ego and the virtue of love:

> To empty ourselves of our false divinity, to deny ourselves, to give up being the center of the world in imagination, to discern that all points in the world are equally centers and that the true center is outside the world, this is to consent to the rule of mechanical necessity in matter and of free choice at the center of each soul. Such consent is love. The face of this love, which is turned toward thinking persons, is the love of our neighbor.[48]

Charity offers recovery, the prospect of "regaining a clear view," of "seeing things as we were meant to see them—as things apart from ourselves."[49] Pascal thus offers a thoroughgoing critique of the project of making the ego, or self, the foundational principle of philosophy.

---

[46] I am indebted to Pierre Manent for this marvelous way of capturing Pascal's account of reason.
[47] Weil, "Forms of the Implicit Love of God," in *Waiting for God*, 99.
[48] Weil, "Forms of the Implicit Love of God," in *Waiting for God*, 99.
[49] J. R. R. Tolkien, *The Tolkien Reader* (New York: Ballantine Books, 1966), 77.

morale chrétienne

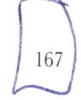

Weil's observations dovetail nicely with Pascal's. To regulate our self-love, Pascal urges us to "imagine a body full of thinking members" (368).[50] The sense of part and whole that we have stressed as essential to Pascal's thought resurfaces in a dramatic way in Pascal's famous discussion of the community of believers, the Christian republic, as a "body full of thinking members," a type of friendship that repudiates autonomy. The reference to a "body of members" calls to mind not only Paul's notion of the mystical body but also the classical pagan notion of the body politic. As Pierre Manent has urged, the Christian community, the city of God, creates a bond that is more intimate than that of the city, the locus of Aristotle's conception of friendship, and more extensive than that of the empire, the other dominant form of political life in antiquity.

Pascal goes on to recapitulate the entire story of the conversion of the human soul in terms of the body of thinking members:

> To be a member is to have no life, no being and no movement except through the spirit of the body and for the body. The separated member, no longer seeing the body to which it belongs, has only a wasting and moribund being left. However, it believes itself to be a whole, and seeing no body on which it depends, believes itself to be dependent only on itself and tries to make itself its own centre and body. But, not having in itself any principle of life, it only wanders about, and becomes bewildered at the uncertainty of its existence, quite conscious that it is not the body and yet not seeing that it is member of a body. Eventually, when it comes to know itself, it has returned home, as it were, and only loves itself for the body's sake. It deplores its past aberrations.
>
> It could not by its very nature love anything else except for selfish reasons and in order to enslave it, because each thing loves itself more than anything else.
>
> But in loving the body it loves itself, because it has no being except in the body, through the body, and for the body. (372)[51]

---

[50] *Pour régler l'amour qu'on se doit à soimême, il faut s'imaginer un corps plein de membres pensants* (474).

[51] *Etre membre est n'avoir de vie, d'être et de mouvement que par l'esprit du corps et pour le corps. Le membre séparé, ne voyant plus le corps, auquel il appartient, n'a plus qu'un être périssant et mourant. Cependant il croit être un tout, et ne se voyant point de corps dont il dépende, il croit ne dépendre que de soi, et veut se faire centre et corps luimême. Mais n'ayant point en soi de principe de vie, il ne fait que s'égarer, et s'étonne dans l'incertitude de son être, sentant bien qu'il n'est pas corps et cependant ne voyant point qu'il soit membre d'un corps. Enfin, quand il vient à se connaître, il*

The image of a body of thinking members manifests the unity of the human race, a unity that engenders in each part a conscious willingness to serve the good of the other as its own good. Conversely, sin fosters the illusion that we are isolated, autonomous units or monads. The recovery of unity is made possible by the redemptive descent of Christ to the level of human persons. Here the horizontal union of persons is rooted in the vertical relationship to the divine. The parts of the body thus come to act as mediators for one another whose activity participates in the archetypal mediation of Christ. That is precisely what the narrator confesses at the end of the wager in his admission that he has abased himself in supplication before God on behalf of the gambler.

Pascal here addresses a central preoccupation of premodern literature, philosophy, and theology. The recognition of the human as an intermediate realm, between the divine and the bestial, was common to poets and philosophers. Both the poets and the philosophers make claims to mediation, to be able to provide a path, an avenue of communication, between the human and the divine. The poems of Homer and the dialogues of Plato, most notably the famous ascent passage in the *Symposium*, aim to do precisely this. In the *Confessions*, the crucial justification for moving beyond the authoritative teaching concerning the good life found in the "books of the Platonists" is the failure of the spiritual exercises to enable Augustine to ascend from the human to the divine. Having been admonished by the books of the Platonists, Augustine turned within and encountered there not only soul but also God. Yet he could not remain there and lapsed back into a world of confusion with a will divided against itself. He goes on to report that it was not until he embraced Christ, the true mediator between God and man, that his will was healed and his path to God made sure. Into this theological reflection on mediation, Pascal incorporates Montaigne's dictum that we must keep to the middle way, the way that maintains rather than erases what is properly human. In contrast to Montaigne, Pascal stresses and stretches the extremes, the twin infinities, cosmological and moral, and seeks the mean that would hold together the

---

est comme revenu chez soi, et ne s'aime plus que pour le corps. Il plaint ses égarements passés. Il ne pourrait pas par sa nature aimer une autre chose, sinon pour soimême et pour se l'asservir, parce que chaque chose s'aime plus que tout. Mais en aimant le corps, il s'aime soimême, parce qu'il n'a d'être qu'en lui, par lui, et pour lui: qui adhaeret Deo unus spiritus est [1 Cor 6:17] (483).

furthest reaches of the spectrum of the human condition. That mean is Christ.

§3. The Problem of Hope

The sense of nothingness is compounded and in a sense infected by the vanity or nothingness of sin, experienced for most human beings as diversion, a frustrated wandering in search of satisfaction that brings only distress. But this paradoxically prompts an objection to the wager itself. The chief strategy for avoiding self-knowledge is diversion. Why not construe the act of faith, particularly as articulated in the wager, as the grandest diversion of all? What could possibly provide a more effective means of diverting ourselves from our wretched condition than to accept the teaching that wretchedness is all part of a divine plan from which we will be rescued at the end of time? If, as Pascal asserts, faith teaches that the "only good thing in this life is the hope of another life," then does not faith constitute a sustained diversion from the present and from reckoning with our true condition?

Variants on this objection can be found in Nietzsche, who sees in the Christian celebration of paradise a denigration of this world as empty and meaningless. Another version of this objection is a shibboleth of twentieth-century atheistic existentialism, in the writings of both Martin Heidegger and Jean-Paul Sartre, the latter of whom calls this "bad faith" the unwillingness to embrace one's freedom and its consequences.[52] Indeed, an existentialist might well see in Pascal's writings a remarkably penetrating analysis of the human condition, of the way in which the traditional sources of moral authority are shown to be unreliable and incapable of replacing the human sense of being cast off in the universe, bereft of any secure guidance. The silence of God, the disorder of nature, the conventional status of justice and natural law, and the arbitrary roots of the political order—Pascal repudiates all these foundations. Pascal gives us reason to doubt whether there is any human nature to which we could appeal in deciding how we ought to live. We are thrown back upon ourselves, condemned to a freedom that we cannot understand or cede to anyone else. However repellent, the human condition is, according to Sartre, to be embraced rather than excused, erased, or corrected. The objection is not new. We

---

[52] Jean-Paul Sartre, *Existentialism and Human Emotions* (New York: Philosophical Library, 1957), 56.

have already seen the germ of this argument—that in the focus on the immortality promised in the Gospel, there is a diversion from a direct acknowledgment of death—in Montaigne.

Pascal's response is that the encounter with the divine mediator enables us to live mindful of our condition. As we have already noted, Pascal holds that the philosophic means of knowing God renders us oblivious of our wretchedness, while "those "who have known God through a mediator know their own wretchedness" (190). The mediator counters our temptation to vacillate between the equally debilitating passions of pride and despair by offering to us the virtues of humility and hope. The grace of the incarnation thus liberates us from our multiform alienation and allows us to live in the present in relation to eternity. As Pascal comments, misery induces despair, pride induces presumption. The incarnation shows man the greatness of his misery by the greatness of the remedy required to free us from our wretchedness.[53] More pointedly, he writes, "Knowing God without knowing our own wretchedness makes for pride. Knowing our own wretchedness without knowing God makes for despair. Knowing Jesus Christ strikes the balance because he shows us both God and our own wretchedness" (192).[54] Furthermore, it is not the case that the believer lives in time with a blind and empty hope of eternity; instead, the "Christian's hope of possessing an infinite good is mingled with actual enjoyment as well as with fear, for . . . Christians hope for holiness, and to be freed from unrighteousness, and some part of this is already theirs" (917).[55] The life of the believer here and now is ordered, in hope, to future fulfillment. Believers are not surrounded by darkness waiting for they know not what. They are on a journey, a pilgrimage.

One of the working assumptions of the wager is that "at every step . . . along this road" the pilgrim will see more clearly the truthfulness and goodness of the Christian way of life. The gap between

---

[53] *La misère persuade le désespoir. L'orgueil persuade la présomption. L'incarnation montre à l'homme la grandeur de sa misère, par la grandeur du remède qu'il a fallu* (526).

[54] *La connaissance de Dieu sans celle de sa misère fait l'orgueil. La connaissance de sa misère sans celle de Dieu fait le désespoir. La connaissance de Jésus-Christ fait le milieu, parce que nous y trouvons et Dieu et notre misère* (527).

[55] *L'espérance que les chrétiens ont de posséder un bien infini est mêlée de jouissance effective aussi bien que de crainte; car ce n'est pas comme ceux qui espéraient un royaume, dont ils n'auraient rien, étant sujets; mais ils espèrent la sainteté, l'exemption d'injustice, et ils en ont quelque chose* (540).

faith and vision, in the quest both before and after the acceptance of the Christian faith, underscores the future-oriented character of the Christian life. That gap highlights in yet another way the narrative character of human existence, its shape as a quest. As Josef Pieper observes, we are wanderers or wayfarers: this is the "core of our creaturely existence."[56] The general object of hope is a difficult future good (*bonum arduum futurum*). The need for hope signifies both our "absence of fulfillment" and our "orientation to fulfillment."[57] As a virtue, hope stands between the twin vices of despair and presumption.[58] It is thus related to the virtues of magnanimity, which urges us to pursue difficult goods, and humility, which counsels us not to claim as our autonomous possession goods that exceed our capacity or merit. As Pascal would put it, we are situated between presumption and despair. Although presumption is a "false similitude of hope" and involves a "perverse security," despair is the greater vice. The former, while dangerous, retains a simulacrum of the virtue of hope, whereas the latter abandons the power of divine grace altogether. The consequence of the loss of hope is an atrophying of the soul.

From the perspective of Pascal's apology, we cannot help but notice a link between hopelessness and diversion. One of the symptoms of the latter is restlessness and dissipation of the soul. The relevant vice is sloth (*acedia*), which is the root of despair or hopelessness. The classical definition of sloth has to do with despair of the divine good, a failure to take delight in true leisure and divine worship. Sloth exhibits a "perverted humility" that wishes to be left alone by God rather than to undertake the demanding task of becoming what by nature and divine grace we are called to be.[59] As Pascal has the potential seeker say, "What good would seeking do me?" (418).

In modernity, the idea of progress replaces that of the quest. That turn is implicitly operative in Descartes' great boast that his method will bring about scientific, technological, and medicinal improvement. Such a linear conception of progress means indefinite extension and delay of the realization of that for which we long. With its sense of directedness and its accentuation of improvement, progress mimics the quest even as

---

[56] Josef Pieper, *Faith Hope Love* (San Francisco: Ignatius, 1997), 93.
[57] Pieper, *Faith Hope Love*, 93.
[58] Pieper, *Faith Hope Love*, 113.
[59] Pieper, *Faith Hope Love*, 117–20.

it alleviates the uncertainty and risk associated with it. Long before the nineteenth-century romantic reaction against modern science and the postmodern critique of the Enlightenment, Pascal was acutely aware of the potential for the Enlightenment dream of universal rationality to become a nightmare of unreason. As Sara Melzer explains, Pascal seeks to demystify modern science, which itself reposes upon a demystification of ordinary experience and received theology. She writes,

> From Pascal's perspective, Descartes and the believers in the "new science" sought to reverse the effects of the Fall and create a human-made paradise that would eliminate the notion of a lack and thus eliminate desire.... The new science provided humans with the tools that would allow them to measure, to weigh, to explain, and ultimately to manipulate the world around them.[60]

Underlying the project of modern science is a conception of progress as infinite improvement, a conception that both presupposes and fosters an understanding of human desire as serial and horizontal, rather than hierarchically ordered and vertical.[61] Thus does the infinite surface in another way for Pascal in his analysis of the modern condition of desire. Modernity promises satisfaction of desire in a linear fashion, but this, Pascal insists, results not in satisfaction but rather in the indefinite postponement of satiety. By making inordinate promises for the amelioration of the human condition, modernity exacerbates our sense of alienation, even as it deprives us of a vocabulary for expressing that sense of loss. The gap between promise and realization creates an unbearable tension. Modern society has thus of necessity become as effective at diverting us from thinking about our ills as it is at eliminating the ills. Present unhappiness combined with the natural desire for happiness is at the root of our restlessness and our sense that the next pursuit, the next promotion, the next experience of love, will remedy our wretchedness and make us happy: "What causes inconstancy is the realization that present pleasures are false, together with the failure

---

[60] Sara E. Melzer, *Discourses of the Fall: A Study of Pascal's Pensées* (Berkeley: University of California Press, 1986), 100–101.

[61] Pascal agrees with the modern repudiation of a hierarchically ordered ascent, with its intelligible stages, but he does not reject the vertical thrust of desire for transcendent satisfaction.

to realize that absent pleasures are vain" (73).[62] This is Pascal's way of accounting for the phenomenon of repetition, the apparently senseless and self-lacerating habit of recurring, destructive behavior.

The false promise of modern, progressive liberalism thus undermines itself: in place of freedom, there is a new servitude; in place of progress, there is regression; in place of knowledge and enlightenment, there is ignorance and darkness. But Pascal would likely accuse Montaigne as much as Descartes of contributing to this state. We might here recall Schaefer's thesis that Montaigne's strategy is to "redirect human concerns from transcendent goods to earthly ones." The counseling of endless diversion exalts "private, pacific, and bodily" goods as a means of "uprooting the very desire for mastery and self-transcendence from people's souls."[63] Pascal's analysis of the nihilistic state to which endless diversion reduces the human soul anticipates Tocqueville's prognosis of the new physiognomy of servitude. As Sheldon Wolin puts it, promising freedom from the past, modernity "fetishizes the future."[64] "Instead of development or fulfillment of potential," we experience in modernity the "exhaustion of time in the conquest of space by beings in a hurry." The result is culture as "end-less process, the formalized method by which artifacts are produced continuously."[65] Following Tocqueville, Wolin identifies one of the chief strategies for combating liberalism: "To enlarge modernity's understanding of progress to include the experience of loss."[66] Otherwise, we have not hope but empty, anxious longing for what we do not yet possess. Although he does not share Tocqueville's principally political goals, Pascal does indeed aim to exacerbate the human person's sense of loss—not just the sense of having lost this or that but the sense of being at a loss, indeed lost in a cosmos that is at best indifferent to human desire.

In the absence of any sense of a telos to human desire, a recognition that the longing for transcendent happiness is woven into the human heart, hope for the integral good becomes transformed into linear

---

[62] *Le sentiment de la fausseté des plaisirs présents, et l'ignorance de la vanité des plaisirs absents causent l'inconstance* (110).

[63] David Lewis Schaefer, *The Political Philosophy of Montaigne* (Ithaca. N.Y.: Cornell University Press, 1990), 308 and 395.

[64] Sheldon Wolin, *Tocqueville between Two Worlds* (Princeton, N.J.: Princeton University Press, 2001), 566.

[65] Wolin, *Tocqueville between Two Worlds*, 568.

[66] Wolin, *Tocqueville between Two Worlds*, 566.

expectation, the fleeting fulfillment of the satisfaction of one desire after another satisfied. Pieper puts the bind in which modernity finds itself succinctly: "If earthly existence is pervasively structured toward what is 'not yet in being,' and if a man, as a *viator*, is truly 'on the way to' something right up to the moment of death, then this hope, which is identical with our very being itself, either is plainly absurd or finds its ultimate fulfillment on the other side of death."[67] Modernity's failure to fulfill the hopes that modernity itself has fostered in humanity generates forms and degrees of despair peculiar to modernity. The response of Pascal and Pieper is not to deny the natural human longing for happiness and justice but to insist that hope can be a real and vigorous virtue only if it is grounded in eternity, not merely in the flow of time. Both Montaigne and Descartes seek to solve the problem of hope in the flow of time. Montaigne does so by an embrace of the flow that in a paradoxical way renders fluidity static: he is always who he is and has no ground for regret or hope for alteration in the future. Descartes seeks instead to offer through his method a way of controlling the flow of the future and thus of detecting in it the clear marks of progress. Pascal thinks that both strategies fail to acknowledge the truth about the longings of the human heart. As C. S. Lewis puts it when describing our experience of beauty and happiness:

> The books or the music in which we thought the beauty was located will betray us if we trust to them; it was not *in* them, it only came *through* them, and what came through them was longing. These things—the beauty, the memory of our own past—are good images of what we really desire; but if they are mistaken for the thing itself they turn into dumb idols, breaking the hearts of their worshippers. For they are not the thing itself; they are only the scent of a flower we have not found, the echo of a tune we have not heard, news from a country we have never yet visited.[68]

This is another way of putting Pascal's claim that, despite our failures to achieve happiness, we continue to seek for it because we retain a trace of a happiness that was once ours. This is, of course, a Socratic and Platonic theme, namely, that any particular experience of beauty calls to mind, and awakens in the soul a longing for, an ideal, pure beauty.

---

[67] Josef Pieper, *Hope and History* (San Francisco: Ignatius, 1991), 107–11.
[68] C. S. Lewis, "The Weight of Glory," in *The Weight of Glory and Other Addresses* (New York: HarperOne, 2009), 3–19; emphasis in original.

§4. Neither Deism nor Voluntarism

The accent on hope and on history as an arena for the dramatic interaction between human freedom and divine grace puts Pascal deeply at odds with early modern deism. As he observes, deism is "almost as far removed from the Christian religion as atheism." Pascal most certainly had Descartes in mind, but in this Pascal seems to anticipate and repudiate in advance the distinctively modern project of natural religion with its assumption of the transparency of nature and of nature's God to human scrutiny. The problem is that pure reason demands lucid clarity, while the rational evidence for the existence of God is decidedly mixed.

Something like this argument is at work in Susan Neiman's *Evil in Modern Thought: An Alternative History of Philosophy*, in which she argues that recovering a sense of the peculiarly modern problem of evil is essential to understanding the history of modern philosophy.[69] Much more than ancient and medieval thought, the Enlightenment rests on a conviction that the law-like behavior of nature and human nature is, or would soon be, transparent to human investigation. The peculiarly modern problem of evil is thus a result not of the teachings of revealed religion but of the natural religion of deism. Although Neiman argues that the problem of evil, in one guise or another, is coterminous with human existence, she also shows that modern philosophers—whether they defend or repudiate theodicy—elevate the status of the problem of evil. And their specific way of framing the problem arises from a specific conception of the divinity, a deistic conception. Neiman explains:

> In asserting a clear and certain link between moral and natural evils, the idea of Providence denies the notion of grace as well as that of atheism. Both grace and atheism leave the connection of virtue and happiness up to chance. Reason demands that the connection be systematic. . . . If the link between virtue and reward were accidental, the watch wouldn't work—to use another favorite Deist metaphor. What watchmaker would

---

[69] Susan Neiman, *Evil in Modern Thought: An Alternative History of Philosophy* (Princeton, N.J.: Princeton University Press, 2004). Neiman initially focuses on the remarkable response to the Lisbon earthquake of 1755. Philosophers as diverse as Voltaire, Rousseau, and Kant took this to be a signal event in the modern world; Goethe, at age six(!), was alleged to have experienced "doubt and consciousness for the first time." Why was this event so important? Not the "weight of the disaster but the increased expectation" rendered the quake salient.

design a mechanism in which the wheels and cogs turned randomly one way then sometimes another, without any warning whatsoever?[70]

Pascal would resist the conflation of providence and deism. But he does share Neiman's concern to separate deism from the Christian understanding of God as offering grace. Indeed, he worries that most of those who demand proofs of the Christian religion are thinking not of the Christian God but of a deistic divinity:

> And on this basis they take occasion to blaspheme against the Christian religion, because they know so little about it. They imagine that it simply consists in worshipping a God considered to be great and mighty and eternal, which is properly speaking deism, almost as remote from the Christian religion as atheism, its complete opposite. And thence they conclude that this religion is not true, because they cannot see that all things combine to establish the point that God does not manifest himself to men as obviously as he might.
>
> But let them conclude what they like against deism, their conclusions will not apply to Christianity, which properly consists in the mystery of the Redeemer, who, uniting in himself the two natures, human and divine, saved men from the corruption of sin in order to reconcile them with God in his divine person. (449)[71]

Just as the modern, scientific project of theodicy was getting off the ground, Pascal insisted, on scriptural grounds, on the "hiddenness of God," that whatever evidence there is of God's presence points not to the truth of deism but to a redeeming God who enters history to take evil upon himself. Simply to proclaim the hiddenness of God is not sufficient; one must explain why it is appropriate for God to be hidden: "God being thus hidden, any religion that does not say that God is

---

[70] Neiman, *Evil in Modern Thought*, 87.
[71] *Et sur ce fondement, ils prennent lieu de blasphémer la religion chrétienne parce qu'ils la connaissent mal. Ils s'imaginent qu'elle consiste simplement en l'adoration d'un Dieu considéré comme grand et puissant et éternel; ce qui est proprement le déisme. Presque aussi éloigné de la religion chrétienne que l'athéisme, qui y est tout à fait contraire. Et de là ils concluent que cette religion n'est pas véritable, parce qu'ils ne voient pas que toutes choses concourent à l'établissement de ce point, que Dieu ne se manifeste pas aux hommes avec toute l'évidence qu'il pourrait faire. Mais qu'ils en concluent ce qu'ils voudront contre le déisme, ils n'en concluront rien contre la religion chrétienne, qui consiste proprement au mystère du Rédempteur, qui unissant en lui les deux natures, humaine et divine, a retiré les hommes de la corruption du péché pour les réconcilier à Dieu en sa personne divine* (556).

hidden is not true, and any religion which does not explain why does not instruct. Ours does all this. Verily thou art a God that hidest thyself" (242).[72] Like Kierkegaard and Dostoevsky after him, Pascal agrees in advance with Neiman's concluding note that "the picture of reason as inherently systematic is fatal to any form of philosophy we will want to preserve."[73] Yet, however much she might want to criticize the dominant modern project, she remains caught in its grips and fails to envision a serious, theological alternative.

If Neiman does not say what form of philosophy or of divinity supplies a viable alternative to systematic philosophy and the God of deism, Pascal does. As we have noted, Pascal was aware of the deist option from his reading of Descartes. Pascal aligns Descartes' idea of divinity with deism, which, according to Pascal, is almost as distant from Christianity as is atheism, because neither conceives of God as personal and active in history. Sometimes it is assumed that the only alternative to a deistic and utterly impersonal conception of God is a voluntarist one, in which the principal attribute of God is his omnipotence. This God is present in Descartes in the form of the evil genius whose arbitrary will threatens our hold on any claims to knowledge of the world.[74] Pascal does not see voluntarism as the only alternative to deism. What else is there? Pascal's response involves a conception of God as practicing an ironic pedagogy, to which Socratic irony is analogous.

The task for the Christian is to carve out a conception of God, an alternative to deism, distinguishable from the arbitrary God of voluntarism. Pascal's focus on divine irony is an attempt to do just that. Ironic pedagogy, as we have noted, is designed in part to force upon an interlocutor a self-awareness that he would otherwise lack, an awareness of his own ignorance. Instead of marching forward, confident in one's understanding and one's capacities, the inquirer is invited to retreat, in order to examine where he stands with regard to the pursuit of truth and whether, and to what extent, he is equipped to pursue a particular line of inquiry.

---

[72] *Dieu étant ainsi caché, toute religion qui ne dit pas que Dieu est caché n'est pas véritable; et toute religion qui n'en rend pas la raison n'est pas instruisante. La nôtre fait tout cela: Vere tu es Deus absconditus* [Isa 45:15] (585).

[73] Neiman, *Evil in Modern Thought*, 150.

[74] For an argument that traces the modern phenomenon of nihilism to the late medieval conception of a voluntarist deity, see Michael Allen Gillespie, *Nihilism before Nietzsche* (Chicago: University of Chicago Press, 1996).

From this perspective, Pascal's critique of natural theology takes on enriched significance. Daniel Fouke rightly contrasts Pascal's positive use of nature with its deployment in traditional arguments in natural theology. Pascal's critique of natural theology is twofold: nature cannot "provide the certainty aimed at in deductive proofs of God's existence," and deductive proofs "misrepresent the epistemological claims of Christianity," by making "God's personal agency" irrelevant to our coming to know him.[75] These proofs also dispense with the appropriate role of human agency, that is, with the ethical presuppositions of faith. Another way to put Fouke's point is to say that Pascal repudiates natural theology because it eliminates the conditions of divine irony: a personal mode of discourse that illumines the ignorance of the human inquirer and turns him back upon himself in a searching investigation of the ways in which he is disposed and ill disposed, equipped and ill equipped, to embark on the quest for the good. That does not mean it is incompatible with every conception of natural theology.

The quest here is for an encounter between creature and creator. As Ralph McInerny puts it:

> How could any character in the human drama fail to search in some way for his author? We are to God as characters to their author. . . . For us it is all but inevitable that, however momentarily, we feel ourselves to be part of a vast cosmic drama and our thoughts turn to the author, not merely of our roles, but of our existence. Natural theology is one version of that quest.[76]

To understand the inquiry into the whole of nature as a quest to encounter the author of the drama in which we are actors transforms the nature of the inquiry. The most obvious difficulty in the quest is that God elects to hide, or at least to determine the conditions under which he is manifest. God himself is a cipher; the evidence of nature is mixed, at best paradoxical. On first glance, the claims of the Christian faith seem contradictory (two natures in the person of Christ), irrational (the necessity of reason submitting to divine authority), merely a matter of chance (the crucial role of historical events), or unjust (the impact of

---

[75] Daniel Fouke, "Argument in Pascal's *Pensées*," *History of Philosophy Quarterly* 6 (1989): 57–68.

[76] Ralph McInerny, *Characters in Search of Their Author: The Gifford Lectures Glasgow 1999–2000* (Notre Dame, Ind.: University of Notre Dame Press, 2003), 4.

original sin on the entire human race). Investigated further, the objections can be shown to be inconclusive; more importantly, the set of teachings proclaimed by the church illumines the human condition in a way superior to that of any other religion or any philosophical school. Thus, ironic pedagogy leads to a manifestation of the intelligibility of the whole.

Now, admittedly there are passages in which Pascal seems to be a thoroughgoing voluntarist: "God wishes to move the will rather than the mind. Perfect clarity would help the mind and harm the will" (234).[77] The passage fits with his claim that knowledge of God without humbling self-knowledge move us further from God. As he puts it elsewhere, "What a long way it is between knowing God and loving him" (377).[78] Since we cannot love God unless he first gives us the gift of faith and repentance, the wager itself cannot hope to produce faith in us: "We shall never believe, with an effective belief and faith, unless God inclines our hearts, and we shall believe as soon as he does so" (380).[79] However, as Pascal makes clear in many ways, love and the heart are not merely matters of will; they have cognitive dimensions; they are vehicles of perception, bestowing capacities for seeing the world anew.

The last point eludes Erec Koch, whose critique of Pascal focuses on the mode of divine revelation by means of charity. Revelation, he supposes, works not by proof or intelligible argument but exclusively by a force "visible in its effects." It is not received by an act of understanding but is "produced by a force that acts upon the will." Accordingly, the entire "truth of the logos" is found in its "style," its manner of working on the human subject, not in its "content."[80] Hyperbolic dialectic combines with radical voluntarism to erase all intelligibility. It is instructive to note that a sympathetic exegete such as Thomas Parker reaches nearly the same conclusion. He concurs with Koch that because "reason is unable to dissolve through synthesis the obscurity created through contrasting images," the will must "take over." Yet,

---

[77] *Dieu veut plus disposer la volonté que l'esprit. La clarté parfaite servirait à l'esprit et nuirait à la volonté. Abaisser la superbe* (581).

[78] *Qu'il y a loin de la connaissance de Dieu à l'aimer!* (280).

[79] *On ne croira jamais d'une créance utile et de foi, si Dieu n'incline le coeur; et on croira dès qu'il l'inclinera* (284).

[80] Erec Koch, *Pascal and Rhetoric: Figural and Persuasive Language in the Scientific Treatises, "The Provinciales," and the "Pensées"* (Charlottesville, Va.: Rookwood Press, 1997), 145, 163–64.

without taking the measure of, much less answering, Koch's conclusion, Parker goes on to speak blithely of the new unity established through grace and the will.[81]

Even if Pascal insists that we cannot make sense of our strange duality apart from the instruction of the Gospel, he also holds that the teaching of Scripture lends intelligibility to an otherwise inscrutable set of paradoxes. We have already rehearsed the basic tenets of his view of faith and reason: "Religion is not contrary to reason, but worthy of reverence and respect . . . because it really understands human nature" (12).[82] The Gospel sheds light on the "confused plan buried out of sight in the depths" of the human soul (136).[83] Without this accent on intelligibility, Pascal could not speak of, or invite others to a quest for, the "true religion." Pascal distinguishes true religion from both superstition and rationalism: "Two excesses: to exclude reason, to admit nothing but reason" (183).[84] Pascal does not argue, as proponents of natural theology might, that reason can demonstrate a portion of what is revealed, but he does argue that reason and faith cannot conflict. Pascal affirms Augustine's claim that "reason . . . judge[s] that there are cases when it ought to submit" (174).[85] How does reason know that religion is not contrary to reason, and on what grounds does it judge that it ought to submit to the assertions of revelation? That, as we have seen, is the burden of Pascal's scripturally informed account of the human condition.

Pascal seeks—and finds in Christ—the intelligibility of the whole, an intelligibility made manifest only retrospectively from the vantage of the reception of the Christian hypothesis. Of course, none of this constitutes a philosophical demonstration of the truth of the Christian faith. To offer such a proof would be to deny the very nature of faith, which

---

[81] Thomas Parker, *Volition, Rhetoric, and Emotion in the Work of Pascal* (New York: Routledge, 2008), 189, 194.

[82] *Les hommes ont mépris pour la religion; ils en ont haine et peur qu'elle soit vraie. Pour guérir cela, il faut commencer par montrer que la religion n'est point contraire à la raison: vénérable, en donner respect; La rendre ensuite aimable, faire souhaiter aux bons qu'elle fût vraie; et puis montrer qu'elle est vraie. Vénérable, parce qu'elle a bien connu l'homme; Aimable, parce qu'elle promet le vrai bien* (187).

[83] *Un projet confus, qui se cache à leur vue dans le fond de leur âme* (139).

[84] *Deux excès: exclure la raison, n'admettre que la raison* (253).

[85] *Saint Augustin: la raison ne se soumettrait jamais si elle ne jugeait pas qu'il y a des occasions où elle se doit soumettre* [Ep. 122, 5]. *Il est donc juste qu'elle se soumette quand elle juge qu'elle se doit soumettre* (270).

is an unmerited gift. Yet, unlike subrational myths, Christian faith does not evaporate in the face of, or retreat from, rational discourse.

For our understanding of charity, the crucial section, noted by von Balthasar but overlooked by Koch, concerns the three orders: body, mind, and charity. Although ranked in a hierarchy, the three orders are different in kind. The lower knows nothing of the higher and provides no access to what is above. "The greatness of intellectual people is not visible to kings, rich men, captains, who are all great in a carnal sense. The greatness of wisdom, which is nothing if it does not come from God, is not visible to carnal or intellectual people" (308).[86] Pascal underscores the incommensurability of the orders in unrestrained hyperbole: "The infinite distance between body and mind symbolizes the infinitely more infinite distance between mind and charity, for charity is supernatural" (308).[87] Pascal does work out a sort of analogy—as the order of mind is to the level of the body, so is the order of sanctity to the level of the mind: "Philosophers: they surprise the ordinary run of men. Christians: they surprise the philosophers" (613). Here there emerges a hierarchy of wonder or bafflement, of wisdom mistaken for folly. The rational satisfaction of the inquiry into the truth about man can be seen only from above and in retrospect; there is no possibility of a smooth transition or ascent from body to mind or from either of these to charity. As Jean-Luc Marion comments, "In the course of descending the hierarchy," however, "continuity is reestablished, since the superior order evaluates and judges the inferior orders. Thus is opened the possibility that charity might judge each and every thing."[88] There is no dichotomy between knowing and loving, no gap between intellect and will or between inclination and apprehension. Pascal speaks of the "impulse" of charity and accentuates the role of the will and love at the third level; yet the teaching on the heart governs here especially. Charity "opens eyes so that the mark of truth is everywhere apparent." Or again, "faith is God apprehended by the heart." The order of charity is the order of Christ.

---

[86] *La grandeur de la sagesse, qui n'est nulle sinon de Dieu, est invisible aux charnels et aux gens d'esprit. Ce sont trois ordres différents de genre. Les grands génies ont leur empire, leur éclat, leur grandeur, leur victoire, leur lustre, et n'ont nul besoin des grandeurs charnelles, où elles n'ont pas de rapport* (793).

[87] *E la distance infiniment plus infinie des esprits à la charité, car elle est surnaturelle* (793).

[88] Jean-Luc Marion, *On Descartes' Metaphysical Prism* (Chicago: University of Chicago Press, 1999), 314.

Pascal brings together the peculiar role of divine and human agency in his brilliant analysis of the hiddenness of God, a scriptural doctrine that directly counters Descartes' insistence that the idea of God is "maximally clear and distinct." That God is hidden is clear from our experience of the world and from the endless philosophic disputes over whether he exists. Why it is appropriate for God to be hidden has to do with the ethical presuppositions of belief in the Christian divinity. The reception of certain truths presumes appropriate dispositions on the part of the receiver. Is God bound to compel those who are smugly indifferent and who resolutely refuse to search? Obscurity, combined with a complex ethical pedagogy, ill suits the deist conception of the deity, but it befits the Christian account, according to which nature is corrupt and in need of a redeemer (449).

Far from marking a tragic impasse in the human progress toward the divine, the insistence on divine hiddenness, on God as at once present and absent, has a precise pedagogical and medicinal function in divine providence. True knowledge of God is inseparable from self-knowledge, a recognition of our own wretchedness. Yet true knowledge must not leave us despairing over our condition; it must offer the hope of a cure. The passage we cited earlier bears repeating here: "Knowing God without knowing our own wretchedness makes for pride. Knowing our own wretchedness without knowing God makes for despair. Knowing Christ strikes the balance because he show us both God and our own wretchedness" (192). The religion of a humiliated, crucified God—inconceivable to natural reason—accounts for the paradoxes of human nature. The truths of Christianity are not propositions that can be detached from a way of life, a way of life that takes its bearings from the comprehensive narrative of creation, fall, and redemption. The chief authority in theology, according to Pascal, is memory.

The strange combination of ineradicable craving and inevitable failure proclaims that there was once in man a true happiness, of which "all that remains now is the empty print and trace" (148).[89] The craving for bliss is a remnant of our original state, but the repeated failure to achieve happiness and—what is more important—our ignorance of the cause of our failure result from our primordial rebellion against God.

---

[89] *Dont il ne lui reste maintenant que la marque et la trace toute vide* (425).

§5. Christ as Eucharistic Cipher

Pascal seeks not just a cure but also an explanation of the seemingly incomprehensible paradoxes of the human condition. We can see in yet another way that Pascal's dialectical mode of inquiry, understood in its classical, Aristotelian sense, seeks to save the phenomena of the human condition by sorting out and critically appraising the received opinions of both the many and the wise concerning the nature and destiny of the human person.[90] The inquiry of Pascal's apology as we have it is unfinished, but even in its fragmented form we can detect his eagerness to investigate popular opinions about happiness, philosophical debates about the ultimate end of human life, and the accounts of the human condition proffered by the world religions.

As much merit as there is to this approach, all this talk about dialectical reasoning as the path to an adequate account of the phenomena can be misleading, and in two ways. First, it might seem that Pascal considered dialectic inquiry sufficient to arrive at the truth about the human condition, as if the sorting of opinions and the investigation of the phenomena would allow for the intelligibility of the phenomena to emerge organically or immanently. But Pascal thinks that the more carefully we examine the human condition and the received opinions about it, the more clearly we see that explanation evades us. Second, it might seem as if the dialectical sorting of opinions could provide sufficient evidence of the truth of Christianity. In place of the received view of Pascal as an antirationalist, we would end up substituting a picture of him as the greatest of Christian rationalists. There is no smooth transition from a set of observations about the human condition to the truths of Christianity. Instead of an account accessible to reason through its analysis of universal nature, Christianity predicates its account of wisdom on singular, contingent, unrepeatable historical events.

As we have indicated already, the influence of Socrates on Pascal extends beyond an appreciation of Socratic ignorance and the way of

---

[90] For two quite different interpretations of dialectical inquiry in Aristotle, see Martha Nussbaum, "Saving Aristotle's Appearances," in *The Fragility of Goodness* (New York: Cambridge University Press, 1986), 240–63; and Kurt Pritzl, "Aristotle: Ways of Truth and Ways of Opinion," *American Catholic Philosophical Quarterly* 67 (1993): 241–52. See my discussion of Aristotle and Thomas in *Dialectic and Narrative in Aquinas: An Interpretation of the "Summa Contra Gentiles"* (South Bend, Ind.: University of Notre Dame Press, 1995), 23–30.

life congruent to it. Revelation itself, which invites human persons to participate in a way of life that involves friendship with Wisdom Incarnate, communicates in and through irony. In this and other ways, revelation resists the attempts of philosophy to refute, dismiss, marginalize, or subordinate theology to philosophy. Willing and eager to engage philosophy on its own terms—on the basis of its claim to enact the best way of life—revelation both underscores the limits to philosophy's achievement of the sovereign good and proffers an alternative path. The "religion of a humiliated God" is certainly baffling to the philosophers, who are nonetheless invited to discern in that life the wisdom of God, the satisfaction of that for which philosophy longs but cannot provide.

Pascal enthusiastically embraces the most ambitious of philosophical goals, wisdom about the whole, but he seeks to show that philosophy is incapable of achieving this goal, which is available only through revelation. There is irony here, of course. To the philosopher, the Christian way can thus become a puzzle, not so much to be solved and dismissed, as a source of ever-increasing wonder. As Pascal writes of figurative statements in the Old Testament, a "figure includes absence and presence" (265).[91] If the philosopher insists that whatever is intelligible ought to be immediately accessible to philosophical reason, then he risks mimicking the sort of misunderstanding characteristic of commonsensical folks in relation to the discourse of philosophy. What revelation presents to the philosopher is a cipher, a phenomenon with two meanings. Pascal writes:

> A cipher has two meanings. When we come upon an important letter, whose meaning is clear but where we are told that the meaning is veiled and obscure, that it is hidden so that seeing we shall not see and hearing we shall not hear, what else are we to think but that this is a cipher with a double meaning? (260)[92]

---

[91] "*Figure porte absence et presence*" (677), but "once the secret" to the deciphering of the figure is revealed, "it is impossible not to see it [*Dès qu'une fois on a ouvert ce secret il est impossible de ne le pas voir*]" (267; 680).

[92] *Le chiffre a deux sens. Quand on surprend une lettre importante où l'on trouve un sens clair, et où il est dit néanmoins que le sens en est voilé et obscurci, qu'il est caché, en sorte qu'on verra cette lettre sans la voir et qu'on l'entendra sans l'entendre; que doiton penser, sinon que c'est un chiffre à double* (678).

Pascal is speaking explicitly about Scripture, but he could also be talking about the human condition, a set of double meanings that generate widely variant interpretations. In either case, the key to deciphering is Christ. In its prophecies and veiled utterances, the Old Testament points to Christ; in the New, he is revealed as the one who comes in the fullness of time to enact a plan devised before all ages. With the incarnation of the Son of God, the entire flow of history is radically altered, given purpose and direction. In Christ, the paradoxes of the human condition, their source and remedy, are made intelligible. Never a matter of mere conceptual insight, the deciphering offered in and through Christ is identical to the third order, that of charity, which is the teaching to which all of Scripture points. Anything that does not lead directly to charity in Scripture is figurative (270).

But reading the cipher aright does not make everything clear and distinct. Instead, it gives definition and shape to mystery. As Pascal writes in one of his most important letters, whenever God appears, he appears veiled.[93] Pascal traces the history of divine hiddenness, even as he underscores the role of hiddenness as pedagogical, mystical, and sacramental. God is veiled in created nature, in Scripture, then in Christ, and finally in the sacrament of the Eucharist. How is this so? Christ, key to unlocking the ciphers of nature and of the Jewish scriptures, is himself a cipher. Now, one might suppose that in the incarnation, divinity is made manifest. In one sense, this is true. The word of God takes on flesh and, as John's Gospel puts it, pitches his tent in our midst. In another sense, it is still possible to "see and not see," to look at the life of Christ and not recognize the divinity. Both during and after the incarnation, we experience the "presence of a hidden God." Pascal defends the paradoxical claim that the more visible God is, the less evident he is. The gap, in the incarnation of the divine Word, between appearance and reality, between surface and depth, is what led Erasmus to revive an ancient image of the Silenus, traditionally applied to Socrates. For Erasmus, both Socrates and Christ are "figures hiding divine wisdom within unpromising exteriors."[94] This is yet another basis for Christian Socratism.

---

[93] The *Lettre IV à Mlle de Roannez* is discussed in some detail in Virgil M. Nemoianu's essay, "Pascal on Divine Hiddenness," *International Philosophical Quarterly* 55, no. 3 (2015): 325–43.

[94] M. A. Screech, *Erasmus: Ecstasy and the Praise of Folly* (London: Duckworth, 1980), 35. Screech is glossing Erasmus' work *Sileni Alcibiadis*.

Pascal ends the discussion of divine hiddenness with a reflection on mode of presence of Christ in the sacrament of the Eucharist, the centerpiece of Catholic sacramental life. The focus on the sacrament calls to mind a number of themes prominent in our analysis of Pascal's thought. First, we might recall the proposal toward the end of the wager that the one who desires belief should "learn from those who were once bound like you and. . . . [F]ollow the way by which they began. They behaved as if they did believe, taking holy water, having masses said, and so on" (418).[95] We have already noted that something more is going on here than a commendation of rote behavior designed to bring about external conformity. We can now see that Pascal is proposing an initiation into the rites and practices of the church. In the accent on the imitation of others who show the way, Pascal highlights the way in which wagering on the Christian God is not a matter of a single act of faith, made at a moment in time, by an isolated individual; instead, it is a matter of incorporation into a body, the church. As much as Pascal may have found himself in conflict with members of the church hierarchy, he is unwavering in his affirmation. "The history of the Church," he writes, "should properly be called the history of truth" (776).[96] In marked contrast to his observations about the futility and misery of human life apart from grace, he describes life in the church thus: "There is some pleasure in being on board a ship battered by storms when one is certain of not perishing. The persecutions buffeting the Church are like this" (743).[97]

So, second, the passage on the Eucharist calls to mind Pascal's memorable image of the church, the community of redemption, as a body of thinking members. He does not choose an image from the order of mind but rather from that of body to signify the church. Instead of the movement toward God involving progressive abstraction and repudiation of the order of matter, the movement is toward the concrete and the material. At the center of the life of the body of thinking members is the eucharistic body. The perception operative here is akin to that of *finesse* rather than to that of the mathematical mind.

---

[95] *Apprenez de ceux qui ont été liés comme vous. . . . Suivez la manière par où ils ont commencé: c'est en faisant tout comme s'ils croyaient, en prenant de l'eau bénite, en faisant dire des messes, etc.* (233).

[96] *L'histoire de l'Eglise doit être proprement appelée l'histoire de la vérité* (858).

[97] *Il y a plaisir d'être dans un vaisseau battu de l'orage, lorsqu'on est assuré qu'il ne périra point. Les persécutions qui travaillent l'Eglise sont de cette nature* (859).

Concrete mysticism is a nice way of capturing Pascal's teaching on the Eucharist. The mystical element here entails a qualification of Grasset's language of vision and seeing. Thus, third, the mystical dimension of divine hiddenness, we should recall, highlights the seeing that is a not seeing. Of course, there are two ways to see and not see. One way entirely misses what is present. Another is aware of what is present but experiences it in the mode of mystery. For Pascal, the presence of the hidden God is nowhere more dramatically at work than in the Eucharist.

And that, fourth, calls to mind the enduring analogy between Socratic ignorance, a wise ignorance that knows itself, and Pascal's theology. Just as Socrates counsels the practice of learned ignorance, so Pascal urges us to cultivate a growing awareness of the absence of God. As C. S. Lewis puts it, "to practice the absence of God" is "to become increasingly aware of our unawareness till we feel like men who should stand beside a great cataract and hear no noise, or like a man in a story who looks in a mirror and finds no face there, or a man in a dream who stretches out his hand to visible objects and gets no sensation of touch." Lest we think this is mere negation, Lewis adds, "To know that one is dreaming is to be no longer perfectly asleep."[98]

In his emphasis on the continuing interplay of absence and presence, of seeing and not seeing, Pascal implicitly distinguishes between an iconic and an idolatrous approach to God. The experience of the idol is an experience of an object that is put at our disposal, fully present to the viewer and amenable to manipulation by the autonomous will. Because meaning and purpose are here bestowed on objects by the desires of the viewer, idolatrous experience ultimately gives way to vacuity and vanity. The nihilism just beneath the surface of pleasure, understood as the serial satisfaction of one desire after another, permeates Pascal's account of the wretchedness of the human condition. Its characteristics are familiar: the distention of desire in empty time, the fantastical projection of our lives into times that no longer are or are not yet, the illusion of defining ourselves by reference to how we are seen by others. These futile ways of defining, establishing, and asserting ourselves throw us back on ourselves. The result is what modern philosophers and poets have described as ennui. Pascal's description is fertile:

---

[98] C. S. Lewis, *The Four Loves* (Boston: Houghton Mifflin, 1960), 141.

> Boredom. Man finds nothing so intolerable as to be in a state of complete rest, without passions, without occupation, without diversion, without effort.
>
> Then he faces his nullity, loneliness, inadequacy, dependence, helplessness, emptiness.
>
> And at once there wells up from the depths of his soul boredom, gloom, depression, chagrin, resentment, despair. (622)[99]

The alternative to these self-defeating attempts at self-definition and self-assertion is not some new project of self-actualization. Rather, the task is to realize one's own nothingness in a way that is receptive of a gift. "Be comforted; it is not from yourself that you must expect it, but on the contrary you must expect it by expecting nothing from yourself" (202).[100]

Pascal's account of the Christian life undermines and reverses idolatry, even as it heals the vanity that engenders boredom and despair. Instead of an idolatrous distancing of the observer from the comprehended object of the gaze, vision here undergoes a decentralization, a reversal in which the achievement of the inquiring heart is realized precisely in a recognition of the distance between observer and observed and of the subversive process whereby the one seeking and looking finds himself discovered and beheld. As Jean-Luc Marion puts it:

> Here our gaze becomes the optical mirror of that at which it looks only by finding itself more radically looked at: we become a visible mirror of an invisible gaze that subverts us in the measure of its glory. . . . Thus, as opposed to the idol, . . . the icon displaces the limits of our visibility to the measure of its own—its glory. It transforms us in its glory by allowing this glory to shine on our face as its mirror.[101]

In the Eucharist not only are we seen rather than seeing, but we are also incorporated into the body that we eat. On one level, the reception of

---

[99] *Ennui.—Rien n'est si insupportable à l'homme que d'être dans un plein repos, sans passions, sans affaire, sans divertissement, sans application. Il sent alors son néant, son abandon, son insuffisance, sa dépendance, son impuissance, son vide. Incontinent, il sortira du fond de son âme l'ennui, la noirceur, la tristesse, le chagrin, le dépit, le désespoir* (131).

[100] *Consolez-vous! ce n'est pas de vous que vous devez l'attendre, mais au contraire, en n'attendant rien de vous, que vous devez l'attendre* (517).

[101] Jean-Luc Marion, *God without Being*, trans. Thomas A. Carlson (Chicago: University of Chicago Press, 1991), 22.

the eucharistic host would seem to fit the ordinary model of eating, of consuming what is other as a way of satisfying human desire. Yet, on another level, the taking of the host into our body takes us, incorporates us, into the body of Christ. The motif and activity of incorporation is central to the Christian life, as it awakens us to the reality of our existence not as isolated monads but as parts of a larger whole. The body of Christ as cipher is not so much a puzzle to be pondered as it is a mystery to be received, a mystery that, in entering us, transforms us and enters us into a communal body, a body of thinking, loving, and worshipping members.

One might wonder, beyond the shared language of presence and absence, what connection there is in Pascal between his lengthy exegesis of Scripture and his teaching on the Eucharist? An answer can be had in Marion's reflections on the passage toward the end of Luke's Gospel, chapter 24, in which the disciples on the road to Emmaus encounter, without knowing him, the risen Christ on the road. Discussing the events surrounding the life and death of Jesus, the stranger adduces passages from the Jewish scriptures about the coming of the Messiah. Still, the disciples remain unknowing. They neither recognize Christ nor acknowledge the force of his exegesis. Only at the meal, when he offers a blessing, do they come to recognize him and their eyes are opened. As soon as they do, he vanishes. For Marion, this means that mere reading is not enough. One must reach through the text to the Word.[102] In this decisive passage, the abrupt shift from exegesis to Eucharist "accomplishes, as it central moment, the hermeneutic. It alone allows the text to pass to its referent, recognized as the nontextual Word of the words." In the Event of the Eucharist, the Word "interprets in person."[103]

* * *

Where does this study leave us, contemporary readers and inquirers? As a study in early modern philosophy, it opens up new way of seeing the beginnings of modernity, the world we now take for granted. We have examined the philosophical and humanistic foundations of three quite distinct options for pursuing the human good. The first, in Montaigne, exalts the private over the public and urges the pursuit of self-examination and self-expression, without temporal end or ultimate

---

[102] Marion, *God without Being*, 149.
[103] Marion, *God without Being*, 150.

goal. Since all standards and ideals are arbitrary, all claims to transcendence are fraudulent, distorting our self-understanding and damaging our lives. An utterly immanent good, authenticity—understood as rigorous self-examination and exhaustive self-expression—now rivals the classical accounts of the good life. The impotence of reason to command human action in light of some understanding of the good means that reason can but narrate. It can only trace the evanescent appearances of the self and its environs. Thus, a form of literature, the essay, replaces previous genres of philosophical and theological inquiry.

The second, in Descartes, is especially intent on showing that reason can be more than a passive observer. Taking on Montaigne's challenge rather directly, Descartes invents a literary work, a fable as he calls it, a kind of autobiographical sketch that moves through the dark night of skepticism to the light of certitude concerning the mind, God, and the natural world. The resolution of seemingly insoluble questions—in the varied disciplines of metaphysics, mathematics, natural science, ethics, and theology—inspires confidence in the power of reason. If in Montaigne reason is passive and never transcends a kind of wonder at itself and its experiences, in Descartes, reason, freed from the encumbrances of the body and the imagination, becomes persistently and dominantly active, as it shapes a series of technical tools to aid it in overcoming nature's resistance to human will and desire.

The differing attitudes toward reason involve divergent stances toward Socrates. For Montaigne, Socrates embodies the recognition that reason can at best achieve a learned ignorance and must accustom itself to be content in this unknowing; for Descartes, Socrates embodies the honesty of philosophy prior to the modern period, that is, prior to Descartes' discovery of a method that could complete the natural (and Socratic) desire for wisdom. Possession would replace love of wisdom.

Unlike Montaigne and Descartes, Socrates exhibits a voracious appetite for dialogue, for investigating with other seeking souls the truth of the matter about the human good. Moreover, Socrates does not just examine endlessly; he knows the need for action. And, even in the face of inconclusive arguments, as is clear from the *Phaedo*, Socrates insists on reason's discernment of the best hypothesis available as a basis for action.

Pascal affirms the Socratic desire for wisdom, but he wants to return to the original Socratic meaning of wisdom as an understanding of the place of human persons in the whole and of the best way of life for such persons. His view of reason stresses neither its impotent passivity nor its dominating activity. Reason itself reflects the duality of the human condition. Pascal, whose image for human rationality is a "thinking reed," insists that thinking well is the core of human dignity, even as he underscores the difficulty of reaching certitude about any matters, either speculative or practical. Despite our tenuous hold on certain knowledge, Pascal thinks the human intellect naturally desires an understanding of the whole and the human heart naturally desires a happiness that eludes it everywhere in its finite experience. Given our limited knowledge, our desire for happiness, and the imminent threat of death, philosophy is about discerning the best hypothesis concerning these matters and wagering everything on that hypothesis.

All three display strong humanistic tendencies, connected in one way or another with the figure of Socrates. In quite varied stances toward Socrates, each thinker takes up his question of the best way of life. Each thinker, moreover, grounds his account of the human good in the received experience of ordinary life; each begins with an account of the human condition in one literary form or another. Thus do they concede something that modern philosophy always risks forgetting, namely, the requirement that philosophical and scientific systems mediate between their own accounts and the shared human world, that they sketch a path from the world the rest of us inhabit into their systems.

How much more rewarding would our discussions (dare we say our lives?) be if they were informed by the writings of Montaigne, Descartes, and Pascal? These moral ideals—the private life of authenticity, the public goods of science and technology, and the life of religious devotion—continue to inform contemporary life and thought. But they do so in increasingly unreflective ways, articulated in a dangerously vacuous vocabulary, void of rich imaginative insight or a desire for dialectical testing by reference to rival views. How much more rigorous is Montaigne's attention to the authenticity of ordinary life, to the examination and savoring of its exquisite details, than are our lax and self-satisfied assertions of individual self-expression? How much deeper and richer would be our consideration of modern science—with its ambitious intellectual project of mapping nature in mathematical terms and its equally ambitious technological project of mastery—were it informed by Descartes' sustained reflection on the foundations of the project in ordinary human experience and on a new set of virtues constitutive of the sovereign good of happiness? And how much more nuanced and humane would be our religious discourse if it were informed by anything like Pascal's insistence on depicting religion as answering the same questions about the human condition that philosophy aspires to answer and his eagerness to test the religious hypothesis against rival philosophical views?

Pascal shows the resilience of the Christian hypothesis. Countering what would soon become a dogma of enlightened reason, Pascal insists that the power and intelligibility of the Christian claim are more evident in the aftermath of modern science than they were in the comfortable premodern cosmos. Indeed, Pascal's engagement with and deconstruction of Cartesian science take him to the cusp of post-Newtonian science.

The cosmos that Pascal thinks we inhabit is characterized by contingency, chance, and paradoxes at both extremes, in the world of the infinitely small (the subatomic world) and at the limits of space and time. Pascal, who describes human nature as "wholly animal," envisions the reestablishing of a strong link between animal and human. In the human order, Pascal's cosmos is one in which the human person is lost and in which dread alternates with wonder in the face of its vastness and elusive complexity. That is certainly not a universe crafted by the God of deism. But, Pascal insists, neither—if we know how to conduct the search—is it the world of the arbitrary God of voluntarism. The burden of Pascal's apology is to demonstrate that the cosmos exhibits the presence of a hidden, ironic God.

Pascal also opens up a third way between Enlightenment rationalism, with its optimism about intelligibility and progress, and deconstruction, which is always threatened by skepticism and nihilism. His account of irony shares much with the critique of modernity found in some postmodern authors, yet his moderate skepticism is a tool against despair. We simply do not know enough to know that seeking is necessarily futile. And his affirmation of the longings of the human heart means that seeking is our only recourse. Hardly naive in his assumptions about the obscurity that envelops us or the darkness discernible in the depths of the human heart, Pascal reaches out to his readers as an amiable counselor, a friend who wishes to be a partner and guide in the quest.

Taking Pascal's Christian Socratism as their guide, Christians might not only continue to astonish the philosophers, but they might also, given the dreary state of contemporary philosophy, serve to remind philosophy of its origins in the practices of wonder and dialogical inquiry about the human good.

BIBLIOGRAPHY

Primary

Aquinas, Thomas. *Summa Contra Gentiles.* Vols. 1–4. South Bend, Ind.: University of Notre Dame Press 1981.
———. *Summa Theologiae: Treatise on God.* New York: Prentice Hall, 1965.
Aristotle. *The Complete Works of Aristotle.* 2 vols. Edited by Jonathan Barnes. Princeton, N.J.: Princeton University Press, 1984.
Descartes, René. *The Geometry of René Descartes.* Edited and translated by David Eugene Smith and Marcia L. Latham. New York: Dover, 1925.
———. *Meditations on First Philosophy.* Translated by Michael Moriarty. Oxford: Oxford University Press, 2008.
———. *Œuvres de Descartes.* Edited by C. Adam and P. Tannery. Paris: Vrin/C.N.R.S., 1964–1976.
———. *Œuvres et lettres.* Edited by André Bridoux. Paris: Bibliothèque de la Pléiade, 1937.
———. *The Philosophical Writings of Descartes.* Translated by John Cottingham, Robert Stoothoff, et al. 3 vols. New York: Cambridge University Press, 1984–1991.
Montaigne, Michel de. *The Complete Essays.* Translated by M. A. Screech. New York: Penguin Classics, 2003.
———. *Les essais de Michel de Montaigne.* Paris: Libraire Felix Alcan, 1931.
Pascal, Blaise. *Pensées.* Edited by Dominique Descotes and Léon Brunschvicg. Paris: Flammarion, 1976.

———. *Pensées*. Translated by A. J. Krailsheimer. New York: Penguin Classics, 1995.
Plato. *The Dialogues of Plato*. Translated by Benjamin Jowett. Chicago: Encyclopaedia Britannica, 1952.
Xenophon. *Recollections of Socrates and Socrates' Defense before the Jury*. Translated by Anna S. Benjamin. Indianapolis: Bobbs-Merrill, 1965.

Secondary

Abraham, Claude, and Marcia Abraham. "Pascal Rediscovered." In *Pascal*, by Jean Mesnard, i–xii. Translated by Claude and Marcia Abraham. Tuscaloosa: University of Alabama Press, 1969.
Alexandrescu, Vlad. "Descartes and Pascal on the Eucharist." *Perspectives on Science* 15, no. 4 (2007): 434–49.
Amesbury, Richard. "Fideism." In *The Stanford Encyclopedia of Philosophy*, edited by Edward N. Zalta. Fall 2009 ed. http://plato.stanford.edu/archives/fall2009/entries/fideism/.
Ariew, Roger. "Descartes and Pascal." *Perspectives on Science* 15, no. 4 (2007): 397–409.
Arteau-McNeil, Raphael. "L'apologie de Raymond Sebond: Ignorance, savoir et confiance." *De Philosophia* 17, no. 1 (2001): 13–32.
Baird, A. W. S. *Studies in Pascal's Ethics*. The Hague: Martinus Nijhoff, 1975.
Balthasar, Hans Urs von. *Studies in Theological Styles: Lay Styles*. Vol. 3 of *The Glory of the Lord: A Theological Aesthetics*. Translated by Andrew Louth et al. Edited by John Riches. San Francisco: Ignatius, 1986.
Boase, Alan M. *Fortunes of Montaigne: A History of the Essays in France, 1580–1669*. London: Methuen, 1935.
Booth, Wayne. *A Rhetoric of Irony*. Chicago: University of Chicago Press, 1974.
Brunschvicg, Léon. *Descartes et Pascal lecteurs de Montaigne*. Neuchâtel: A la Baconnière, 1942.
Burge, E. L. "The Irony of Socrates." *Antichthon* 3 (1969): 5–17.
Burger, Ronna. "Socratic Eironia." *Interpretation: A Journal of Political Philosophy* 13, no. 2 (1985): 143–49.
Carraud, Vincent. *Pascal et la philosophie*. Paris: Presses universitaires de France, 1992.
———. "Pascal's Anti-Augustinianism." *Perspectives on Science* 15, no. 4 (2007): 450–92.
Carroll, Thomas. "The Traditions of Fideism." *Religious Studies* 44 (2008): 1–22.

Chambers, Frank. "Pascal's Montaigne." *PMLA* 65, no. 2 (1950): 790–804.
Christodoulou, K. "Socrate chez Montaigne et Pascal." *Diotima: Review of Philosophical Research* 7 (1979): 39–50.
Collier, Carol. "The Self in Montaigne and Descartes: From Portraiture to Indigence." *De Philosophia* 13, no. 2 (1997): 249–58.
Corey, David. *The Sophists in Plato's Dialogues*. Albany: State University of New York Press, 2015.
Curley, E. M. *Descartes against the Skeptics*. Cambridge, Mass.: Harvard University Press, 1978.
Davidson, Hugh. *Pascal and the Arts of the Mind*. New York: Cambridge University Press, 1993.
De Man, Paul. "Pascal's Allegories of Persuasion." In *Allegory and Representation*, edited by Stephen Greenblatt, 1–25. Baltimore: Johns Hopkins University Press, 1981.
Derrida, Jacques. "Force of Law: The Mystical Foundations of Authority." *Cardozo Law Review* 11, no. 5 (1990): 920–1045.
Descotes, Dominique. *L'argumentation chez Pascal*. Paris: Presses Universitaires de France, 1993.
Desgrippes, Georges. *Études sur Pascal de l'automatisme à la foi*. Paris: Pierre Téqui, 1935.
Esolen, Anthony. *Ironies of Faith: The Laughter at the Heart of Christian Literature*. Wilmington, Del.: ISI Books, 2007.
Evans, C. Stephen. "Kierkegaard's View of Humor: Must Christians Always Be Solemn?" In *Kierkegaard on Faith and the Self*, 81–92. Waco, Tex.: Baylor University Press, 2006.
———. "The Role of Irony in Kierkegaard's *Philosophical Fragments*." In *Kierkegaard on Faith and the Self*, 67–80. Waco, Tex.: Baylor University Press, 2006.
Filho, Azar. "Montaigne e Sócrates: Cepticismo, conhecimento e virtude." *Revista Portuguesa de Filosofia* 58, no. 4 (2002): 829–45.
Fine, Gail. "Descartes and Ancient Skepticism: Reheated Cabbage?" *Philosophical Review* 109, no. 2 (2000): 195–234.
Fouke, Daniel. "Argument in Pascal's *Pensées*." *History of Philosophy Quarterly* 6 (1989): 57–68.
Frazier, Brad. *Rorty and Kierkegaard on Irony and Moral Commitment*. New York: Palgrave Macmillan, 2006.
Friedrich, Hugo. *Montaigne*. Edited by Philippe Desan. Translated by Dawn Eng. Berkeley: University of California Press, 1991.

Funkenstein, Amos. *Theology and the Scientific Imagination from the Middle Ages to the Seventeenth Century*. Princeton, N.J.: Princeton University Press, 1986.

Gadamer, Hans-Georg. "The Proofs of Immortality in Plato's *Phaedo*." In *Dialogue and Dialectic: Eight Hermeneutical Studies on Plato*, translated by P. Christopher Smith, 21–28. New Haven, Conn.: Yale University Press, 1980.

Gillespie, Michael Allen. *Nihilism before Nietzsche*. Chicago: University of Chicago Press, 1996.

Gilson, Etienne. *Discours de la méthode*. 5th ed. Paris: Vrin, 1976.

Goldmann, Lucien. *Le Dieu caché: Étude sur la vision tragique dans les "Pensées" de Pascal et dans le théâtre de Racine*. Paris: Gallimard, 1959.

———. *The Hidden God: A Study of Tragic Vision in the "Pensées" of Pascal and the Tragedies of Racine*. London: Routledge & Kegan Paul, 1964.

Griswold, Charles. "Irony in the Platonic Dialogues." *Philosophy and Literature* 26, no. 1 (2002): 84–106.

Guéroult, Martial. *Descartes' Philosophy Interpreted According to the Order of Reasons*. Translated by Roger Ariew. 2 vols. Minneapolis: University of Minnesota Press, 1984–1985.

Haakonssen, Knud, ed. *Enlightenment and Religion: Rational Dissent in Eighteenth-Century Britain*. New York: Cambridge University Press, 1996.

———. *Natural Law and Moral Philosophy from Grotius to the Scottish Enlightenment*. New York: Cambridge University Press, 1996.

Hadot, Pierre. *Philosophy as a Way of Life: Spiritual Exercises from Socrates to Foucault*. Edited by Arnold Davidson. Malden, Mass.: Wiley-Blackwell, 1995.

———. *What Is Ancient Philosophy?* Translated by Michael Chase. Cambridge, Mass.: Harvard University Press, 2004.

Hammond, Nicholas. "Pascal's *Pensées* and the Art of Persuasion." In *The Cambridge Companion to Pascal*, edited by Nicholas Hammond, 235–52. New York: Cambridge University Press, 2003.

Hampton, Timothy. "Montaigne and the Body of Socrates: Narrative and Exemplarity in the *Essais*." *Modern Language Notes* 104, no. 4 (1989): 880–98.

Hans, James. "Alexander Nehamas and *The Art of Living*." *Philosophy Today* 44, no. 2 (2000): 190–205.

Hartle, Ann. *Death and the Disinterested Spectator: An Inquiry into the Nature of Philosophy*. Albany: State University of New York Press, 1986.

———. *Michel de Montaigne: Accidental Philosopher.* New York: Cambridge University Press, 2003.

———. "Montaigne and Skepticism." In *The Cambridge Companion to Montaigne*, edited by Ullrich Langer, 183–206. Cambridge: Cambridge University Press, 2006.

Hibbs, Thomas S. *Aquinas, Ethics, and Philosophy of Religion: Metaphysics and Practice.* Bloomington: University of Indiana Press, 2007.

———. *Dialectic and Narrative in Aquinas: An Interpretation of the "Summa Contra Gentiles."* South Bend, Ind.: University of Notre Dame Press, 1995.

———. "Habits of the Heart: Pascal and the Ethics of Thought." *International Philosophical Quarterly* 45, no. 2 (2005): 203–20.

———. "Stanley Cavell's Philosophical Improvisations." *Chronicle of Higher Education* 57, no. 8 (2010): B6–B9.

Hoffmann, George. "The Investigation of Nature." In *The Companion to Montaigne*, edited by Ullrich Langer, 163–82. New York: Cambridge University Press, 2006.

Hunter, Graeme. "Motion and Rest in the *Pensées*: A Note on Pascal's Modernism." *International Journal for Philosophy of Religion* 47, no. 2 (2000): 87–99.

Husserl, Edmund. *The Crisis of European Sciences and Transcendental Phenomenology.* Chicago: Northwestern University Press, 1970.

Jean, B., and F. Mouret. *Montaigne, Descartes et Pascal.* Manchester: Manchester University Press, 1971.

Jesseph, Douglas Michael. "Descartes, Pascal, and the Epistemology of Mathematics: The Case of the Cycloid." *Perspectives on Science* 15, no. 4 (2007): 410–33.

Jones, Matthew L. "Descartes's Geometry as Spiritual Exercise." *Critical Inquiry* 38, no. 1 (2001): 40–71.

———. *The Good Life in the Scientific Revolution: Descartes, Pascal, Leibniz, and the Cultivation of Virtue.* Chicago: University of Chicago Press, 2006.

Keefe, Terry. "Descartes's 'Morale Definitive' and the Autonomy of Ethics." *Romantic Review* 64, no. 2 (1973): 85–98.

Kennington, Richard. "Rene Descartes." In *History of Political Philosophy*, edited by Leo Strauss and Joseph Cropsey, 2nd ed., 395–415. Chicago: University of Chicago Press, 1981.

Khalfa, Jean. "Pascal's Theory of Knowledge." In *The Cambridge Companion to Pascal*, edited by Nicholas Hammond, 122–43. New York: Cambridge University Press, 2003.

Kierkegaard, Søren. *Concluding Unscientific Postscript to Philosophical Fragments.* Vol. 12.1 of *Kierkegaard's Writings*. Translated and edited by H. V. Hong and E. H. Hong. Princeton, N.J.: Princeton University Press, 1992.

Koch, Erec R. *Pascal and Rhetoric: Figural and Persuasive Language in the Scientific Treatises, "The Provinciales," and the "Pensées."* Charlottesville, Va.: Rookwood Press, 1997.

Kołakowski, Leszek. *God Owes Us Nothing: A Brief Remark on Pascal's Religion and on the Spirit of Jansenism.* Chicago: University of Chicago Press, 1998.

Kritzman, Lawrence D. "The Socratic Makeover: Montaigne's 'De la physionomie' and the Ethics of the Impossible." *L'Esprit Createur* 46, no. 1 (2006): 75–85.

Lachterman, David Rapport. *The Ethics of Geometry: A Genealogy of Modernity.* New York: Routledge, 1989.

Lane, Melissa. "Reconsidering Socratic Irony." In *The Cambridge Companion to Socrates*, edited by Donald R. Morrison, 237–59. Cambridge: Cambridge University Press, 2011.

Le Doeuff, Michele. *The Philosophical Imaginary.* Translated by Colin Gordon. Stanford, Calif.: Stanford University Press, 1989.

Lear, Jonathan. *A Case for Irony.* Cambridge, Mass.: Harvard University Press, 2011.

Lefebvre, M. H. ""De la morale provisoire à la générosité." In *Descartes, Cahiers de Royamount*, Philosophie no. 2, 237–72. Paris: Les Éditions de Minuit, 1957.

Lewis, C. S. *The Four Loves.* Boston: Houghton Mifflin, 1960.

———. *Mere Christianity.* San Francisco: HarperCollins, 2001.

———. *The Weight of Glory and Other Addresses.* New York: HarperOne, 2009.

Limbrick, Elaine. "Montaigne and Socrates." *Renaissance and Reformation* 9 (1973): 46–67.

Lyons, John. "Descartes and Modern Imagination." *Philosophy and Literature* 23, no. 2 (1999): 302–12.

MacIntyre, Alasdair. *After Virtue: A Study in Moral Theory.* Notre Dame, Ind.: University of Notre Dame Press, 1981.

———. *Against the Self-Images of the Age.* Notre Dame, Ind.: University of Notre Dame Press, 1978.

---. "What Has Christianity to Say to the Moral Philosopher?" In *The Doctrine of God and Theological Ethics*, edited by Michael C. Banner and Alan J. Torrance, 17–32. New York: T&T Clark, 2006.
Mackie, J. L. *The Miracle of Theism: Arguments for and against the Existence of God*. Oxford: Clarendon, 1982.
Maclean, Ian. "Montaigne and the Truth of the Schools." In *The Cambridge Companion to Montaigne*, edited by Ullrich Langer, 142–62. Cambridge: Cambridge University Press, 2006.
Magnard, Pierre. "L'infini pascalien." *Revue de l'Enseignement philosophique* 31, no. 1 (1980): 2–16.
Manent, Pierre. *The City of Man*. Princeton, N.J.: Princeton University Press, 1998.
---. *Les métamorphoses de la cité: Essai sur la dynamique de l'Occident*. Paris: Flammarion, 2010.
---. *Modern Liberty and Its Discontents*. Edited and translated by Daniel J. Mahoney and Paul Seaton. Lanham, Md.: Rowman & Littlefield, 1998.
---. *Montaigne la vie sans loi*. Paris: Flammarion, 2015.
---. "Pascal's Paradoxical Rationalism." Unpublished essay. Delivered at Boston College, Boston, Mass.
Marion, Jean-Luc. *God without Being*. Translated by Thomas A. Carlson. Chicago: University of Chicago Press, 1991.
---. *On Descartes' Metaphysical Prism: The Constitution and the Limits of Onto-theo-logy in Cartesian Thought*. Chicago: University of Chicago Press, 1999.
Maritain, Jacques. *Three Reformers: Luther, Descartes, Rousseau*. New York: Charles Scribner's Sons, 1929.
McGowan, Margaret. *Montaigne's Deceits: The Art of Persuasion in the "Essais."* London: Hodder & Stoughton, 1974.
McInerny, Ralph. *Characters in Search of Their Author*. Notre Dame, Ind.: University of Notre Dame Press, 2001.
Melehy, Hassan. *Writing Cogito: Montaigne, Descartes, and the Institution of the Modern Subject*. Albany: State University of New York Press, 1998.
Melzer, Sara E. *Discourses of the Fall: A Study of Pascal's "Pensées."* Berkeley: University of California Press, 1986.
Menn, Stephen. *Descartes and Augustine*. New York: Cambridge University Press, 2002.
Mesnard, Jean. *Pascal*. Translated by Claude and Marcia Abraham. Tuscaloosa: University of Alabama Press, 1969.

Miel, Jan. *Pascal and Theology*. Baltimore: Johns Hopkins University Press, 1969.
Miner, Robert. "Pascal on the Uses of Scepticism." *Logos: A Journal of Catholic Thought and Culture* 11, no. 4 (2008): 111–22.
Muecke, D. C. *The Compass of Irony*. London: Methuen, 1969.
Natoli, Charles. *Fire in the Dark*. Rochester, N.Y.: University of Rochester Press, 2005.
Nehemas, Alexander. *The Art of Living: Socratic Reflections from Plato to Foucault*. Berkeley: University of California Press, 1998.
Neiman, Susan. *Evil in Modern Thought: An Alternative History of Philosophy*. Princeton, N.J.: Princeton University Press, 2003.
Nemoianu, Virgil M. "The Insufficiency of the Many Gods Objection to Pascal's Wager." *American Catholic Philosophical Quarterly* 84, no. 3 (2010): 513–30.
———. "The Order of Pascal's Politics." *British Journal for the History of Philosophy* 21, no. 1 (2013): 34–56.
———. "Pascal on Divine Hiddenness." *International Philosophical Quarterly* 55, no. 3 (2015): 325–43.
Nicgorski, Walter. "Cicero's Socrates: Assessment of the 'Socratic Turn.'" In *Law and Philosophy: The Practice of Theory*, vol. 1, edited by J. Murley, R. Stone, and W. Braithwaite, 213–33. Athens: Ohio University Press, 1992.
Nietzsche, Friedrich. *Beyond Good and Evil*. Translated by Walter Kaufmann. New York: Random House, 1966.
Nussbaum, Martha C. *The Fragility of Goodness: Luck and Ethics in Greek Tragedy and Philosophy*. New York: Cambridge University Press, 1986.
O'Connell, Marvin. *Blaise Pascal: Reasons of the Heart*. Grand Rapids: Eerdmans, 1997.
Osborne, Catherine. "Successors of Socrates, Disciples of Descartes, and Followers of Freud." *Apeiron: A Journal for Ancient Philosophy and Science* 34, no. 2 (2001): 181–93.
Parker, Thomas. *Volition, Rhetoric, and Emotion in the Work of Pascal*. New York: Routledge, 2008.
Pavlovits, Tamás. "Admiration, Fear, and Infinity in Pascal's Thinking." In *Philosophy Begins in Wonder: An Introduction to Early Modern Philosophy, Theology, and Science*, edited by Michael Funk Deckard and Péter Losonczi, 119–26. Eugene, Ore.: Pickwick, 2010.
Penelhum, Terence. *God and Skepticism: A Study in Skepticism and Fideism*. Dordrecht: D. Reidel, 1983.

———. "Pascal's Wager." *Journal of Religion* 44, no. 3 (1964): 201–9.
Phillips, Henry. "Pascal's Reading and the Inheritance of Montaigne and Descartes." In *The Cambridge Companion to Pascal*, edited by Nicholas Hammond, 20–39. New York: Cambridge University Press, 2003.
Pichanick, Alan D. "A Case for Irony: An Interview with Jonathan Lear." *Expositions* 6, no. 1 (2012): 1–8.
Pieper, Josef. *Faith Hope Love*. San Francisco: Ignatius, 1997.
———. *Hope and History*. San Francisco: Ignatius, 1991.
Popkin, Richard H. *The History of Skepticism from Erasmus to Spinoza*. Berkeley: University of California Press, 1979.
———. *The History of Skepticism from Savonarola to Bayle*. Oxford: Oxford University Press, 2003.
Pritzl, Kurt. "Aristotle: Ways of Truth and Ways of Opinion." *American Catholic Philosophical Quarterly* 67 (1993): 241–52.
Rée, Jonathan. "Descartes's Comedy." *Philosophy and Literature* 8, no. 2 (1984): 151–66.
Rescher, Nicholas. *Pascal's Wager: A Study of Practical Reasoning in Philosophical Theology*. Notre Dame, Ind.: University of Notre Dame Press, 1985.
Riley, Patrick. *Character and Conversion in Autobiography: Augustine, Montaigne, Descartes, Rousseau, and Sartre*. Charlottesville: University of Virginia Press, 2004.
Rorty, Richard. *Contingency, Irony, and Solidarity*. Cambridge: Cambridge University Press, 1989.
Rosen, Stanley. *The Ancients and the Moderns: Rethinking Modernity*. New Haven, Conn.: Yale University Press, 1989.
Rowe, C. "Platonic Irony." *Nouva Tellus: Anuario del Centro de Estudios Clasicos* 5 (1987): 83–101.
Sayce, Richard A. *The Essays of Montaigne: A Critical Exploration*. London: Weidenfeld & Nicolson, 1972.
Schaefer, David. "Montaigne's Intention and His Rhetoric." *Interpretation: A Journal of Political Philosophy* 5 (1975): 57–90.
———. *The Political Philosophy of Montaigne*. Ithaca, N.Y.: Cornell University Press, 1990.
Schiffman, Zachary S. "Montaigne and the Rise of Skepticism in Early Modern Europe: A Reappraisal." *Journal of the History of Ideas* 45, no. 4 (1984): 499–516.
Schwartz, Jerome. "Montaigne and Deconstruction." In *Approaches to Teaching Montaigne's Essays*, edited by Patrick Henry, 131–37. New York: Modern Language Association of America, 1994.

Screech, M. A. *Erasmus: Ecstasy and The Praise of Folly.* London: Duckworth, 1980.
———. *Montaigne and Melancholy.* Selinsgrove, Penn.: Susquehanna University Press, 1984.
Starobinski, Jean. "The Body's Moment." In *Montaigne: Essays in Reading,* edited by Gerard Defaux, 273–305. New Haven, Conn.: Yale University, 1983.
———. *Montaigne in Motion.* Translated by Arthur Goldhammer. Chicago: University of Chicago, 1985.
Steiner, Gary. *Descartes as a Moral Thinker: Christianity, Technology, Nihilism.* Amherst, N.Y.: Humanity Books, 2004.
Strauss, Leo. *The City and Man.* Chicago: University of Chicago Press, 1964.
———. *Natural Right and History.* Chicago: University of Chicago Press, 1953.
Taylor, Charles. *A Secular Age.* Cambridge, Mass.: Harvard University Press, 2007.
Traverso, Edilia. *Montaigne e Aristotele.* Florence: Le Monnier, 1974.
Tolkien, J. R. R. *The Tolkien Reader.* New York: Ballantine Books, 1966.
Toulmin, Stephen. *Cosmopolis: The Hidden Agenda of Modernity.* Chicago: University of Chicago Press, 1990.
Villey, Pierre. *Les sources et l'évolution des "Essais" de Montaigne.* Vol. 2. Paris: Hachette, 1908.
Vlastos, Gregory. *Socrates: Ironist and Moral Philosopher.* Ithaca, N.Y.: Cornell University Press, 1991.
Warner, Martin. *Philosophical Finesse: Studies in the Art of Rational Persuasion.* Oxford: Clarendon, 1989.
Weil, Simone. *Waiting for God.* Translated by Emma Craufurd. New York: Harper, 2009.
Wertheimer, Roger. "Socratic Scepticism." *Metaphilosophy* 24, no. 4 (1993): 344–62.
Wolin, Sheldon. *Tocqueville between Two Worlds.* Princeton, N.J.: Princeton University Press, 2001.
Yhap, Jennifer. "Pascal and Descartes on First Ideas." *American Catholic Philosophical Quarterly* 69, no. 1 (1995): 39–50.
Zagzebski, Linda. *Virtues of the Mind.* Cambridge: Cambridge University Press, 2002.
Zalloua, Zahi. "Montaigne, Skepticism and Immortality." *Philosophy and Literature* 27, no. 1 (2003): 40–61.

INDEX OF NAMES AND AUTHORS

Anselm, 11
Aquinas, T., 9, 11, 16, 74, 92, 97, 147, 183
Aristotle, 9, 17, 20, 41–42, 45–50, 52–55, 57, 71, 74–76, 79, 96–99, 124, 135–37, 156, 167, 183
Augustine, 10, 16, 18, 24, 41–42, 51, 54–60, 77, 82, 85, 96, 108, 122, 123, 125–27, 131, 139, 152, 168, 180

Bacon, F., 48, 79, 84
Baird, A. W. S., 8–9
Bernard of Clairvaux, 16, 154
Boase, A. M., 43
Booth, W., 11, 34
Braithwaite, W., 23, 48
Burger, R., 17

Carraud, V., 18, 29, 77, 100, 105, 110, 117, 132
Carroll, T., 3
Cavell, S., 44
Cicero, 22–23, 45, 48
Corey, D., 141
Crospey, J., 22, 74

Davidson, H., 34, 35, 135, 140, 148

Descartes, R., 4–7, 10, 13, 18, 20–22, 26–29, 33, 36–37, 40, 45–46, 51, 59, 67–117, 120, 123, 127, 129–33, 138, 144–47, 171–75, 177, 181–82, 190–91
Desmond, W., 163–65
Dostoevsky, F., 145, 177

Elizabeth, Princess of Bohemia, 67, 72
Epictetus, 126
Erasmus, 2, 15, 45, 185
Esolen, A., 2, 11, 32
Evans, C. S., 11

Fouke, D., 178
Friedrich, H., 20, 41, 46, 48, 54–55, 64
Funkenstein, A., 71, 109, 133

Gadamer, H. G., 24–25
God of Abraham, 3, 7, 8, 10, 15–16, 26, 29–33, 36–37, 48, 52, 55–57, 59, 64, 82, 84, 89–90, 92–93, 95–96, 100, 108–10, 114, 124, 126–28, 137–39, 144–52, 154–56, 160–61, 163–71, 175–79, 181–82, 184–90, 192
Goldmann, L., 29, 138, 139, 143, 144, 161, 164

INDEX OF NAMES AND AUTHORS

Griswold, C., 11–12, 16–17, 30, 34

Hadot, P., 7, 10–11, 70, 92
Hammond, N., 2, 18, 35, 102
Hartle, A., 19–20, 44, 62, 65
Hegel, G. W. F., 138, 143, 163
Heidegger, M., 169
Hobbes, T., 98, 99, 109, 115–16, 119, 139
Husserl, E., 72

Ignatius of Loyola, St., 93, 96

Jesus Christ, 30–31, 148–50, 154, 170, 189
John of the Cross, 16
Jones, M., 4–5, 7–8, 27, 70, 72, 105, 107

Kennington, R., 22, 74
Khalfa, J., 34–35, 102, 140, 148
Kierkegaard, S., 11–13, 136, 152, 177
Koch, E., 34, 137, 138, 140, 179–81
Krailsheimer, A. J., 1, 4, 16, 80, 100–101, 144, 156

Lachterman, D., 70–72, 79, 82–83
Lear, J., 11, 12–16, 21, 81
Lewis, C. S., 158, 174, 187
Locke, J., 98–99, 135

Machiavelli, N., 78–79, 98–99
MacIntyre, A., 139, 160, 161
Mackie, J. L., 114–15
Maclean, I., 49
Manent, P., 20, 28, 98–99, 127, 139–40, 166–67, 183
Marion, J. L., 15, 16, 20, 33, 100–102, 127, 138, 144, 181, 188–89
Maritain, J., 113
McInerny, R., 178
Melzer, S., 114, 138, 172
Mesnard, J., 3, 31, 34, 137
Miner, R., 4
Montaigne, M. D., 4–7, 10, 18–20, 26–29, 32, 36–37, 39–69, 75–77, 80, 84–88, 92, 96–98, 100–109, 113, 127–33, 168, 170, 173–74, 189–91

Nehemas, A., 11, 19–20, 30, 41, 43

Nicgorski, W., 22–23, 48
Neiman, S., 175–77
Nietzsche, F., 40, 59, 114–15, 163, 164, 169, 177

O'Connell, M., 7–8

Parker, T., 179–80
Pascal, B., 1–12, 14–19, 22–37, 40, 45, 51, 59, 64, 70, 75, 80, 86, 99–192
Paul, St., 1–2, 37, 57, 167
Pieper, J., 171, 174
Plato, 11–12, 17, 19–21, 23, 24–25, 29–30, 32, 40–42, 44, 47–48, 52–55, 63, 65, 66, 69–70, 72, 74–76, 78–79, 81–82, 96–99, 108, 127, 136, 141, 151–52, 168, 174
Popkin, R., 4, 45

Rée, J., 76–77
Riley, P., 56, 77, 85
Rorty, R., 12–14, 136

Sartre, J. P., 56, 77, 169
Schaefer, D. L., 19, 62, 173
Schopenhauer, A., 163
Shakespeare, W., 40
Socrates, 1, 5, 7, 10–12, 15–25, 27, 29–30, 32–33, 36–37, 39–44, 48, 50–52, 59, 62–63, 65–70, 72, 73–74, 76, 78, 80, 81, 92, 98, 100–103, 141, 183, 185, 187, 190–91
Strauss, L., 7, 9–10, 18, 22, 29–30, 36, 74, 91, 99

Taylor, C., 85–86
Theresa of Avila, 16
Toulmin, S., 5–7, 40

von Balthasar, H. U., 119, 120, 148, 181

Walsh, D., 13, 31–32
Warner, M., 134, 135, 136

Zagzebski, L., 136, 137

status of theology
role of the divine

a new vision of the familiar

Socrates & transcendence

importance of a link
through Augustine

best way of life

vice of amazement

irony as a relation.